Social Sector Spending, Governance and Economic Development

Economic development depends heavily on the growth of social sectors like education, healthcare, gender equality, as well as factors like income, consumption, investment and trade. This book examines the interlinkages between development, good governance and spending on social growth.

The book focuses on different areas of social growth, public welfare and poverty reduction including managing human resources, corruption in public institutions and public spaces as well as health and welfare measures. The chapters in the volume highlight the role of government interventions in boosting human development – particularly in developing countries in Asia and Africa and many developed countries in the post-COVID scenario. The book also examines the foundations of government spending on development and effective governance while underlining the impact which social growth has on the economy.

Rich in theoretical and empirical perspectives, this book will be useful for students and researchers of economics, sociology, political studies, public finance, development studies as well as for policymakers and think tanks working in the areas of human development.

Ramesh Chandra Das is Professor of Economics at Vidyasagar University, West Bengal, India.

Social Sector Spending, Governance and Economic Development

Perspectives from Across the World

Edited by
Ramesh Chandra Das

LONDON AND NEW YORK

First published 2023
by Routledge
4 Park Square, Milton Park, Abingdon, Oxon OX14 4RN

and by Routledge
605 Third Avenue, New York, NY 10158

Routledge is an imprint of the Taylor & Francis Group, an informa business

© 2023 selection and editorial matter, Ramesh Chandra Das; individual chapters, the contributors

The right of Ramesh Chandra Das to be identified as the author of the editorial material, and of the authors for their individual chapters, has been asserted in accordance with sections 77 and 78 of the Copyright, Designs and Patents Act 1988.

All rights reserved. No part of this book may be reprinted or reproduced or utilised in any form or by any electronic, mechanical, or other means, now known or hereafter invented, including photocopying and recording, or in any information storage or retrieval system, without permission in writing from the publishers.

Trademark notice: Product or corporate names may be trademarks or registered trademarks, and are used only for identification and explanation without intent to infringe.

British Library Cataloguing-in-Publication Data
A catalogue record for this book is available from the British Library

ISBN: 978-1-032-13813-8 (hbk)
ISBN: 978-1-032-15819-8 (pbk)
ISBN: 978-1-003-24579-7 (ebk)

DOI: 10.4324/9781003245797

Typeset in Sabon
by SPi Technologies India Pvt Ltd (Straive)

To my parents-in-law
Niltu Kumar De and Ila De

Contents

List of Figures x
List of Tables xi
List of Contributors xiii
Foreword xviii
Preface xx
List of Abbreviations xxii

Introduction 1
RAMESH CHANDRA DAS

1 Political Economy Underlying Corruption and Its Macroeconomic Implications: An Introspection 9
SANGHITA GHOSH AND MAINAK BHATTACHARJEE

2 Social Credibility and Institutional Informality in the Governance of Public Space: The Commons Perspective 22
PASCHALIS ARVANITIDIS AND GEORGE PAPAGIANNITSIS

3 Governance, Social Sector Development and Employment in European and Sub-Saharan African Countries 41
NWOKOYE STELLA EBELE, IFEOMA AUGUSTA EBOH,
EBIKABOWEI BIEDOMO ADUKU AND
PRISCA CHIBUZO EGBUCHULAM

4 Effectiveness of Good Governance on Human Development: Empirical Evidence from Selected Countries in the World 58
KISHOR NASKAR, SOURAV KUMAR DAS AND TONMOY CHATTERJEE

5 Linkages between Social Sector Spending, Governance and Economic Growth: Case Study of India and China 74
RAJIB BHATTACHARYYA

6 Governance, Social Sector Spending and Sustainable
   Growth in Selected African Countries   92
   EBIKABOWEI BIEDOMO ADUKU, RICHARDSON KOJO EDEME AND
   OGOCHUKWU CHRISTIANA ANYANWU

7 Is Fiscal Decentralization a Means to Poverty and
   Inequality Reduction? An India–China
   Comparative Study   111
   SOVIK MUKHERJEE

8 The Culture of Corruption in Pakistan and Afghanistan:
   Impacts on Socio-Economic Profiles   126
   DEBASISH NANDY

9 Do Emerging Market Economies Have Sustainable
   Development? A Panel Vector Autoregression Analysis   140
   ADEM GÖK AND NAUSHEEN SODHI

10 Governance Reforms from a Global Perspective:
   Some Dimensions   158
   ASIM KUMAR KARMAKAR AND SEBAK KUMAR JANA

11 Effectiveness of Social-Sector Expenditure and Governance
   on Economic Development: A Comparative Study between
   Developing and Developed Economies   173
   MADHABENDRA SINHA, DURLAV SARKAR, ANJAN RAY CHAUDHURY AND
   ARINDAM METIA

12 Some Issues on Health, Urbanization and Wage Inequality
   in the Aftermath of the Pandemic: An Introspection   188
   DEBASHIS MAZUMDAR AND MAINAK BHATTACHARJEE

13 Healthcare in India with Respect to Sustainable
   Development Goals: A Comparative
   Study within South Asian Countries   205
   BAPPADITYA BISWAS AND ROHAN PRASAD GUPTA

14 Transformation of Microfinance and
   Financial as well as Social Inclusion in India   221
   SUDHAKAR PATRA

15 Knowledge Deprivation Index: Measurement
for the UG Students in Purulia and Paschim
Bardhaman Districts of West Bengal, India   233
SAPTARSHI CHAKRABORTY AND CHANDAN BANDYOPADHYAY

Index   249

Figures

2.1	Urban open space governance: the general framework	28
2.2	Modes of UOS governance	32
4.1	Functional relationship between good governance and HDI	65
4.2	Screenplot of eigenvalues after PCA	68
5.1	GDP growth rates in India and China	76
5.2	Comparison of health and educational expenditure in India and China	77
5.3	Stability test results for China	82
5.4	Stability test results for India	82
9.1	Pillars of sustainable development	151
9.2	Impulse response functions	152
10.1	Trends of different governance indicators	170
14.1	Trends in rural–urban share of MFI borrowers	227

Tables

2.1	Expected levels of effectiveness according to governance attributes of ideal governance structures	33
3.1	Im, Persaran and Shin (IPS) unit root test and Pedroni's test for cointegration	51
3.2	GMM estimates of the effects of governance on employment and social sector development	53
4.1	Indicators of HDI	62
4.2	Correlation matrix	67
4.3	Principal components analysis	67
4.4	Principal components (eigenvectors)	68
4.5	Regression result of effect on human development	69
5.1	Results of unit test (ADF)	80
5.2	Results for serial correlation (LM Test) and stability analysis (CUSUM Test)	81
5.3	Long-run association between variables (Wald test)	83
5.4	Short-run causality (Wald test)	84
6.1	Results of Breitung and Im, Pesaran and Shin (IPS) unit root test and Pedroni's test for cointegration	102
6.2	Estimated results of the effect of governance and social sector spending on sustainable growth	104
6.3	Estimated results of the interaction effects of governance and social sector spending on sustainable growth	106
7.1	Impact on poverty (India and China)	120
7.2	Impact on income inequality	121
9.1	Statistical results	151
10.1	Estimates of governance indicators for India (ranges from –2.5 (weak) to 2.5 (strong) governance performance)	169
11.1	Results of LLC (2002) and IPS (2003) panel unit root tests	181
11.2	Results of dynamic panel GMM estimations for developing countries	182
11.3	Results of dynamic panel GMM estimations for developed countries	183
12.1	Global scenario of health spending and COVID-19 pandemic	189
12.2	Associations between COVID mortality and health spending	198

xii *Tables*

12.3	Associations between COVID mortality and health spending & urbanization	199
12.4	Linear regression analysis of the causality of COVID-19 pandemic across the Indian states	200
12A.1	Health infrastructure equivalence of military expenditure	202
12A.2	Post-COVID fiscal stimulus package across countries	202
12A.3	Incidence of COVID across the Indian states vis-à-vis health spending and urbanization	203
13.1	Correlation and regression analysis	212
13.2	Single-factor ANOVA table	215
13.3	Mean ranks of indicators of SDG 3 (2000–2001 to 2020–2021)	216
14.1	Operational highlights of SHG model	225
14.2	Industry growth and market share by lender type from FY16 to FY20	225
14.3	Portfolio outstanding trends – Top 10 states	226
15.1	Deprivation index across sex and areas	245

Contributors

Ebikabowei Biedomo Aduku is a researcher. He is the general overseer of the Opportunity Research Team, Bayelsa State, Nigeria. He has attended several national and international conferences. He has publications in books and journals of reputation. He has research interests in governance, social sector and development economics.

Ogochukwu Christiana Anyanwu is a Lecturer in the Department of Economics, University of Nigeria, Nsukka, Nigeria. She is currently a PhD student in the same department. She has attended several national and international conferences. Her areas of research interest include Development and Environmental Economics.

Paschalis Arvanitidis is an Associate Professor of Institutional Economics in the Department of Economics, University of Thessaly (Greece) and visiting scholar on Commons at the Hellenic Open University, Patras, Greece. His specialization is in institutional economics, urban development and real estate. His current recent research interests focus on issues of urban commons, social and solidarity economy, public space, civic engagement and immigration.

Chandan Bandyopadhyay, PhD, is currently an Associate Professor of Economics at Asansol Girls' College, India. He obtained his MA in Economics from The University of Burdwan, securing the Gold Medal in 1994 and PhD from the same university in 2007. He has research interests in Gender economics, Environmental Economics, Development Economics, etc.

Mainak Bhattacharjee is presently an Assistant Professor in Economics at Loreto College, Kolkata, India. He has also worked in the same post at The Heritage College, Kolkata. He has obtained an M.Phil and MA in Economics from Jadavpur University. He has been working in the areas of Macroeconomics and International Trade. He has produced many research articles published in reputed journals.

Rajib Bhattacharyya, PhD, is an Associate Professor of Economics at Goenka College of Commerce and Business Administration, Kolkata,

India. He obtained his PhD in Economics from the University of Calcutta. His fields of interest are International Trade, Finance, Indian Economic Development and Women Empowerment. He has published many articles in journals/books viz. IGI Global, Emerald, Springer and Taylor & Francis.

Bappaditya Biswas, PhD, is presently an Assistant Professor in the Department of Commerce, University of Calcutta, India, with 12 years of teaching experience in undergraduate and postgraduate courses. Dr. Biswas has published more than 35 articles in different journals and edited volumes of repute. He has successfully completed one UGC Minor Research Project and presently is a Co-Investigator in two Major Research Projects under UGC-UPE Program.

Saptarshi Chakraborty, PhD, works as a Professor of Economics in the Department of Commerce and is the Principal of Panchakot Mahavidyalaya, Purulia, India. He has several papers and chapters published in journals and books, besides the completion of two Minor Research Projects of The University Grants Commission, Government of India, to his credit.

Tonmoy Chatterjee, PhD, is an Assistant Professor in Economics at Ananda Chandra College, West Bengal, India. He has worked as Research Assistant at the Centre for Studies in Social Sciences, Kolkata, India, for a World Bank project (under CTRPFP). Also, he obtained Prof. M. J. Manohar Rao Award from the Indian Econometric Society for the best research paper in 2012. He has published numerous research articles in several international and national journals and books.

Anjan Ray Chaudhury is a Senior Assistant Professor at the Department of Economics, Durgapur Government College, India. He has obtained MSc and PhD in Economics from the University of Calcutta. He has the credit of 22 years of research and teaching experience. Some of his papers on welfare economics, development economics, etc., have been published in reputed journals of Elsevier, Springer, Routledge, Sage, Emerald, IGI Global, etc.

Sourav Kumar Das, PhD, is currently teaching Economics at Lalbaba College, Howrah, India. His area of interest includes rural development, tribal livelihood, consumption pattern and terrorism. He also edited books on refugee crisis, tribal development and issues on globalization. He has contributed to numerous reputable national and international journals and books.

Ifeoma Augusta Eboh is a researcher. She is presently a research assistant to Prof. U. Nwaoguogu, the Dean, School of Social Sciences, Nnamdi Azikiwe University, Awka, Nigeria. She has publications in books and journals of reputation. Her research areas lie in development economics and quantitative economics.

Contributors xv

Richardson Kojo Edeme, PhD, is an Associate Professor at the Department of Economics, University of Nigeria, Nsukka, Nigeria, and is a Research Fellow at Institute of Business Research, University of Economics, Ho Chi Minh City, Vietnam, and is Visiting Lecturer, Pan African University (African Union Commission), Institute of Governance, Humanities and Social Sciences. He has published in reputable journals and books in areas such as public expenditure policy, infrastructural development, trade policy analysis and poverty.

Prisca Chibuzo Egbuchulam is a researcher and a public policy analyst. She has attended several national and international conferences. She has publications in books and journals of reputation. She is part of the Department of Political Science, University of Nigeria, Nsukka, Nigeria.

Adem Gök is currently an Associate Professor in the Department of Economics at Kırklareli University, Turkey. He holds a PhD in Economics from Marmara University, Istanbul, Turkey, since 2016. His research areas include economics of governance, environmental economics, economics of education and financial economics.

Sanghita Ghosh is presently associated with Jadavpur University, India, as Junior Research Fellow in Economics. She obtained M.Phil and MA degrees in Economics from the same institution. Her research interest lies in the area of Development Economics and Econometrics.

Rohan Prasad Gupta is currently perusing M.Phil in Commerce from the Department of Commerce, University of Calcutta, as a Junior Research Fellow. He has published more than ten research papers and articles in national and international journals and edited volumes.

Sebak Kumar Jana, PhD, is currently a Professor of Economics at Vidyasagar University, West Bengal, India, with more than 20 years of teaching and research experience. His area of research includes environmental and resource economics and economics of education.

Asim Kumar Karmakar, PhD, is an Assistant Professor, Department of Economics, School of Professional Studies, Netaji Subhas Open University, Kolkata, India. Having diversified research interests, he has published more than 100 papers at home and abroad, written books and edited books of high repute. He has received two national and three international awards.

Debashis Mazumdar, PhD, presently is working as a Professor of Economics at The Heritage College, Kolkata, India. He is also acting as visiting faculty in the Post Graduate Department of Commerce at Nababullygunge Mahavidyalaya, Kolkata, and in the PG (Economics) Section of Indira Gandhi National Open University (IGNOU), Muralidhar Girls' College Center, Kolkata. He has written a good number of textbooks on Managerial Economics and contributed articles in many national and international journals.

xvi   *Contributors*

Arindam Metia is an Assistant Professor in the Department of Management at Raiganj University, West Bengal, India. He received his PhD degree from the University of North Bengal. He has a total teaching experience of more than 12 years. He has the credit of a couple of research publications in reputed journals.

Sovik Mukherjee is presently an Assistant Professor in Economics and the Academic Coordinator of the Department of Commerce (Morning Section) at St. Xavier's University, Kolkata, India. He is former Visiting Research Fellow (2019–2020) at NISPAcee, Bratislava, Slovak Republic. His current research interests are in the areas of Applied Game Theory, Applied Econometrics, Public Economics and International Economics.

Debasish Nandy is an Associate Professor, Department of Political Science, Kazi Nazrul University, Asansol, India. He is the Visiting Faculty in the Department of International Relations, Tajik National University, Dushanbe, Tajikistan. Dr. Nandy has published 40 research papers in national and international well-reputed journals and he also contributed 38 book chapters in edited volumes.

Kishor Naskar, PhD, is an Assistant Professor in Economics at Budge Budge College, India. His area of interest includes rural development and tribal livelihood. Dr. Naskar has contributed to numerous reputable national and international journals.

Nwokoye Stella Ebele is an Associate Professor, Department of Economics, Nnamdi Azikiwe University, Awka, Nigeria, having research interests in social economics, development economics and applied economics.

George Papagiannitsis is a freelance Architect. Apart from his main diploma in Architectural Engineering, he holds an M.Sc in Urban Planning alongside an M.Arch in architectural design. He is also a PhD candidate studying the city as a commons and the role of ICT in the institutions of democracy.

Sudhakar Patra, PhD, is presently the Professor of Economics at Berhampur University, Odisha, India. He has published research papers in international and national journals and in edited books. Dr. Patra has completed four major research projects and has participated in workshops at the Asian Institute of Technology, Bangkok, Thailand and Kathmandu.

Durlav Sarkar is presently working as the Registrar of Raiganj University, West Bengal, India. Formerly, Dr. Sarkar served as Associate Professor in Management at the Royal University of Bhutan and prior to that, he worked as a Professor and Director at the Delhi School of Professional Studies and Research, New Delhi, India.

Madhabendra Sinha is an Assistant Professor at the Department of Economics & Politics, Visva-Bharati (University), Santiniketan, India; and prior to that, he served as an Assistant Professor at the Department of Business Administration, Raiganj University, West Bengal, India. He obtained PhD from the National Institute of Technology Durgapur, India. He has several publications in Scopus/ABDC/Web of Science listed journals/books from Elsevier, Springer, Wiley, Routledge, Sage, etc.

Nausheen Sodhi is a senior research fellow (UGC-SRF) pursuing PhD in the Department of Economics, Panjab University, India. Her area of research is economics of governance and public policy, and she is currently researching on good governance at the sub-national level in India. She has six years of teaching and research experience.

Foreword

The role of the social sector in any economy – developed or emerging – cannot be overemphasized. The sector plays an important role both in the short run and in the long run, and it is vital for sustained growth. Social sector is a very broad term and its coverage also varies from country to country. Health and Education are at the core of it, but there are many more services that it provides or can provide, such as supporting women, vulnerable groups, people with disabilities, etc. In most countries, both the private and the public sectors provide those services, with the exact mix varying widely between countries. However, even in countries like the US, the public sector plays a very important role, particularly in education. A lack of investments by the public sector in education or health can sometimes be compensated by investments by the private sector. But the private sector more often than not caters only for rich people, and without public investments, the poorer sections of the population get deprived of access to such services. In India, for example, the lack of investments in health and education has led to a dualistic system, with rich people relying almost exclusively on the private sector and the poor people depending on a very poorly served public sector, resulting in increased inequality in healthcare and education provisions.

There are many theoretical issues relating to the provision of social services. Why is there an under-provision of such services in most emerging countries? It is not always the lack of resources; often, it is the lack of political will that is to blame. Moreover, the provision of such services comes with a significant amount of corruption which draws away the limited funds that are allocated to them.

In this volume titled *Social Sector Spending, Governance and Economic Development: Theoretical and Empirical Perspectives from Across the World* and in another related volume (titled *Social Sector Development and Governance: Empirical Investigations for Countries and Groups*), the editor, Dr. Ramesh Chandra Das of the Department of Economics, Vidyasagar University, India, has brought together a large number of researchers and their studies on this very important and under-researched area. In this volume, there are a number of chapters that deal with many of the theoretical issues, and it also has empirical studies on country comparisons in the performance of the social sector. The range of topics covered is really extensive and the chapters are developed in a very rigorous way.

The editor has attempted to write broadly on the subject matter of the book and the quality of his proficiency in the area is mirrored in the quality of the individual chapters that he has accumulated.

Sajal Lahiri
Vandeveer Chair Professor of Economics and Distinguished Scholar
Southern Illinois University Carbondale, Carbondale, Illinois, USA

Preface

The role of good governance in expanding the economy's output and maintaining proper development in an economy has been considered by political economists as inevitable. Further, different historical good and bad shocks have proved that the government of any country should provide social sectors' development packages to stand by the affected people in the society. However, there is the problem of making transfer of funds for these social heads from the government exchequers to the people entitled for. The issue of bad or weak governance matters much in these distributive losses. Good governance involves the appropriate use of political power and reflects the success of the political institutions within a society. On the other hand, weak or bad governance leads to an imbalance between the processes of acquisition of positions of political power in a society and the rights of citizens to control the use of that power. The ultimate effects of good governance are low inequality and high development and that of weak governance is the high inequality and low level of development. The present book titled *Social Sector Spending, Governance and Economic Development: Perspectives from Across the World* cover the implications of good governance in relation to social sector spending and economic development in the world's different economies and groups. Making theoretical developments and empirical verification, the chapters in general justify the importance of good governance upon different heads of social sector spendings and their impacts on economic developments of the groups of countries. Good governance allows low levels of corruption, allowing more funds to the less privileged classes of a society, uplifting them from the poverty trap, reducing inequality, and encouraging sustainable development. The governments of the countries having poor or weak governance should thus focus on strengthening the level of governance and make their common people happy in order to reach a proper level of development. The book is expected to be beneficial to the students and researchers from the disciplines such as Economics, Public Economics, Sociology, Political Economics, Administrative Sciences, Public Finance and other social sciences, and will open the scope of further researches in the related fields at the global level.

In completing the book project, the collaborations and supports of several organizations and academicians are required to be recognized. I first acknowledge the unstoppable support and cooperation of Routledge, the publisher, for their continuous efforts from processing the project to its final acceptance. Second, I am highly grateful to Prof. Sajal Lahiri for writing the valuable foreword for this volume and the contributing authors for their valuable research articles and for maintaining patience for the project taking such a long duration. Finally, I am beholden to my family members for sharing the stress and sacrificing the household's time for consociation. Of course, no one other than me, as the editor, discloses to remain utterly accountable for any errors that still persist in the book.

Ramesh Chandra Das
Editor

Abbreviations

NGO	Non-Governmental Organization
UOS	Urban Open Space
PSGF	Public Space Governance Framework
GMM	Generalized Method of Moments
ILO	International Labour Organization
IMF	International Monetary Fund
IPS	Im, Persaran and Shin
OLS	Ordinary Least Square
SDI	Index of Social Development
SSA	Sub-Saharan African
UNDP	United Nations Development Programme
WDI	World Development Indicators
CC	Control of Corruption
COE	Council of Europe
FEM	Fixed Effect Model
GDP	Gross Domestic Product
GE	Governments Effectiveness
GVI	Governance Index
HDI	Human Development Index
PCA	Principal Component Analysis
PSAV	Political Stability and Absence of Violence/Terrorism
REM	Random Effect Model
RL	Rule of Law
RQ	Regulatory Quality
VA	Voice and Accountability
WGI	Worldwide Governance Indicators
ADF	Augmented Dickey–Fuller
ARDL	Autoregressive Distributed Lag Approach
CPI	Corruption Perceptions Index
CUSUM	Cumulative Sum
ECM	Error Correction Model
ECT	Error Correction Term
EE	Educational Expenditure
HE	Health Expenditure

LML	Lagrange Multiplier
MDGs	Millennium Development Goals
ARDL	Autoregressive Distributive Lag
SDGs	Sustainable Development Goals
VAR	Vector Auto-Regressive
CEIC	Census and Economic Information Center
DA	Debt Autonomy
ER	Expenditure Ratio
GE	Generalized Entropy
LOO	Leave-One-Out
MFDI	Modified Fundamental Index of Fiscal Decentralization
NITI	National Institution for Transforming India
OECD	The Organisation for Economic Co-operation and Development
PPP	Purchasing Power Parity
RA	Revenue Autonomy
TD	Transfer Dependency Ratio
USSR	Union of Soviet Socialist Republics
KESC	Karachi Electric Supply Corporation
NAB	National Accountability Bureau
NGOs	Non-Governmental Organizations
NUG	National Unity Government
TI	Transparency International
CO_2 Emissions	Carbon Dioxide Emissions
GDP per capita	Gross Domestic Product per Capita
GOV	Governance Indicator
NSDP	Net State Domestic Product
Panel VAR	Panel Vector Autoregression
IMF	International Monetary Fund
AIC	Akaike information criterion
DCF	Domestic Capital Formation
EU	European Union
FDI	Foreign Direct Investment
GEX	Government Expenditure on the Social Sectors
HCF	Human Capital Formation
LLC	Levin-Lin-Chu
PCI	Per Capita Gross Domestic Product
SAARC	South Asian Association for Regional Cooperation
TRD	Volume of International Trade
VECM	Vector Error Correction Model
AB GMM	Arellano and Bond Generalized Method of Moments
FE	Fixed Effect
RM	Random Effect
USAID	United States Agency for International Development
WHO	World Health Organization
CMIE	Centre for Monitoring Indian Economy

SMEs	Small and Medium Enterprises
ANM	Auxiliary Nurse-Midwife
ANOVA	Analysis of Variance
ASEAN	Association of Southeast Asian Nations
ASHA	Accredited Social Health Activist
AWW	Anganwadi Worker
DTP	Diphtheria, Tetanus Toxoids and Pertussis
GCF	Gross Capital Formation
ICDS	Integrated Child Development Services
OBC	Other Backward Classes
SC	Scheduled Castes
ST	Scheduled Tribes
UN	United Nations
MFI	Micro Finance Institutions
MFIN	Microfinance Institutions Network
MUDRA	Micro Units Development and Refinance Agency
NABARD	National Bank for Agriculture and Rural Development
NBFC	Non-Banking Financial Corporations
SFB	Small Finance Bank
SHG	Self-Help Group
SIDBI	Small Industries Development Bank of India
ITU	International Telecommunication Union
MHRD	Ministry of Human Resource Development
SMS	Short Message Service
UNICEF	United Nations Children's Fund

Introduction

Ramesh Chandra Das

Policymakers in all economies, developed or less developed, aim to reach ultimate development in the long run through making growths in all the associated sectors over the different short runs. Over time, the respective factors of development improve in their quantities and qualities to mark a footprint in the long-run trajectory of development. The other sectors – economic, social, political, environmental, etc. – have their own styles of progress and have interlinks with each other as well. Out of all the sectors, the role of the social sectors deserves special emphasis as it constitutes the sub-sectors such as health, education, and gender as the source of human and intellectual capital formation, the lagging of which will ultimately defer the goal of ultimate development. But history says that the growth and development of these sectors are mostly brought by the governments of the countries, even in the so-called developed economies. The outbreak of COVID-19 has proved that well beyond any doubt. The private or corporate bodies, who are the drivers of growth in these economies, have not been seen to act on the frontline to fight against the pandemic. Thus, the role of government interventions in different social sectors' developments cannot be wiped out, particularly in developing countries and in post-COVID developed countries. It is to further add that some studies in the existing literature have pointed out that social sector development is highly correlated to poor governance in the means of corruption in particular and other forms of governance in general. The political parties and the governments of the countries capitalize the social sector spending for their election purpose when the scenario of weak governance prevails. A strong governance in any country prevents public servants to practice unfair means in terms of rent-seeking activities. Hence, social sector spending, economic development, and governance are interlinked in developing countries in general and developed countries in particular. Whether the economic development due to noticeable social sector development is sustainable is a big issue of discussion in development economics.

Economic development in a true sense depends on different social sectors' developments like education, healthcare, and gender equality besides economic factors like income, consumption, investment, and international trade. The United Nations' Sustainable Development Goals (SDGs) has a

DOI: 10.4324/9781003245797-1

17-point agenda. The SDGs were set up in 2015 by the United Nations General Assembly (UN-GA) and are intended to be achieved by the year 2030. They are included in a UN-GA resolution named the 2030 Agenda (United Nations, 2017). Out of the 17 goals, Goals 3, 4, 5, 8, and 16 cover the social sector components of health, education, gender, good practice, and proper justice, respectively. Goal 3 mainly targets the reduction of the global maternal mortality ratio to less than 70 per 100,000 live births, culminating in escapable deaths of new-borns and children under 5 years of age; eradicating epidemics such as AIDS, tuberculosis, malaria, and neglected tropical diseases; and combating hepatitis, water-borne diseases, and other communicable diseases by the year 2030. Besides, it is targeted to attain universal health coverage, including financial risk protection, access to quality essential healthcare services, and access to harmless, effective, high-quality, and affordable vital medicines and vaccines for all. The principal targets of Goal 4 include warranting that all girls and boys complete free, equitable, and high-quality primary and secondary education, leading to relevant and effective learning outcomes, ensuring that all girls and boys have access to quality early childhood, care, and pre-primary education and guaranteeing equal access for all women and men to reasonable and quality technical, vocational, and tertiary education, including the university levels by the year 2030. Goal 5 aims to achieve the principal targets such as eliminating all forms of discrimination against all women and girls everywhere, ending all forms of violence against all women and girls in the public and private spheres, including trafficking and sexual and other types of exploitation and finishing all destructive practices, such as child-, early-, and forced marriage and female genital mutilation. Goal 8 focuses on the targets such as endorsing development-oriented policies that support productive activities, decent job creation, entrepreneurship, creativity, and innovation; improving progressively, global resource efficiency in consumption and production and attempting to dissociate economic growth from environmental degradation; achieving full and productive employment and decent work for all women and men, including for young people and persons with disabilities, and equivalent pay for work of equal value by the year 2030. Goal 16 covers targets such as encouraging the rule of law at the national and international levels, guaranteeing equal access to justice for all, reducing significantly the illicit financial and arms flows, strengthening the recovery and return of stolen assets, combating all forms of organized crime, lessening considerably the corruption and bribery attitudes of all forms, developing active, accountable, and transparent institutions at all levels, mostly by the year 2030.

As the worldwide economy experiences a broad-based consolidation of growth, the narrative is shifting toward fastening economic policy to medium-term sustainability which is often sought to be attained by re-orienting public expenditure toward growth-promoting capital and social sector expenditures, particularly for the nations with limited fiscal space. The general approach is to entrench macroeconomic stability by reaping benefits for medium-term growth through the accumulation of physical and human capital and extenuating inequality. Human capital development is investment-intensive, and returns aren't instant. Theoretically, public provision of merit goods like education and health services is justified by the idea of externalities and therefore the difference between private and social returns (Musgrave, 1996). It's this non-rivalry and non-excludability characterizing consumption and investment of human capital which makes it a core responsibility of the general public sector. Moreover, there's no guarantee of an equitable provision of those basic services under the free market mechanism as postulated by a group of economists (Fredrickson, 1990; Musgrave, 1996; Harrow, 2002).

Economists and social scientists generally argue that if you throw a coin from the top of a hill, it will ultimately reach the mainland. Transforming the essence of this sentence into economic and social aspects, if there is growth and development of the upper stratum of a society, then the impact of that will be trickled down to the baselines comprising the poorest of the poor, destitute, and moderately poor. If this is so, then any heavy investment in the name of public projects helping business houses and agricultural farmhouses should make positive impacts on the people in high need. And then, the ultimate objective of a development planner should be achieved by reducing the inter-class inequalities in incomes, consumption, and opportunities. But the reality tells the opposite in many instances. To counter such negative aspects of this type of developmental goal, the policyholders opt for another way of reducing the inter-class inequalities in the name of Inclusive Growth which is based upon spending directly upon the highly needy people of the society that will pull up their levels of standards of living and ultimately the gap between the rich and poor can be minimized. Social sector spending is crucial because it is likely relatively to benefit the poor more than the rich and because, defensibly, it improves the human capital in the economy, which can have a direct sustainable growth effect and indirect spillover advantages for the rest of the economy. While little empirical work exists on examining the determinants of government spending in these sectors, a common view is that good governance could be leading to higher participation of the less privileged in the political process, leading to results that will be beneficial to the poor. One such result is the amount of government supports or resources allocated to the provision of education and health. This could lead to a positive sustainable growth effect as a result of human capital externalities. Social sector spending can be crucial for sustainable growth and sustainable growth manifests in social sector spending. Good governance will play a key role in ensuring prudent social sector spending, which is necessary for sustainable growth.

Sustainable economic process is apparent as a growth process whereby there's no reduction of economic activities over time and, there's no decrease in social welfare as a result of the misconduct of economic resources or a fall in production and consumption activities; it's a financial condition which is such that the per capita income of a countryside demonstrates a bent to expand over a period of time; nonetheless, the method could have sporadic periods of declination and stagnation almost like that caused by the trade cycle. That is, a sustainable economic process is an economic process where a rise in per capita material output is to such a level that the economic welfare doesn't display a probability of decline over time (Roy, 2019). It is to be noted further that the concept of sustainable economic process differs from that of sustainable development. According to Giraldo (2019), sustainable development refers to each sort of growth in preserving the requirements of the present generation without compromising future generations. Sustainable development also refers to maintaining a balance between natural resource usage and therefore the proper functioning of the natural system. In developing countries especially countries within the low- and middle-income regions like Africa and South Asia, growth seems not to be sustainable as most of the economies frequently experience impoverishment of economic activities with increasing unemployment rates and inequality.

Coming to the governance factor, as recently as 35 years ago, the word had remained almost unexploited. For an extended time, the term 'governance' was deserted by economists, perhaps because they expected the government to supply it proficiently. Though understanding of less-developed countries and restructuring economies, and explanations from economic history have led economists to review non-governmental institutions of governance (Frederickson & Smith, 2003; Kaufmann, 2005, 2008; Kaufmann & Kraay, 2002; Kaufmann et al., 2010). It had been the former British Prime Minister Harold Wilson who brought it back to general passage, by enabling his 1976 chronicles. Since then, it's moved rapidly from obscurity to the limelight. Governance is now utilized in various fields of studies, disciplines, and authorities. The concept of 'governance' was introduced on the agenda by the planet Bank in 1989 because it was needed to elucidate why a variety of nations did not develop despite the very fact that they had adopted the neo-liberal adjustment policies which was forced upon them by the IMF and the International Bank for Reconstruction and Development. The solution was 'bad' or 'weak' governance. If it is now questioned: What can explain the differences in the levels of development between Argentina and France while both were at an equivalent level of development and among the richest countries in the world at one time? The answer is bad governance for Argentina and good governance for France.

The 2030 Agenda for Sustainable Development was adopted by the United Nations Summit in New York in September 2015. The agenda was a broad and universal policy schedule, with 17 SDGs, with 169 associated targets which are united and attached. Building on the Millennium Development Goals (MDGs), the 2030 Agenda pursues to guide Member States to rework their approach to realize inclusive, people-centered, and sustainable development with nobody left behind.

Against the backdrop, the present volume aims to discuss the implications of good governance in relation to the social sector expenditure and economic development for the groups of economies in the world through theoretical developments and empirical verifications. The book titled *Social Sector Spending, Governance and Economic Development: Theoretical and Empirical Perspectives from Across the World* contains 15 chapters which deal with the main themes of the book. The essences of the individual chapters are as follows.

Chapter 1 explores theoretically the political and economic aspects of corruption, a failure of good governance, by addressing its fallout on the overall state of economic activities in touch with potential implications for distributive justice. It finds that the rising incidence of corruption and institutional malpractices lead to a recession in the economy and thereof will have further destabilizing consequences for the economy as a whole. Besides, it observes that as corruption is getting more pronounced, there will be an adverse redistribution of income from workers to capitalists which leads to the problem of income inequality.

Chapter 2 addresses the issues of social credibility and institutional informality in the governance of public space from the perspective of the commons. It aims to advance conceptualization on public space governance which allows shifting focus from 'institutional formality', strict 'legal credibility', and 'exogenous regulation', to 'institutional informality', 'functional user-based credibility', and 'endogenous ordering', highlighting them as prominent and valid elements of sustainable asset governance. The discussions show that the '*commons*' emerges as a key concept and tool that enables us to better comprehend reality and to assess the institutional organization of asset governance in a more pragmatic, meaningful, and useful way.

Chapter 3 examines the issues of governance, social sector development, and employment in European and Sub-Saharan African (SSA) countries from 1996 to 2020 to ascertain if there were significant differences in the effects of governance on social sector development and employment. Using the generalized method of moments, it finds that control of corruption, safety and rule of law, government effectiveness and political stability, and absence of violence/terrorism significantly increased employment and significantly improved social sector development in European and SSA countries. Significant differences in the effects of governance on social sector development and employment were found between European and SSA countries which forward the study to recommend that SSA countries should set good governance on a top priority basis.

Chapter 4 explores the impact of good governance on human development in some selected countries in the world using panel data econometric model and Principal Component Analysis. It finds that there is a significant relationship between good governance and human development and among the six factors, government effectiveness is most effective to induce good governance.

Chapter 5 aims to establish the linkages between social sector spending, good governance, and economic growth with reference to two of the fastest-growing emerging nations, China and India. Using time series analysis, the results show that not only social sector expenditures (particularly in health and education) in these two countries are below the world average, but poor governance has also been responsible for the decline in growth in these two countries in recent times.

Chapter 6 examines the role of governance upon social sector spending and sustainable growth in selected African countries for the period 1981–2020 using the generalized method of moment estimation technique and the main finding suggests that governance promotes sustainable growth. Further, among the components of governance, control of corruption is the most effective in stimulating growth.

Chapter 7 tries to examine the relationship between fiscal decentralization reforms, poverty reduction, and income inequality reduction in the presence of control variables like the modified fundamental index of fiscal decentralization (MFDI), the size of the government, the logarithm of per capita GDP, adult literacy rate, mortality rate, religious fragmentation, share of urban population, and trade openness ratio using GMM Kernel estimations on data for the period 2006–2019 for the two highly growing economies, China and India. Also, it tested to what extent is fiscal decentralization effective in combating social tension arising out of absolute (poverty) and relative (income inequality) deprivations. Remarkably, the study finds that fiscal decentralization reduces poverty levels while it deteriorates the inequality in the distribution of income below a threshold size of the government.

Chapter 8 examines the nexus between administration and politics and explores the reasons for corruption in Pakistan and Afghanistan. The study observes the existence of such a nexus and shows that due to the nexus between administration and politics, the degree of corruption has intensified in both countries. The reasons for corruption in both countries have been laid on societal and administrative culture.

Chapter 9 analyzes the prevalence of sustainable development in emerging market economies over the period of 1996–2017 using panel vector auto regression analysis. The study brings forth a theoretical perspective that a country or a country group has sustainable development only if it meets three hypotheses simultaneously. First, development should be self-reinforcing, second, there should be lower income inequality, better governance quality, and higher environmental quality, and third, an increase in the level of development should reduce income inequality and improve governance and environmental quality. Results show that although Hypothesis 1 is valid for emerging market economies, Hypotheses 2 and 3 are not valid. Hence, it is concluded that development is not sustainable for emerging market economies.

Chapter 10 attempts to reflect on the nexus between good governance and economic development and on some essential characteristics of good economic governance by grouping them into three heads: rule of law; accountability for actions and results; and combating corruption. Considering only governance in its economic aspect, it also shows how some simple and basic ideas from economic theory give useful suggestions for the reform of economic governance. It appears that there is no optimal model of economic governance since diverse governance arrangements can lead to economic growth and increasing welfare.

Chapter 11 investigates the effects of social sector expenditure of government and governance on economic development with a comparative analysis between the developing and developed countries across the world during the era of globalization. Using the dynamic panel difference GMM method for the period 2000–2019, the outcomes show that governance is more effective than the social sector expenditure of government to promote economic development in developing nations as compared to developed nations.

Chapter 12 makes an extensive review of the key socioeconomic perspectives on the issue of the pandemic caused by the coronavirus of late by developing a theoretical model in line with an open general equilibrium framework comprising tradable and non-tradable sectors as well as empirical verifications. It clearly indicates a wide tailspin in real economic activities in what can be apprehended as the inevitable fallout of the pandemic featuring a rise in unemployment and creating excess capacity and burgeoning income inequality, particularly in the form of widening the wage gap between skilled and unskilled workers. To make the response more effective and reduce the cost of the crises, strong coordination and cooperation among governments are needed which will help to enhance governance and build public trust inside and across borders.

Chapter 13 aims to investigate the relationship between social infrastructure financing and SDG 3 targets achievements in India along with an evaluation of various government schemes supporting the achievement of the targets on the one hand and make a cross-country analysis among South Asian Countries to measure the performance of South Asian Countries in achieving SDG 3 goals on the other. It is revealed that efforts made by both the central and state governments in the form of health sector expenditure had helped to improve the overall health and well-being of the masses in India. However, cross-country analysis shows that countries with smaller populations and resources are in a better position as compared to India and other similarly populated countries.

Chapter 14 analyzes the evolution and transformational journey of the microfinance sector and financial as well as social inclusion in India comprising its impact on the socio-economic development of the poor people. The study finds that meaningful financial and social inclusion could be achieved only through a collaborative effort of all the stakeholders involved in the entire process and using good governance practices.

The final chapter, Chapter 15, starts by raising a question on the recent pandemic, how far the students have been able to adapt and accept the new regime of online learning, and how far they find themselves or are deprived of being in the pre-COVID era. It goes for formulating an index, the amount by which the students were deprived owing to the challenges faced by them over and above the opportunities enjoyed on experiencing this new method of learning and reveals that the shift of learning mode from 'campus' to 'online' not only increased 'deprivation of knowledge' but also widened the intra-group, viz. male–female, rural–urban, etc., inequality, making it a socially unsustainable solution.

Summary

Having attempted to discuss the implications of good governance in relation to the social sector expenditure and economic development for the groups of economies in the world through theoretical developments and empirical verifications the chapters, in general, justify the importance of good governance upon different heads of social sector spending and their impacts upon economic developments of the groups of countries. Good governance allows low levels of corruption, allowing more funds to the less-privileged classes of a society, uplifting them from the poverty trap, reducing inequality, and encouraging sustainable development. The governments of the countries having poor or weak governance should thus focus on strengthening the level of governance and making their common people happy in order to reach a proper level of development.

References

Frederickson, H. G. & Smith, K. B. (2003). *The Public Administration Theory Primer*, Boulder, Colorado, West View Press.

Fredrickson, H. G. (1990). Public administration and social equity. *Public Administration Review*, 50(2), 228–237.

Giraldo, A. (2019). Sustainability and 5 examples of economic growth. Available at: https://ideasforus.org/sustainability-and-5-examples-of-how-it-helps-economic-growth/

Harrow, J. (2002). New Public Management and social justice: Just efficiency or equity as well?, in K. McLaughlin, S.P. Osborne and Ferlie, E. (eds.) *New Public Management: Current Trends and Future Prospects*. London, Routledge.

Kaufman, D. (2005). Back to basics-10 myths about governance and corruption. *Finance and Development*, 42(3).

Kaufmann, D. (2008). Irrational Exuberance vs. 'Afro-Pessimism': *Lessons from an Empirical Perspective on Governance in Africa*, World Bank.

Kaufmann, D. & Kraay, A. (2002). *Growth without Governance*, World Bank, July. Published by Latin American and Caribbean Economic Association (LACEA), Madrid.

Kaufman, D., Krray, A. & Mastruzzi, M. (2010). The worldwide governance indicators: Methodological and analytical issues. World Bank Policy Research Working Paper, Washington, DC.

Musgrave, R. (1996). The role of the state in fiscal theory. *International Tax and Public Finance*, 3(3), 247–258.

Roy, S. (2019). Sustainable growth. *Fundamental Economics*, II, 1–10. Available at: https://www.eolss.net/sample-chapters/c04/e6-28b-05-01.pdf

United Nations (2017). SDG indicators — Global indicator framework for the sustainable development goals and targets of the 2030 agenda for sustainable development. *United Nations Statistics Division (UNSD)*.

1 Political Economy Underlying Corruption and Its Macroeconomic Implications

An Introspection

Sanghita Ghosh and Mainak Bhattacharjee

1.1 Introduction

Corruption occurs in every civilisation and is present in every economy and is constant in every society. However, in the last 20 years, researchers have begun to seriously explore the term Corruption. The term corruption is derived from the Latin word "corruptus" which means corrupted. The concept of corruption is considered to be complex and complicated (Huberts, 2010). Corruption is the misuse of government power for personal gain. So, corruption is a by-product of government activity, and the larger the public sector, the greater the opportunity for corruption. Transparency International (2020) defines corruption as "the abuse of entrusted power for private gain." It is believed that corruption in developing countries arises due to the conflict between traditional values and modern norms. In an economy, there are different types of corruption (Shleifer and Vishny, 1993; Sun, 2004; Wedeman, 1997; Ades and Di Telia, 1999; Blackburn and Puccio, 2004; Rose-Ackerman, 1997) and it has various effects both on the economy and society at large.

Bureaucratic corruption is a major problem for an economy. Huntington (1968) states, "the only thing worse than a society with a rigid, overcentralized, dishonest bureaucracy is one with a rigid, overcentralized, honest bureaucracy." In order for government policies to be effective, bureaucrats play an important role and, actually, they implement these policies. So, it becomes crucial that officials must not deviate from their appointed task. In the early 1960s, researchers devoted significant effort to examining bureaucratic corruption in developing countries and its impact on economic growth and development. Studies like Mauro (1995) indicate that countries mired in poverty are inundated by corruption (Zaire, Indonesia, and Haiti are notorious examples), whereas rich countries (Switzerland, Canada, and the United States) are less susceptible. Researchers Alam (1989) and Bayley (1966) consider bureaucratic corruption as an unavoidable outcome of modernisation and development.

Bureaucratic corruption allows civil servants the opportunity to raise their compensation above what the law prescribes. Through the practice of corruption, private entrepreneurs are able to capture and maintain monopoly positions in the economy. Corruption allows inefficient producers to

DOI: 10.4324/9781003245797-2

remain in business, encourages governments to pursue perverse economic policies, and provides opportunities for bureaucrats and politicians to enrich themselves by extorting bribes from those seeking government favours. Thus, corruption distorts economic incentives, discourages entrepreneurship, and slows economic growth (Mbaku 1992, Gould 1980).

David Osterfeld (1992) has said that in a heavily regulated economy, there are two distinct types of corruption: "expansive corruption," which involves activities that improve the competitiveness and flexibility of the market; and "restrictive corruption," which limits opportunities for a productive and socially beneficial exchange. According to Osterfeld, this latter type of corruption is characterised by the redistribution of income and wealth in favour of individuals or groups. Most public-sector corruption falls in the restrictive category and involves the illegal appropriation of public resources for private use (e.g. outright embezzlement by a civil servant) or the illegal use of an individual's public position for his own personal enrichment. Public-sector corruption hinders the proper functioning of the market system, retards economic growth, and thus is restrictive corruption. As examples of expansive corruption, Osterfeld mentions the bribing of judges, politicians, and bureaucrats by members of the private sector. The payment of bribes to the right officials, he argues, can help mitigate the harmful effects of excessive government regulation and improve economic participation. But international institutions such as The World Bank have identified corruption as the single greatest obstacle to economic and social development and have given priority to anti-corruption initiatives in their strategies for improving the quality of governance.

In this study, the main objective is to develop a game-theoretic model to explore the process of bureaucratic corruption and its impact on the economy.

1.2 Literature Review

In the fair wage–effort hypothesis, Akerlof and Yellen (1990) said that civil servants may willingly forego opportunities for corruption if they were paid proper wages. Tanzi (1994) reports that "unrealistically low wages always invite corruption and at times, lead societies to condone acts of corruption." On the other hand, studies like Goel and Rich (1989) and Rauch and Evans (2000) suggest that the proportion of bureaucrats convicted of bribery is negatively related to the difference between government wages and the average income of the private sector group of white-collar professionals. Researchers like Mbaku (1996) argue that incompetence and inefficiency among government officials may also lead to bureaucratic corruption. A study by Leys (1965) reveals that pervasive and chronic poverty, extremely high levels of material deprivation, and severe inequalities in the distribution of resources also have been advanced as major determinants of corruption in African countries. Various researchers believe that corruption in Africa and other developing regions arises from the existence of defective

Political Economics of Corruption from a Macroperspective 11

cultural norms and behaviours (Jabbra 1976). The public choice theory contends that bureaucratic corruption is related primarily to government control and regulation of economic activities (Mbaku, 1996).

> To foster inequality by compromising the effectiveness of redistributive policy, and in Blackburn and Sarmah (2008) who show how corruption can influence demographic outcomes (life expectancy in particular) through its impact on the provision of public health expenditures.

A study by Blackburn and Forgues-Puccio (2007) reveals how corruption can foster inequality by compromising the effectiveness of the redistributive policy. Blackburn and Sarmah (2008) examine how corruption can influence demographic outcomes (life expectancy in particular) through its impact on the provision of public health expenditures. Mauro (1997) presents evidence that corruption distorts public expenditures away from growth-promoting areas (e.g. education and health) towards other types of projects (e.g. large-scale infrastructure investment) that are less productivity-enhancing.

Rose-Ackerman (1993) suggests that competition between politicians and also between bureaucrats minimises corruption in government. McChesney (1987) shows that political competition is posited to reduce corruption in two additional ways. First, the freedom of information and association characteristic of democracies helps to monitor public officials, thereby limiting their opportunities for corrupt behaviour. Second, the possible turnover of power in democracies implies that politicians cannot always credibly promise that particular laws and regulations will continue in the future. This minimises the size of bribes that rent-seekers are willing to pay.

Ades and Di Tella (1997) provide some support for those public choice theories that stress the importance of market competition for minimising corruption and the importance of institutional arrangements, such as an independent judiciary, capable of minimising government officials' incentives and opportunities to engage in corruption.

According to the efficiency-enhancing view, some researchers argue that corruption may improve the efficiency of government bureaucracy (Leff, 1964). But many researchers disagree with this view as this theory considers rigid bureaucracy and anti-business regulation as given (Kaufmann and Wei, 2000; Svensson, 2005).

1.3 Objective of the Study

In this chapter, the main objective remains in developing a macro-theoretic model to explore the very regime of the political economy characterised by institutional corruption, in form of collusion or implicit contract or undertable agreement between government agents or law enforcement personnel or administrative official, on the one hand, and private economic agent on the other, by addressing its fallout on the overall state of economic activities in touch with potential implication for distributive justice.

1.4 The Baseline Theoretical Model

Here, in this chapter, the aforementioned objective envisages framing an aggregative model in Keynesian paradigm distilled with the flavour of structural macroeconomic perspective, owing to Kalecki (1954) and Ghosh and Ghosh (2019), which evinces the overall economic system as a dichotomous structure comprising workers and the capitalist (with the workers being in the role net lending owning the economy's aggregate stock of debt while the capitalist being in the net borrowers) along with the government. The musing on corruption as elucidated in this chapter essentially takes on the very case of capitalists having nexus with the government on account of political reasons, say, in terms of the former being instrumental as bankrolling entity behind the political force or part in rule, as one possibility, while other being the bureaucratic malfeasance in form of bribe-seeking behaviour of government officials mediated through the imposition of red tape cost and discretionary tax treatments as much as possible under the existing lapses in tax structure and administration. In the first case, corruption has been perceived to take shape through tax immunity enjoyed by few selected business entities that are at the helm of the business ecosystem in terms of commercial hegemony and financial clout and having a portion of such accumulation being diverted as donation or tribute to the political force in rule. On the other hand, the second case has to do with bureaucratic corruption of the portion of wealth accumulated by the capitalist through undue tax breaks and redemption from red tape cost is parted away as bribes to officials engaged in the functioning of the administration. However, in both scenarios, the cost of corruption is ultimately charged from the public exchequer and thereof, its brunt comes to fall on the mass section represented by workers and marginal business entities and entrepreneurs.

The model developed here ligers essentially on the aggregate goods market wherein, aggregate output is determined from the equilibrium between planned aggregate demand and planned aggregate supply as delineated by the following condition.

$$Y = C_w\left[\left(\frac{\overline{W}lY + Dr_0}{P}\right)(1-t)\right] - C_c\left[\left(Y - \frac{\overline{W}lY + Dr_0}{P}\right)(1-t)\right]$$
$$+ I\left(r(r_c), \varepsilon\right) + G \ldots \ldots \quad (1.1)$$

Let us now explain the above equation. The right-hand side of Equation (1.1) signifies the planned aggregate demand as consisting of the aggregate consumption of workers (C_w), of capitalists (C_c), aggregate private investment (I), and overall government spending (G). The aggregate income generated in a given period of time aggregate production is Y which denotes NNP at factor cost. Now, the aggregate real disposable income of workers (denoted by $\left[\left(\dfrac{\bar{W}lY + Dr_0}{P}\right)(1-t)\right]$) derives from the total wage income from aggregate production $\left(\bar{W}lY\right)$ (where $\bar{W}$ stands for institutionally given money wage and l denotes the inverse of average productivity of labour being given by the underlying production technology) and interest income from holding of economy's aggregate stock debt outstanding in a given period of time (D) and interest rate averaged over time (r_0), deflated by the price level (P), with the "t" being the rate of direct tax. On the other hand, the aggregate real disposable income accruing to the workers is the residual of Y over total wage payment and interest payment on outstanding debt owed to the workers, taken in real terms, net of the direct tax. Besides, the aggregate private investment depends on the interest rate (r) which is determined solely by the policy rate $\left(r_c\right)$ as administered by central bank or monetary authority and overall expectation about future profit (ε) as well. Now, in the backdrop of this dispensation, we attempt to introduce the incidence of corruption by assuming the profiteers represented by the giant capitalist or large business houses at large, to be concealing a fraction (denoted by θ) of gross profit income from the government which they get to do either by harnessing insidious political liaison or by dint of bribing taxman, which in turn constitutes a compromise on public exchequer and henceforth, can have a potential adverse implication on fiscal capacity. Thus, to this end, the goods market condition goes to be rephrased as

$$Y = C_w\left[\left(\dfrac{\bar{W}lY + Dr_0}{P}\right)(1-t)\right] + C_c\left[\left(Y - \dfrac{\bar{W}lY + Dr_0}{P}\right)(1-\theta)(1-t)\right.$$
$$\left. + (1-\beta)\left\{\theta\left(Y - \dfrac{\bar{W}lY + Dr_0}{P}\right)\right\}\right] + I(r(r_c),\varepsilon) + G\ldots\ldots \quad (1.2)$$

The rephrased goods market equilibrium condition brings to the fore some alterations to the consumption by the capitalist in terms of widening up of their disposable income by the illicit accumulation made through the undue immunity from tax obligation to the tune of $\left\{\theta\left(Y - \dfrac{\bar{W}l + Dr_0}{P}\right)\right\}$ units, of which some fraction β gets channelised to the corrupt bureaucrats as bribes or surreptitious donations to the political power at the helm. In this regard, one may assume some positive correlation to exist between β and θ, in as much as the increase in illicit accumulation is likely to come against more of tribute to bureaucracy or political part in rule and thus β is supposedly an increasing in θ. Besides, this model unfurls an interesting possibility of having the price level being linked to the degree of tax evasions and income concealment and, this is such that an increase in the incidence of such corruption will syphon more resources off the fiscal reserve and which in turn may induce the government to raise indirect tax meet the deficit thus created, causing an increase in the price level. Hence, the price level can be considered as being rising in θ.

1.5 Recession, Corruption, and Macroeconomic Stability

A plausible proceeding from the baseline model discussed so far can come on how the persistence of corruption affects the economy's resilience to adverse macroeconomic shock from the demand side and thereby impact the overall economic order. In other words, we shall move on to examine how the system of corruption can turn into a potential element of destabilising the economy when it grapples with recession and thereby can cause the recession to deepen. This particular analysis has been tailored by using the conventional comparative static exercise as on Y with respect to θ in what follows.

$$\frac{dY}{d\varepsilon} = \frac{I_\varepsilon}{1 - \left[C'_w\left(\frac{\bar{W}l}{P}\right)(1-t) + C'_c\left(\left(1 - \left(\frac{\bar{W}l}{P}\right)\right)\{(1-\theta)(1-t) + (1-\beta)\theta\}\right)\right]} \dots$$

(1.3)

Let us now explain the multiplier effect of an exogenous fall in private investment on aggregate output and how it got a bearing on the incidence of corruption. Following a contraction of private-investment-led worsening profit expectation by $d\varepsilon$ units, the aggregate demand shrinks by $(I_\varepsilon\, d\varepsilon)$ units and with the aggregate output remaining unchanged, excess surplus comes into being, thereby calling for a downward adjustment in Y. Now, for a unitary fall in Y, the aggregate real disposable income accruing to the workers comes down by $\left\{\left(\frac{\bar{W}l}{P}\right)(1-t)\right\}$ units and, consequently, their consumption expenditure dips by $\left\{C'_w\left(\frac{\bar{W}l}{P}\right)(1-t)\right\}$ units. Similarly, the capitalists are also faced with a reduction in accounted real disposable income $\left\{\left(1 - \left(\frac{\bar{W}l}{P}\right)\right)(1-t)(1-\theta)\right\}$ units and so in the unaccounted portion by $\left\{\left(1 - \left(\frac{\bar{W}l}{P}\right)\right)(1-\beta)\theta\right\}$ units so that the overall real aggregate disposable income shrinks by $\left\{\left(1 - \left(\frac{\bar{W}l}{P}\right)\right)(1-t)(1-\theta) + \left(1 - \left(\frac{\bar{W}l}{P}\right)\right)(1-\beta)\theta\right\}$ and consequently, their real consumption narrows by $\left[C'_c \left(\left(1 - \left(\frac{\bar{W}l}{P} \right) \right) \{ (1-\theta)(1-t) + (1-\beta)\theta \} \right) \right]$ units. Now, it is to be noted in this regard that consequent to increase in the incidence of corruption as indicated by the rise in θ, the diversion of resources towards bribery or political donation may increase in as much as the relation between β and θ, (as stated at the outset) is concerned (which in turn opens a possibility for the decline aggregate real consumption by the capitalist to be intensified, particularly when the rate of erosion of accounted or undisclosed profit either through bribery or political donation is larger than the tax rate imposed on the capitalist). This, therefore, leads to the offsetting of excess supply in the goods market, but only at the smaller magnitude for every unitary fall in Y and thus would necessitate the downward adjustment in Y to happen at a greater extent to equilibrate the goods market as a whole, amplifying the degree of recession and making it more prolonged as well. Hence, we have the following proposition.

Proposition 1:

That the rising incidence of corruption and institutional malfeasance mediated through tacit collusion between big-shot enterprises or giant business houses with government or bureaucratic depravity or incestuous behaviour of law-and-order enforcing agents, will happen to debilitate the resilience of the economy to adverse demand shock or recession and thereof, will have further destabilising consequence for the economy.

1.6 A Dynamic Analysis of Destabilising Effect of Corruption during Recession

Let us now explain the adjustment process of aggregate output in connection with the multiplier effect of adverse demand shock in terms of how it affected, with the degree of corruption being prevalent. This is what follows.

To begin with, the exogenous fall in private investment by $(-I_\varepsilon d\varepsilon)$ units following the worsening of future profit expectations causes aggregate demand to contract and consequently, a fall in aggregate output in the same period, as denoted by $dY_1 = I_\varepsilon d\varepsilon < 0$. Now, in period 2, the aggregate real disposable income accruing to workers gets worse by $\left\{ \left(\frac{\bar{W}l}{P} \right)(1-t)dY_1 \right\}$, while the same for the capitalist being $\left\{ \left(1 - \left(\frac{\bar{W}l}{P} \right) \right)(1-\theta)(1-t)dY_1 \right\}$ units, which is however less than $\left\{ \left(1 - \left(\frac{\bar{W}l}{P} \right) \right)(1-t)dY_1 \right\}$, the amount of fall in case there was no corruption. However, the capitalists are also faced with commensurate contraction in illicit income holding by $\left\{(1-\beta)\theta\left(1-\left(\frac{\overline{W}l}{P}\right)\right)\right\}dY_1$ units, so that the overall contraction in real disposable income of capitalists becomes $\left[\left\{\left(1-\left(\frac{\overline{W}l}{P}\right)\right)(1-\theta)(1-t)\right\}+\left\{(1-\beta)\theta\left(1-\left(\frac{\overline{W}l}{P}\right)\right)\right\}\right]dY_1$ units, which may happen to be less than $\left\{\left(1-\left(\frac{\overline{W}l}{P}\right)\right)(1-t)dY_1\right\}$, the amount of fall as what would have been true in case there was no corruption, for a plausible reason of the bribe rate being smaller than the tax rate. It is to be mentioned at this juncture that capitalists find it economically rational to resort to malpractice in terms of bribery if they can command a greater level of real disposable income relative thereby, relative to what they would have been able to do otherwise and thus it is justifiable to claim that $\left[\left(Y-\left(\frac{\overline{W}lY+Dr_0}{P}\right)\right)\left\{(1-\theta)(1-t)+(1-\beta)\theta\right\}\right]$ is greater than $\left[\left(Y-\left(\frac{\overline{W}lY+Dr_0}{P}\right)\right)(1-t)\right]$. Thus, it clearly elicits that contraction in aggregate real disposable income would be larger in presence of corruption than what would be otherwise and hence contraction in the overall consumption forthcoming from the fall in the aggregate disposable income will be more pronounced, leading to further contraction of demand and consequently, so is aggregate real output at the end of period 2 as:

$$dY_2 = \left[C'_w\left(\frac{\overline{W}l}{P}\right)(1-t)+C'_c\left[\left\{\left(1-\left(\frac{\overline{W}l}{P}\right)\right)(1-\theta)(1-t)\right\}\right.\right.$$
$$\left.\left.+\left\{(1-\beta)\theta\left(1-\left(\frac{\overline{W}l}{P}\right)\right)\right\}\right]\right]dY_1 < 0$$

The narrowing of aggregate output coming up at the end of period 2 spills into the next period by replicating the developments emanating from the fall in Y at the end of period 1 and thereof will give rise to further contraction of aggregate output at the end of period 3 in what follows.

$$dY_3 = \left[C'_w\left(\frac{\overline{W}l}{P}\right)(1-t) + C'_c\left[\left\{\left(1-\left(\frac{\overline{W}l}{P}\right)\right)(1-\theta)(1-t)\right\}\right.\right.$$
$$\left.\left.+\left\{(1-\beta)\theta\left(1-\left(\frac{\overline{W}l}{P}\right)\right)\right\}\right]\right]^2 dY_1 < 0$$

$$dY_4 = \left[C'_w\left(\frac{\overline{W}l}{P}\right)(1-t) + C'_c\left[\left\{\left(1-\left(\frac{\overline{W}l}{P}\right)\right)(1-\theta)(1-t)\right\}\right.\right.$$
$$\left.\left.+\left\{(1-\beta)\theta\left(1-\left(\frac{\overline{W}l}{P}\right)\right)\right\}\right]\right]^3 dY_1 < 0$$

and so on.

This is how the bout of contraction in aggregate output will go on happening in subsequent periods until the goods market gets to revert back to equilibrium, with the magnitude of fall in Y coming up at the end period being more and more pronounced on account of corruption.

1.7 Corruption, Redistribution of Income, and Economic Pie

In this section, we shall elucidate the case of corruption as an instrument of redistribution of income and wealth away from the workers towards the capitalist in a disproportionate manner, consequently shrinking the economic pie. To this end, we shall introduce the case of price level being increasing in θ which is so because increased incidence of corruption leads to the erosion of direct tax base, so much so that the government is induced to raise indirect tax in order to keep its commitment to fiscal restraint by having to limit the fiscal deficit to a certain percentage of GDP. Thus, we have the following result:

$$\frac{dY}{d\theta} = \frac{\begin{bmatrix}-\left(C'_w(1-t)-C'_c\{(1-\theta)(1-t)+(1-\beta)\theta\}\right)\left(\frac{\overline{W}lY+Dr_0}{P^2}\right)P'\\ +C'_c\left(Y-\frac{\overline{W}lY+Dr_0}{P}\right)\{(1-\beta)-(1-t)-\beta'\theta\}\end{bmatrix}}{1-\left[C'_w\left(\frac{\overline{W}l}{P}\right)(1-t)+C'_c\left(\left(1-\left(\frac{\overline{W}l}{P}\right)\right)\{(1-\theta)(1-t)+(1-\beta)\theta\}\right)\right]}\ldots\ldots$$

(1.4)

The above-mentioned expression indicates that the impact of proliferation or intensification of corruption, as epitomised by an increase in θ, on the magnitude of economic activities, the nature of which can be elicited from the sign of the term in the numerator, signifying the extent of adjustment in aggregate demand, forthcoming thereof. Thus, following the spike in the incidence of corruption led by an increase in the fraction of profit income concealed by the capitalist there, the government gets to lose out on its tax base and in turn, has its total proceeds from the direct tax being comprised in a proportionate manner, and is thereby forced to raise the indirect tax, leading to a rise in price level by P' units per unit rise in θ. As result, there happens a redistribution of income from workers to the capitalist and consequently, we get to see a contraction in real consumption expenditure of the workers by $\left[C'_w(1-t)\left(\dfrac{\overline{W}lY + Dr_0}{P^2}\right)P'\right]$ units contrary to the rise in real consumption expenditure of the capitalist by $\left[\left(C'_c\{(1-\theta)(1-t)+(1-\beta)\theta\}\right)\left(\dfrac{\overline{W}lY + Dr_0}{P^2}\right)P'\right]$ units. However, the other side of the story rests on the extent of change in leakage from illegal holding by the capitalist as a consequence of increased payment of bribes or political donations weighed against the increase in illegal holding by capitalist by dint of rise in the rate of non-disclosure. To elaborate, the increased concealment rate raises the holding of unaccounted profit income by $\left[\left(Y - \dfrac{\overline{W}lY + Dr_0}{P}\right)\{(1-\beta)-(1-t)\}\right]$ units, as against an increase in outflow in the same to the tune of $\left[\left(Y - \dfrac{\overline{W}lY + Dr_0}{P}\right)\beta'\theta\right]$ units and thus the net increase in illicit income accruing to capitalists as a whole comes up as $\left[\left(Y - \dfrac{\overline{W}lY + Dr_0}{P}\right)\{(1-\beta)-(1-t)-\beta'\theta\}\right]$ units, which adds to their aggregate real consumption expenditure by $\left[C'_c\left(Y - \dfrac{\overline{W}lY + Dr_0}{P}\right)\{(1-\beta)-(1-t)-\beta'\theta\}\right]$ units. Thus, given that the workers have greater to consume than the capitalist, the redistribution effect of corruption is likely to be negative on the aggregate real consumption expenditure, so that $\left[\left(C'_w(1-t) - C'_c\{(1-\theta)(1-t)+(1-\beta)\theta\}\right)\left(\dfrac{\overline{W}lY + Dr_0}{P^2}\right)P'\right]$ is positive in sign. Now, in case the adverse redistribution effect dominates the increase in real consumption expenditure by capitalists attributable to the net increase in illicit income holding, then the overall real consumption spending would end up plummeting to cause a contraction in the aggregate demand and thereof, a plummeting of real aggregate output. Hence, we have the following proposition.

Proposition 2:

In event of corruption getting more pronounced, there happens an adverse redistribution of income from workers to capitalists which intensifies the problem of income inequality, leading to the worsening of distributive justice. Moreover, in case this adverse redistribution effect becomes relatively preponderate when compared to the degree of material wellbeing of the capitalist in terms of consumption, the economy's overall demand condition will worsen so as to bring about a contraction of economic activities at the aggregate level, causing a shrinkage of the overall economic pie and thereby, a further escalation of inequality malady led by the intensification of economic misery of the workers. Thus, the persistence of corruption in the economy led by the insidious nexus between capitalists and government or the ruling political force can prove to be detrimental to economic growth and distributive justice by setting in adverse loop dynamics between the size of the economic pie and inequitable change in its composition.

1.8 Conclusion

Political economy and corruption are two phases that have drawn increasing attention from academicians and researchers from the past. This chapter considers the case of capitalists having nexus with the government on account of political reasons while another being the bureaucratic malfeasance in form of bribe-seeking behaviour of government officials mediated through the imposition of red tape cost and discretionary tax treatments as much as possible under the existing lapses in tax structure and administration. The theoretical model developed in the chapter evinces that the rising incidence of corruption and institutional malfeasance channelised through the collusion between big-shot enterprises with government or bureaucratic depravity or insidious behaviour of law-and-order enforcing agents will happen to debilitate the resilience of the economy to recession and thereof, will have further destabilising consequence for the economy as a whole. Besides this, it is also found that as corruption gets more pronounced, there will be an adverse redistribution of income from workers to capitalists, which leads to the problem of income inequality. Therefore, the persistence of corruption in the economy between the capitalists and government can be harmful to economic growth also.

References

Ades, A., and Di Telia, R. (1999). Rents, Competition, and Corruption. *American Economic Review*, 89(4), 982–993.

Ades, A. and Di Tella, R. (1997). The New Economics of Corruption: A Survey & Some New Results. *Political Studies*, 45.

Akerlof G.A. and Yellen J. (1990). The Fair Wage Effort Hypothesis and Unemployment. *Quarterly Journal of Economics*, 105(2), 255–283.

Alam, M.S. (1989). Anatomy of Corruption: An Approach to the Political Economy of Underdevelopment. *American Journal of Economics and Sociology*, 48(4), 441–56.
Bayley, D.H. (1966). The Effects of Corruption in a Developing Nation. *The Western Political Science Quarterly*, 19(4), 719–32.
Blackburn, K. and Forgues-Puccio, G.F. (2007). Why is Corruption Less Harmful in Some Countries Than in Others? *Journal of Economic Behavior and Organization*, 72(3), 797.
Blackburn, K. and Puccio, F.G. (2004). Distribution and Development in a Model of Misgovernance. *European Economic Review*, 51(6), 1534–1563.
Blackburn, K. and Sarmah, R. (2008). Corruption Development and Demography. *Economics of Governance*, 9(4), 341–362.
Ghosh, C. and Ghosh, A. (2019). *Keynesian Macroeconomics Beyond the IS-LM Model*. Springer.
Goel, R. and Rich, D. (1989). On the Economic Incentives for Taking Bribes. *Public Choice*, 61(3), 269–275.
Gould, D.J. (1980). *Bureaucratic Corruption Underdevelopment in the Third World: The Case of Zaïre*. New York: Pergamon Press.
Huberts, L.W.J.C. (2010). A multi approach in corruption research: towards a more comprehensive multi-level framework to study corruption & its causes In G. D. Graaf, P.V. Maravic, and P. Wagenaar (eds.), *The Good Cause: Theoretical Perspectives On Corruption* (pp. 146–165). Opladen: B. Budrich. https://nbn-re-solving.org/urn:nbn:de:0168-ssoar-368896
Huntington, Samuel P. (1968). *Political Order in Changing Societies*. New Haven, CT: Yale University Press.
Jabbra, J.G. (1976). Bureaucratic Corruption in the Third World: Causes and Remedies. *Indian Journal of Public Administration*, 22, 673–91.
Kalecki, M. (1954). *Theory of Economic Dynamics*. London: Allen and Unwin, 1951.
Kaufmann, D. and Wei, S.J. (2000). Does Grease Money Speed Up the Wheels of Commerce? NEBR Working Paper No. 7093, *National Bureau of Economic Reseach*, Cambridge MA.
Leff, N.H. (1964). Economic Development through Bureaucratic Corruption. *The American Behavioral Scientist*, 8(3), 8–14.
Leys, C. (1965). What is the Problem About Corruption? *Journal of Modern African Studies*, 3(2), 215–24.
Mauro, P. (1997). The Effects of Corruption on Growth, Investment and Government Expenditure: A Cross-country Analysis. In K.A. Elliott (ed.), *Corruption and the Global Economy*, Washington DC, Institute for International Economics.
Mauro, Paolo (1995). Corruption and Growth, *Quarterly Journal of Economics* 110, 681–712.
Mbaku, J.M. (1992). Bureaucratic Corruption as Rent-Seeking Behavior. *Konjunkturpolitik (Germany)*, 38(4), 247–65.
Mbaku, J.M. (1996). Bueaucratic Corruption in Africa: The Futility of Cleanups. *The Cato Journal*, 16(1), 99–108.
McChesney, F.S. (1987). Rent Extraction and Rent Creation in the Economic Theory of Regulation. Journal *of Legal Studies*, 16(1), 101–118.
Osterfeld, D. (1992). *Prosperity Versus Planning: How Government Stifles Economic Growth*. New York: Oxford University Press.

Rauch, J. and Evans, E. (2000). Bureaucratic Structure and Bureaucratic Performance in Less-developed Countries. *Journal of Public Economics*, 75(1), 49–71.

Rose-Ackerman, S. (1997). The Political Economy of Corruption. In K.A. Elliott (ed.), *Corruption and the Global Economy*. USA: Institute for International Economics.

Shleifer, Andrei and Vishny, Robert W. (1993). Corruption. *Quarterly Journal of Economics*, 108, 599–617.

Sun, Y. (2004). *Corruption & Market in Contemporary China*. Ithaca NY: Cornell University Press.

Svensson, J. (2005). Eight Questions About Corruption. *Journal of Economic Perspectives*, 19(3), 19–42.

Tanzi, V. (1994). Corruption, Government Activities and Markets, IMF working paper no. 94/99.

Transparency International (2020). What is Corruption? 0041vailable at https://www.transparency.org/en/what-is-corruption

Wedeman, A. (1997). Looters, Rent-Scrapers, and Dividend-Collectors: Corruption and Growth in Zaire, South Korea and Phillipines *The Journal of Developing Areas*, 31(4). 457–78.

2 Social credibility and institutional informality in the governance of public space

The commons perspective

Paschalis Arvanitidis and George Papagiannitsis

2.1 Introduction

Urban public space constitutes the underlying fabric upon which social and economic life thrives, whereas the needs for efficient management and provision of such spaces become more pressing over time given the uninterrupted urbanization of the world and the limitations in available urban land. The provision of such spaces is, in modern democracies, a constitutional obligation of the state towards its citizens and they are seen as public goods. Yet, affected by a number of structural, economic and political changes and challenges worldwide, alongside the gradual retreat of the welfare state, the quality and quantity of urban public spaces seem to decline (Haas and Mehaffy, 2019), despite the contrary policy prescriptions of various organizations (e.g. UN-Habitat et al., 2015) and the growing needs and demands of the urban inhabitants.

Although the study of public space provision has traditionally been a planning discipline, the general recognition of the high complexity of the process has turned the attention of scholars to other perspectives looking for a more holistic approach. From this point of view, the provision and management of urban, public (as well as semi-public and generally 'open') space has been reframed and seen as a dynamic governance issue. Yet, the overall discussion and approach in the academic literature remain state-centric and formality-imbued, in the sense that the public sector is perceived to be the pivotal coordinator around which a number of additional players (e.g. private sector, NGOs and community organizations) revolve, whereas state regulation and formality are regarded as key parameters for successful provision of such spaces.

Breaking out of this kind of thinking, the current chapter aims to advance discussion on an alternative way to conceptualize urban open space (UOS) governance. It advocates the adoption of a user-centric approach, placing the end-user at the forefront of the analysis as the ultimate arbiter and driver of the various governance modes that can be applied in order of requirements so as to provide the functional and socially credible UOS. Consequently, the chapter introduces 'the commons' as a distinct mode of governance that draws its strength on the user-based, function-driven

DOI: 10.4324/9781003245797-3

credibility it incorporates. Overall, the argument the chapter upholds is the need to shift focus from legal ordering and institutional formality to a different rationale that incorporates institutional informality and function-based credibility as valid and prominent elements of sustainable asset governance.

The chapter proceeds as follows. Section 2.2 outlines the debate over the issue of UOS provision to indicate where the existing literature converges and to introduce our perspective. Section 2.3 deploys our conceptual building block, the commons, which is employed in Section 2.4 to discuss three exemplar UOS governance modes (the public, the private and the commons). Last, Section 2.5 concludes.

2.2 Framing the issue of urban open space provision

2.2.1 *The urban open space management*

UOS constitutes the underlying fabric upon which cities exist. It includes spaces of movement from one activity to another and places in which civic activities take place in a planned or unplanned manner. It is in a sense the interface of all those activities that define and constitute the urban as such, encompassing '…all the streets, squares and other rights of way, whether predominantly in residential, commercial or community/civic uses; the open spaces and parks; and the 'public/private' spaces where public access is unrestricted (at least during daylight hours)' (Carmona et al., 2008: 4; Carmona, 2021). In a similar spirit, Arvanitidis and Nasioka (2017) use the term to essentially convey the same idea, placing however a stronger emphasis on users' requirements and perceptions. Thus, UOS refers to an over-arching term encompassing a variety of public, semi-public and even private spaces of the urban frame that are generally open, freely accessible and available to people aiming to satisfy their multiple and growing needs for common space (for interaction, socialization, recreation and amenity purposes).

Such an explicit emphasis on users' perspective is justified by the fact that citizens increasingly acknowledge the important role these spaces play in their lives. This is because such spaces: (1) advance human health, by encouraging physical exercise, sports and outdoor events, and reducing stress levels thus improving the psychological well-being of urban residents, (2) meliorate environmental conditions, through air purification, reduction of heat island effects and water run-off, while simultaneously creates conditions for urban wildlife to flourish, (3) increase social capital and social cohesion, by providing opportunities for social interaction and a vibrant community life, thus further reducing incidents of anti-social behaviour and crime and (4) improve the economic conditions of the respective area, by attracting economic activities and investment. Thus, by corresponding to the physical, psychological, ecological, social and economic needs of the people, UOS seems to be of critical importance for urban dwellers' quality of life and well-being (Arvanitidis et al., 2009; Carmona et al., 2008;

Wolch et al., 2014). This in turn informs citizens' demands for such services and consequently for policies and actions required on the part of the governments, affecting politics in general.

Yet, despite the growing needs and demands of the urban population and the corresponding policy prescriptions of various organizations, the quality and quantity of UOS seem to decline over the years (Banerjee, 2001; Haas and Mehaffy, 2019). This situation has been driven by a number of structural (economic, political and technological) changes and challenges worldwide, alongside the gradual retreat of the welfare state and has been expressed as a process of privatization and over-management (commodification, enclosure and homogenization) that gave rise to exclusionary spaces (Harvey, 2012), or as a problem of state under-investment and under-management (poor design, inadequate maintenance and protection, etc.), creating a degraded environment and disadvantaged communities (Carmona et al., 2008; Jacobs, 1961). Obviously, not all the respective spaces are poorly developed and maintained.

With the above under consideration, the overall urban policy agenda has increasingly taken into account issues of urban sustainability, resilience, competitiveness, etc., acknowledging that UOS, in addition to typical urban functions as a meeting place, amenity space and connecting tissue between private spaces, performs a lot of other complex roles towards social inclusion, civic involvement, community revitalization, urban regeneration and economic development (Carmona et al., 2008; Fainstein and Campbell, 2001; Low and Smith, 2006; Whitehead et al., 2006). This general recognition of the plurality of functions and impact of UOS has turned urban planners' attention to more advanced theories and holistic perspectives in approaching UOS. Consequently, the question of 'how to provide better such spaces' has been reframed not as a planning or design matter but rather as an overall management issue.

Along these lines, Carmona et al. (2008: 66) defined UOS management as '...[t]he set of processes and practices that attempt to ensure that public space can fulfil all its legitimate roles, whilst managing the interactions between, and impacts of, those multiple functions in a way that is acceptable to its users', developing also a conceptual model to elucidate further these processes on the basis of four basic interlinked dimensions (regulation, investment, maintenance and coordination). According to it, UOS management needs to be informed by both stakeholders' aspirations and the specificities and constraints of UOS delivery, that is, the existing policies and higher-level regulations. Once such aspirations and policies are identified, the first delivery process concerns regulation. This determines how UOS should be used, setting a framework for solving conflicts and establishing rules of access and acceptable behaviour. The maintenance routines and practices constitute another interrelated management process, required to ensure the sustainability and functionality of the delivered UOS. These are linked to the number of resources (financial, human and material) devoted to these activities necessitating significant investments to be made (to cover daily duties, regular tasks or extraordinary contingencies). Finally, because the aforementioned processes involve directly or indirectly a wide spectrum of actors in UOS management, there is a necessity for coordinating mechanisms to ensure that those involved pull in the same direction. Needless to say, that nowadays, coordination becomes even more critical (also more complicated), due to the fragmentation of the public hierarchy, the retreat of the state from direct service provision, the increasing engagement of other players and the emergence of various forms of multi-actor collaboration (e.g. public–private partnerships).

Although one may argue that the pursuit of high-quality UOS should remain the same as contexts (socio/economic and physical/spatial) change, in reality, the relative emphasis on different dimensions and aspects of management varies from one place to another (Carmona et al., 2008). Contextual factors therefore act as a filter to this highly complex (multi-actor, multi-level) and dynamic (repetitive, continual) process of UOS provision giving rise to different organizational forms that can be applied in UOS management. These forms develop different institutional configurations to cope with all these issues, and the qualities they incorporate afford them to tackle these complexities with a different degree of success. The relevant literature (e.g. Adams and Tiesdell, 2013; Carmona et al., 2008; Healey, 2010; Tiesdell and Adams, 2011) has pointed out three models of organizational structure and agency that have been engaged in the complex process of UOS provision: the state-centred (where the public sector has the lead), the market-centred (where responsibilities are transferred to the private sector) and the community-centred (where responsibilities pass over to voluntary bodies and community organizations). Comparative analysis (see, inter alia, Carmona et al., 2008) highlighted that although these models are guided by different fundamentals and have their own intrinsic advantages and disadvantages, there is no moral or practical superiority of one over the others since all can provide solutions to particular UOS challenges in the particular contexts in which they are applied.

2.2.2 *From management to governance*

As discussed above, the contemporary urban planning literature has converged to the view that UOS provision is a complex, dynamic and contextual process needed to be approached holistically. Nevertheless, even this line of argument falls short of addressing the complexity of stakeholders' motivations, interests and degree of engagement in UOS, and the multiplicity of their relationships and roles in UOS provision (Zamanifard et al., 2018). Issues related to how the legitimate function of public space is defined and by whom, what kind of connection exists between actors and place, whether and how stakeholders can participate in decision-making processes, how responsibilities among participants are shared, and the like, cannot be effectively addressed from the UOS management approach.

In an attempt to address such questions Carmona (2014) proposed a new model of UOS governance, called the placing-shaping continuum that puts urban design at a central position. Acknowledging the significance of contextual factors and power relationships, he argues that UOS provision is a continuous and dynamic process by which places are shaped 'for use' and 'through use', indicating that even unselfconscious interventions, such as those of ordinary users, are part of the shaping and reshaping processes of space. The model distinguishes four key place-shaping processes: design, development, space (or place) in use and management, which are explored through the lenses of power relationships and the spatiotemporal context in London to argue that '...structure trumps agency' since '...power relationships sit at the heart of the urban design—place-shaping—process, dictating the flow and function of the process itself, and the nature of its outcomes' (Carmona, 2014: 30).

The proposed theory, although insightful, has been criticized by Zamanifard et al. (2018) for its limitations in addressing the nuances of relationships and roles among different stakeholders, something which leads to assuming a unanimous perception of space and action related to UOS provision and management. In turn, Zamanifard et al. (2018: 158) draw on Pierre (2005) to conceptualize governance as a socio-political 'processes of control, coordination and regulation' by which a range of formal and informal actors, institutions and organizations imbued by certain cultures and perceptions come to steer urban society towards collectively defined goals and to propose a Public Space Governance Framework (PSGF) that identifies four major components: governance structure; actors and stakeholders; governing tools; and governing tasks, along with contextual factors and external (economic) conditions. The governance structure is the linchpin of the framework. It is the dynamic outcome of stakeholders' requirements and power relationships. As such, every process and action are informed by and informs the governance structure.

As becomes clear, the governance structure is the central element that directly or indirectly pervades the entire governance process. This is a finding that runs through all this literature (Adams and Tiesdell, 2013; Carmona, 2014, 2016; Healey, 2010, 2015; Tiesdell and Adams, 2011; Zamanifard et al., 2018) which comes to converge on two further points concerning UOS governance. First, governance is perceived as a state-sanctioned process of coordination between the many different actors involved in their production, management and development of the place. The process operates: (1) in the public interest; (2) through multiple means and tools and (3) as ultimately a responsibility of the state.

Second, three pure-type governance structures are generally acknowledged: (1) the state, where power is concentrated in the public sector (2) the market, where a shrunken state apparatus gives way to the private sector and (3) a hybrid, where community-based or collaborative arrangements among public, private and voluntary agencies attempt a middle way. These exemplar governance forms, Carmona (2016) maintains, may co-exist in time and space, giving rise to various UOS governance modes, all informed by a triad of fundamental characteristics: the mode of operation (whether ideological or managerial in style), the relative concentration of public authority (whether centralized or disaggregated) and the power to deliver (whether public or market-oriented). In addition, empirical evidence suggests that there is not necessarily a superior form and that different settings could equally deliver outcomes of high quality, which means that any approach should rather focus on what actually works best on a pragmatic, contextual basis (Royal Town Planning Institute, 2014).

Assessing this line of thought a few remarks should be made. First, although this literature has clearly addressed place-shaping as a significant dimension of UOS provision acknowledging the key role ordinary users play in this process, UOS governance remains orchestrated by the state which is presumed to act for the benefit and in the interest of the users. In short, the overall conception ascribes to the state a pivotal coordinating and regulating function, downgrading and subordinating users' needs, wants and roles and underestimating their capacity for collective action and self-governance. In addition, this state-centric approach is prescribed by formality, in the sense that state regulation, legal ordering and institutional/structural formality are regarded as key parameters for successful provision of such spaces, leaving marginal space for the informal in the praxis of UOS governance. Second, even though the literature makes an elaborate discussion of the governance structures advancing our capacity for exploratory and explanatory analysis on how UOS is provided and place is shaped and reshaped through time, it falls short in pinpointing and specifying this 'hybrid' type of governance, which is seen rather as a kind of leftover or residual area of governance (seen to emerge mainly when neither the state nor the market undertakes the lead) without distinct identity and content. Third, the aforementioned literature makes a valuable contribution to the theory of public space provision establishing firmly the argument that UOS governance is a place-shaping process and so users' values, identities, perceptions and their attachment to place are important determinants of success, but it remains reluctant to articulate in full and employ such criteria in the assessment of governance modes. Overall, it sheds little light on how the different structures of governance can be evaluated to support decision-making and policy formulations. As elements needed to be considered towards this direction, Carmona et al. (2008) admit and concern (1) how priorities are set, (2) how conflicts are resolved and (3) how rights are unfolded in such spaces.

Figure 2.1 outlines the aforementioned discussion of the governance literature (left figure) and the point that our approach seeks to make (right figure). Clearly, UOS provision is a complex, multi-actor, dynamic and contextual process needed to be approached holistically taking into account actors' perceptions, interests and requirements, as well as their power relationships. Three main groups of actors are identified, the public sector, the private sector and the citizens (with users constituting a subgroup of the

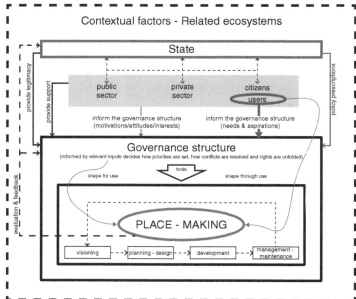

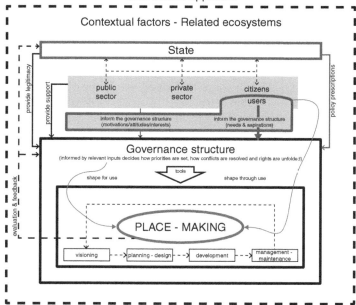

Figure 2.1 Urban open space governance: the general framework.
Source: Sketched by the authors.

latter), reflecting also different types of agencies, that come to formulate a governance structure informed by contextual factors and the state's regulatory/institutional framework (which dictates actors' options and choices and legitimize the final configuration). The governance structure deploys suitable tools in order to perform the necessary tasks towards place-making, the latter of which is fine-tuned by the acts of users through use. Along this way, the governance structure specifies priorities, addresses conflicts and prescribes rights distributed among stakeholders. As stated, our perspective (right figure) advances this thinking to articulate a user-centric approach, placing the end-user at the forefront of the analysis. We argue that since the purpose of UOS is to satisfy end-user's needs and aspirations, they should be the driver and the ultimate arbiter of the various governance modes that can be applied in order of requirement to provide functional and socially credible UOS. In addition, governance should elaborate and promote the modes that accomplish better this task by incorporating a degree of informality which enables flexible, cost-effective adjustments to be made. Yet, all governance structures may provide solutions to particular UOS challenges in the particular contexts in which they apply. This indicates the need to put forth a methodology that enables to assess the governance structures in a meaningful, pragmatic and useful way, something which is addressed in Section 2.3.

2.3 From formality to user-centric functional credibility

2.3.1 *The commons as an UOS governance structure*

Section 2.2 presented the very recent developments in the analysis of UOS provision, seen as a complex governance issue. This however is a rather new, but growing, body of literature. Given that historically, urban public space was the prominent field of urban planning and design (Carmona, 2019), much of the earlier literature adopts the view that UOS is a public resource and focuses upon the constituent components of such space as physical entities which under rationalized formally designed processes (exogenously imposed) could provide the necessary conditions for human activities to flourish. This line of thought, although it has significantly contributed and still does (according to Batty, 2013), to our understanding about how cities function, takes as given many urban aspects that are rather dynamic and crucial. To start with, a series of structural changes and challenges worldwide (globalization, population movements, urbanization, climate change, depletion of natural resources, increase of inequalities, etc.) highlights the fact that physical resources, and urban ones in our case, are under competition and in limited or distorted (e.g. segregated, privatised) supply (Carmona, 2010; Sorkin, 1992; UN-Habitat III, 2017). Second, in an ever-evolving urban environment, contemporary UOS needs and uses have increased and differentiated dramatically, while the intensity with which many spaces are used throughout the day have also multiplied

(Carmona, 2008; Moroni and Chiodelli, 2014). This inevitably gives rise to conflicts between different uses which are hard to resolve and which undermine the overall urban quality and levels of citizen satisfaction. Third, the widespread perception, held in most modern democracies, that the provision and maintenance of the UOS is a responsibility of the public sector is rather myopic (Carmona, 2014, 2015) given the multiplicity of stakeholders.

In an attempt to incorporate the developments discussed above into their analysis, subsequent urban design and planning studies reached for adequate solutions to UOS provision through the lenses of formality. Typical approaches to the matter ascribe the state with a regulatory power to define and enforce strong **property rights** on these spaces, attributed either to public institutions (state stewardship) or to private agency (through privatization), giving the involved parties the incentives and the authority to safeguard and guarantee resource sustainability and efficiency (Demsetz, 1967; Hardin, 1968; Libecap, 2009). However, these approaches have been criticized on the basis that they restrict the rights and activities of real users, destroying the social relations and values that characterize local communities (i.e. the social capital), to the detriment of both these communities and the long-term viability of the resource. The most well-known exponent of this view is the 2009 Nobel laureate in economics, Elinor Ostrom, who, drawing on a number of empirical cases across the world, established that communities can successfully manage common resources by themselves, at least when certain qualifications (or 'design principles') are met (Ostrom, 1990, 1992, 1999, 2000, 2008). On these grounds, a third, more socially acceptable management solution is proposed, 'the commons', where the community of users, overcoming collective-action problems, forms indigenous institutions for the sustainable appropriation and provision of the common resource.

Overall, the management of UOS as a commons institution concerns a system of endogenous arrangements (rules, norms, mechanisms, etc.) that regulate the appropriation and governance of the resource by its own users. These institutions are developed collectively by a community of local participants who rely on the resource for their well-being, having the support (Iaione, 2016; Parker and Schmidt, 2017) or, at least, the tolerance (Arvanitidis and Papagiannitsis, 2020) of the state and the other stakeholders. Membership in the community may be defined formally or according to ex post criteria, such as residence or acceptance by existing members. The interest groups participating in the governance regime play different roles and have different sets of (de jure or de facto, formal or informal) rights that are unlikely to be either exclusive or easily transferable. It is important to note that the practical management of the resource constitutes a critical feature of the commons governance regime and as such, its success depends not so much on formal/legal ownership per se, but on the provision and allocation of diverse (many times, informal) rights to those involved (Arvanitidis and Papagiannitsis, 2020; Colding et al., 2013;

Shah and Garg, 2017). The way in which these rights are structured and used has a great impact on the benefits generated, on equity issues and, ultimately, on the sustainability of the resource (Colding and Barthel, 2013).

The Ostromian perspective of UOS as a commons, with locally understood boundaries (design principle no 1), clearly brings the end-user at the forefront, allowing collective-choice arrangements – mainly informal (design principle no 3). As such, arrangements will tend to match local needs and conditions avoiding disproportionate equivalence between benefits and costs (design principle no 2). What is more, informality allows for rapid, low cost, conflict resolution mechanisms (design principle no 6) and graduated (peer-imposed and collectively agreed) sanctions (design principle no 5), based on a locally framed monitoring system (design principal no 4). Yet, the previous can only be realized when higher level authorities recognize (explicitly or tacitly) the right of the community for self-governance (design principle no 8). The latter subtly brings back the issue of formality which troubles the current debate on UOS governance (see inter alia: Adams and Tiesdell, 2013; Carmona et al., 2008; De Magalhães and Carmona, 2009; Hambleton, 2015; Healey, 2015; Zamanifard et al., 2018).

2.4 Modes of urban open space governance

Having articulated a revised framework of UOS governance that explicitly draws on the commons to incorporate informality, the discussion now turns to explore the three ideal modes of governance and evaluate their expected level of effectiveness to deliver quality UOS based on their structural characteristics. Figure 2.2 depicts this analysis placing these governance modes within the overall framework of UOS governance discussed earlier. Overall, the criteria to assess (Table 2.1) reflect the evaluation criteria proposed by Carmona et al. (2008). These are: (1) 'user priorities', in terms of representation, accountability, transparency, social legitimacy or support, fairness and justice, that structures should exhibit; (2) resolution of 'conflict' situations generated both internally and externally, in relation to other systems, to actors or to the external environment in general and (3) 'property rights – *placeing*', on the basis of how the unfolded property rights deviate or converge with the actual practice and needs. We start with an overview of the general characteristics of each governance structure and its key agents.

2.4.1 *The public governance structures*

'The public' is a state-based bureaucratic structure characterized by legal-statutory power, hierarchical chain of command, control through state authority and coordination via 'formal ordering'. The public agency, in its ideal, is an impersonal, impartial, complex and technically proficient organization, possessing specialized and diverse expertise and exhibiting unity, continuity, stability and security. It is driven by formal authority and statutory rules, rather than personal, more intimate or informal, routines

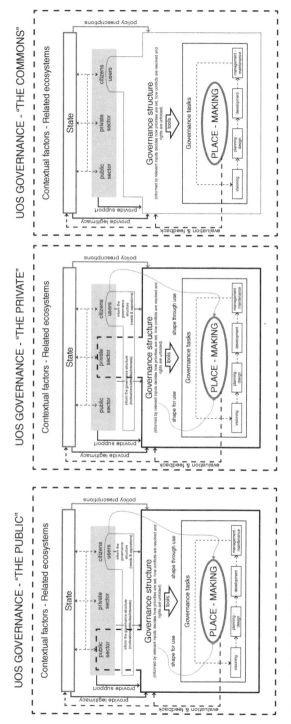

Figure 2.2 Modes of UOS governance.
Source: Sketched by the authors.

Table 2.1 Expected levels of effectiveness according to governance attributes of ideal governance structures

Governance attributes determine how:	Criteria to assess	Expected level of effectiveness and variance due to structural characteristics		
		Governance structures (Governance agency)		
		Public	Private	Commons
priorities are set	• representation • accountability • transparency • social support • social fairness and justice	(−) medium (+)	(−) medium (+)	(−) high
conflicts are resolved	• internally (informally) • externally (formally)	(−) medium (+)	(−) medium (+)	(−) high (certain actions can lead to low)
rights are unfolded	• formally • in relation to actual practice and needs	(−) medium (+)	(−) medium (+)	(−) high (certain actions can lead to low)

Source: Authors' calculations.

(resulted from ties of membership, friendship, or patrimonial or charismatic authority) that are apparent in other types of organization. According to Weber (1978), these defining features afford the public bureaucracy a number of organizational advantages that are based on formality, but also entail elements of organizational disfunction, including low individual incentives, low flexibility and autonomous adaptability, low cooperative spirit, and low user representation and downward accountability, which preclude it from delivering certain goods in a timely and efficient manner.

Compelled by the state, a public structure will deliver UOS in accordance to citizens' demands with relative adequacy, as it is characterized by formality, legal-statutory power procedural regularity, a hierarchical system of accountability and responsibility, specialization of function, and purpose stability and continuity. Yet, given that resources are limited, the structure will have to make prioritization of needs and demands, while preserving certain standards regarding issues of representation, accountability, transparency and social fairness. On the other hand, whatever prioritization will be that will inevitably cause conflicts and so, the specific needs will not be met. Finally, the unfolded rights will probably be equally distributed to all in the most general manner, because it is extremely difficult and costly (due to monitoring and enforcement costs) to unfold different rights on the basis of even specified criteria. The previous, call for a tight formal regulatory framework, with clear lines of bottom-up accountability and quantifiable evaluation procedures. which lead to rigidity and less accuracy in delivering customized, user-oriented goods.

In sum, the public agency will set priorities, regulate conflict and render rights in accordance to the overarching legislative framework, guidelines or directives, in order to satisfy at least minimum requirements, so as decisions can be adequately reasoned. Put it differently, UOS governed by a public agency will meet the thresholds of 'place-making quality' laid down by the higher level of public bureaucracy, in accordance with the constitutional requirements of the state. Furthermore, the retreat of a welfare state and the embracement of economic efficiency as the predominant assessment criterion renders determinants such as users' representation, institutional accountability, social legitimacy, fairness and justice, subordinate or redundant, if not an obstacle towards the achievement of objectively measurable goals. On the other hand, conflicts are to be dealt almost exclusively through formal or court ordering which in most cases means extremely time-consuming procedures which do not conform with the necessary flexibility that modern urban environments command.

2.4.2 The private governance structures

'The private' is a market-based organizational structure in which players count on the price mechanism to deliver goods and services. As a mode of governance, it relies on the forces of competition and on a decentralized, 'invisible hand' kind of 'market ordering' that is driven by agents pursuing their own self-interest. Based upon competition, a market organization agency will seek to make the best use of the available resources, to reduce costs and to deliver the product quality that would enable it to maximize its profits. Appropriate actions are dictated by formal contract law which provides credible (private) property rights ensuring that agents are highly incentivized to act, but basically in an individualistic and opportunistic manner (i.e. perusing in their own personal interest). In this framework, all parties are responsible for their losses or gains and no third party can legitimately redistribute resources or subsidize possible losses. As such, 'the private' is characterized by high-powered individual incentives that are based on legal/formal credibility, and a high degree of flexibility and autonomous adaptability, but low cooperative spirit, user representation, social accountability and fairness, where coordination comes as a natural, spontaneous order based on competition and the working of the price mechanism.

Imbued by a profit-making rationale and incentives a market-based organization will deliver UOS in accordance to citizens' satisfaction as long as such profit is not compromise. Yet, by its nature, the good under delivery indicates a rather small margin of profitability that discourages participation, thus restricts free market competition. Even if the vital, on the part of the market agency, requirements for profitability and contractual security are met, such an organizational actor would be compelled (due to the market imperfections that compress profit margins) to deliver only the necessary minimum of the good under concern. In addition, the high investment required in delivering the good will encourage a disproportionate resource allocation towards those spaces that enable greater profitability, such as locations that facilitate the development of additional (perhaps supplementary) activities (e.g. the provision of a coffee shop inside or next to a park), to the detriment of others.

Overall, the market agency will operate within the boundaries of contractual arrangements and, given the complex and dynamic nature of the good under delivery, it will be rather inadequate. All governance attributes (setting of priorities, regulation of conflict and allocation of rights) will be approached with an economic, profit-maximization perspective. Users' needs for 'place-making' will be satisfied to the extent it can meet certain objectively measurable standards, so as contractual obligation to be satisfied. Issues of representation, accountability, transparency, social legitimacy, fairness and justice are at best irrelevant to a market agency, unless such attributes contribute to profit-making or are specified in contractual terms in a quantifiable manner. On the other hand, a market agency will certainly seek to minimize conflict generation and to resolve them internally, given that conflicts raise costs and thus reduce profitability. Yet, given that conflicts are unavoidable, a market agency will probably employ measures and tools (e.g. surveillance and access control) that directly or indirectly prevent certain uses and users which put at risk its profitability, to the benefit of others. Last, the unfolded rights will be more concerned with issues regarding user-satisfaction, efficiency and optimization, which are closer to real needs, albeit approached through a profit-oriented and opportunistic rationale, which could also lead to the indirect exclusion of undesirable individuals or groups.

2.4.3 The commons governance structure

'The commons' is a collective organizational structure that enables and enhances networking among autonomous and self-interested, yet interdependent participants that constitute a community based on some kind of membership, commitment to shared values, interests and purposes, alongside collaboratively defined, usually informal, rules, arrangements and institutions. Such an organizational structure facilitates groups of participants to solve problems (conflicts) in a self-organizing and 'informal ordering' mode (relying at a low degree on markets or the state), where control and coordination are based on personal and social relations built upon trust and to a low degree on official, formal authority and legitimacy afforded by the state. As such, the commons is characterized by high individual and collective incentives that are based on informality and functionality, a high degree of flexibility and autonomous adaptability, strong representation based on democratic (usually, direct-democratic) processes that afford accountability and distributive fairness, which however are conditioned by the statutory framework and authorities' recognition that commons rely on (see no 7 of Ostrom's design principles).

The commons governance structure involves the formation of adequate institutions (primarily informal) and the active participation of those involved provide adequate safeguards regarding potential disturbances, given that the UOS users coincide with the community. Hence, decision-making and service provision is incentivized due to direct, personal interest for 'place-making quality' on the grounds of its use value. Even though complete satisfaction of individual needs may not be possible (due to resource limitations or conflicting views and uses), deliberation processes can smooth differences, promote mutual gains and provide context and user specific services. On the other hand, it can be argued that problems of collective (in-) action could be in place (especially of large communities or of communities with loose ties and low social capital) putting at risk the provision of the required UOS.

Due to its organizational principals, issues of representation, accountability, transparency, social support, fairness and justice are all incorporated and constitute the foundation of the governance structure. The commons, as a user-governed, collective institutional structure that is organized along the lines of informality following democratic deliberation processes, will accord rights taking into account not only the necessary statutory requisites (the formal) but a rather pragmatic and balanced estimate of what is regarded as user-functional or seen as substantial by the people and what can actually be accomplished. This, however, does not imply that the commons are the absolute solution to the problem in hand. The various interests of participants and the diverging views within the community of what is functional, substantial, or a matter of official (formal) legitimation, means that conflicts and disturbances could be in place. Yet, these disturbances can be resolved endogenously as long as the commons hold the capacity to sustain deliberation, collective action and accessible, low-cost means for dispute resolution. In this sense, the expected level of effectiveness is to be situated high. Yet, lack of recognition and respect by higher-level authorities, can easily disturb balances and jeopardize the institution, pushing effectiveness downwards to lower levels.

The preceding analysis indicates that the commons is the governance mode that in comparison to the other two enjoys higher expected level of effectiveness and ability to deliver place-making UOS; of course, as long as (1) it is able to establish a solid base for collective action taping into internal qualities (mainly informality, trust and democratic deliberation) and (2) it enjoys a minimum level of external acceptance (or at least a degree of tolerance from higher-level authorities, if not state recognition and official support). This is due to the fact that users, who are the main drivers and the ultimate arbiter of these qualities, become an integral part of the governance structure (as Figure 2.2 clearly depicts), undertaken without intermediates the accomplishment of their goals. Nevertheless, this does not imply that the commons constitute the absolute governance structure.

2.5 Conclusions and future research agenda

UOS is increasingly recognized as a vital component of urban life that promotes the well-being of citizens and consequently the society as a whole. Nevertheless, its quality and quantity seem to decline over the years, mainly due to lack of necessary commitment and investment at all fronts (physical, human, organizational, institutional). In the academic sphere, the complexities associated with the sustainable provision of such spaces, alongside the interdisciplinary nature of the subject, gave rise to more holistic approaches which reframe the issue as an UOS governance problem. Yet, the overall discussion and approach of the contemporary literature remains state-centric and formality-imbued, falling short to comprehend and to articulating user-driven, informality-based solutions that are apparent in many real-life contexts, let alone to provide a solid framework to assess the governance models that have been applied in practice.

Aiming to address these deficiencies, the current research proposed an alternative approach to UOS governance that place the end-user (the main driver and ultimate arbiter of UOS quality) at the forefront of the analysis. In doing so, it introduced the commons as a distinct mode of UOS governance that clearly puts the community of users in the spotlight and provides a hint of methodology for assessing governance structures on the basis of their attributes. Overall, the chapter advocates that credible, sustainable and efficient UOS governance can be achieved by incorporating elements of institutional informality, user-based functionality and social credibility. Although such a conceptualization is still in its infancy and requires further exploration, let alone solid empirical research, we hope the chapter has managed to infuse the idea the informal governance structures may perform equally well.

This regards the complexity of regimes that can be employed for the efficient provision (i.e. governance) of goods, especially of public and common ones. The analysis of the three exemplar modes of UOS governance indicates that each of them possesses different qualities and thus it is expected to respond differently in delivering the required good under concern. Whereas the state ('the public', in our terms) is conventionally seen as the pivotal mode in providing the required UOS, our analysis indicates that, under certain conditions or in certain cases, high-quality, place-making, UOS can be delivered by 'the commons' in a way that is socially credible, flexible and, so, less prone to deficiency and failure. Even though this conclusion might seem too obvious, it provides useful insights about what is expected to happen when circumstances change or when different 'legal credentials' are in place, that would allow communities to securely perform such roles.

The study so far has been made purely from a theoretical background. It justifies the role of UOS and the associated good governance factor upon the good livelihood of the citizens. UOS not only improves the local socio-environmental conditions but also put impacts upon the global socio-environmental quality. There thus needs some empirical investigations at different country levels to justify the relevance of the study. The present study preserves it as one of its future research agendas.

References

Adams, D. & Tiesdell, S. (2013). *Shaping Places: Urban Planning, Design and Development*. London: Routledge.

Arvanitidis, P., Lanenis, K., Petrakos, G. & Psycharis, Y. (2009). Economic aspects of urban green space: A survey of perceptions and attitudes. *Environmental Technology and Management*, 11, 143–168.

Arvanitidis, P. & Nasioka, F. (2017). Urban open greenspace as a commons, an exploratory case study in Greece. *The Public Sector*, 43(1), 19–32.

Arvanitidis, P. & Papagiannitsis, G. (2020). Urban open spaces as a commons: The credibility thesis and common property in a self-governed park of Athens, Greece. *Cities*, 97, 102480.

Banerjee, T. (2001). The future of public space: Beyond invented streets and reinvented places. *Journal of the American Planning Association*, 67(1), 9–24. doi:10.1080/01944360108976352.

Batty, M. (2013). *The new Science of Cities*. Cambridge, Massachusetts: The MIT Press.

Carmona, M. (2010). Contemporary public space: Critique and classification, part one: Critique. *Journal of Urban Design*, 15(1), 123–148. doi:10.1080/13574800903435651.

Carmona, M. (2014). The place-shaping continuum: A theory of urban design process. *Journal of Urban Design*, 19(1), 2–36. doi:10.1080/13574809.2013.854695.

Carmona, M. (2015). Re-theorising contemporary public space: A new narrative and a new normative. *Journal of Urbanism: International Research on Placemaking and Urban Sustainability*, 8(4), 373–405.

Carmona, M. (2016). Design governance: Theorizing an urban design subfield. *Journal of Urban Design*, 21(6), 705–730. doi:10.1080/13574809.2016.1234337.

Carmona, M. (2021). *Public Places Urban Spaces: The Dimensions of Urban Design*, Third Edition, New York: Routledge.

Carmona, M., De Magalhaes, C., & Hammond, L. (2008). *Public Space: The Management Dimension*. New York: Routledge.

Carmona, M., Magalhaes, C. & Hammond, L. (2008). *Public Space: The Management Dimension*. London and New York: Routledge.

Colding, J. & Barthel, S. (2013). The potential of 'Urban Green Commons' in the resilience building of cities. *Ecological Economics*, 86, 156–166.

Colding, J., Barthel, S., Bendt, P., Snep, R., van der Knaap, W. & Ernstson, H. (2013). Urban green commons: Insights on urban common property systems. *Global Environmental Change*, 23(5), 1039–1051.

de Magalhães, C. & Carmona, M. (2009). Dimensions and models of contemporary public space management in England. *Journal of Environmental Planning and Management*, 52(1), 111–129.

Demsetz, H. (1967). Toward a theory of property rights. *The American Economic Review*, 57(2) Papers and Proceedings of the Seventy-ninth Annual Meeting of the American Economic Association, 347–359.

Fainstein, S. & Campbell, Sc. (Ed.) (2001). *Readings in Urban Theory*. London: Blackwell Publishers.

Haas, T. & Mehaffy, M.W. (2019). Introduction: The future of public space. *Urban Design International*, 24, 1–3.
Hambleton, R. (2015). Power, place and the new civic leadership. *Local Economy*, 30(2), 167–172. doi:10.1177/0269094215570563
Hardin, G. (1968). The tragedy of the commons. *Science*, 162, 1243–1248.
Harvey, D. (2012). *Rebel Cities: From the Right to the City to the Urban Revolution.* London: Verso.
Healey, P. (2010). *Making Better Places: The Planning Project in the Twenty-first Century.* Basingstoke, UK: Palgrave Macmillan.
Healey, P. (2015). Civic capacity, place governance and progressive localism. In S. Davoudi, & A. Madanipour (Eds.). *Reconsidering Localism*, 105–125. Basingstoke, UK: Palgrave Macmillan.
Iaione, C. (2016). The CO-city: Sharing, collaborating, cooperating, and commoning in the city. *American Journal of Economics and Sociology*, 75(2), 415–455.
Jacobs, J. (1961). *The Death and Life of Great American Cities.* New York: Random House.
Libecap, G. (2009). The tragedy of the commons: Property rights and markets as solutions to resource and environmental problems. *The Australian Journal of Agricultural and Resource Economics*, 53, 129–144.
Low, S. & Smith N. (Eds.) (2006). *The Politics of Public Space.* London: Routledge.
Moroni, S. & Chiodelli, F. (2014). Municipal regulations and the use of public space: Local ordinances in Italy City. *Territory and Architecture*, 1(11), 1–7.
Ostrom, E. (1990). *Governing the Commons: The Evolution of Institutions for Collective Action.* New York: Cambridge University Press.
Ostrom, E. (1992). Community and the endogenous solution of commons problems. *Journal of Theoretical Politics*, 4(3), 343–351.
Ostrom, E. (1999). Coping with tragedies of the commons. *Annual Review of Political Science*, 2, 493–535.
Ostrom, E. (2000). Reformulating the commons. *Swiss Political Science Review*, 6(1), 29–52.
Ostrom, E. (2008). The challenge of common-pool resources. *Environment: Science and Policy for Sustainable Development*, 50(4), 8–20.
Parker, P. & Schmidt, S. (2017). Enabling urban commons. *CoDesign*, 13(3), 202–213. doi:10.1080/15710882.2017.1355000.
Pierre, J. (2005). Comparative urban governance uncovering complex causalities. *Urban Affairs Review*, 40(4), 446–462. doi:10.1177/1078087404273442.
Royal Town Planning Institute (2014). *Making Better Decisions for Places, Why Where We Make Decisions Will be Critical in the Twenty-first Century.* London: RTPI.
Shah, A. & Garg, A. (2017). Urban commons service generation, delivery, and management: A conceptual framework. *Ecological Economics*, 135(C), 280–287.
Sorkin, M. (Ed.) (1992). *Variations on a Theme Park: The New American City and the End of Public Space.* New York: Hill and Wang.
Tiesdell, S. & Adams, D. (Eds.) (2011). *Urban Design in the Real Estate Development Process.* Chichester: Wiley-Blackwell.
UN Habitat III (2017). *New Urban Agenda.* https://unhabitat.org/sites/default/files/2019/05/nua-english.pdf
UN, PPS & Ax: Son Johnson Foundation Habitat (2015). *Key Messages from the Future of Places.* https://unhabitat.org/wp-content/uploads/2015/10/Key-Messages-from-the-Future-of-Places.pdf

Weber, M. (1978). *Economy and Society: An Outline of Interpretative Sociology.* Edited by G. Roth and C. Wittich. Translated by E. Fischoff et al. 2 vols. Berkeley: University of California Press.

Whitehead, T., Simmonds, D. & Preston, J. (2006). The effect of urban quality improvements on economic activity. *Journal of Environmental Management*, 80, 1–12.

Wolch, J.R., Byrne, J. & Newell, J.P. (2014). Urban green space, public health, and environmental justice: The challenge of making cities 'Just Green Enough'. *Landscape and Urban Planning*, 125, 234–244.

Zamanifard, H., Alizadeh, T. & Bosman, C. (2018). Towards a framework of public space governance. *Cities*, 78, 155–165.

3 Governance, Social Sector Development and Employment in European and Sub-Saharan African Countries

Nwokoye Stella Ebele, Ifeoma Augusta Eboh, Ebikabowei Biedomo Aduku and Prisca Chibuzo Egbuchulam

3.1 Introduction

Undeveloped social sector and rising unemployment are twin problems facing developing countries, especially in Sub-Saharan Africa (SSA), as the levels of social sector development and employment are well below expectations years after political independence. Remarkably, social sector development and employment generation remain a vital feature of every country, as such, and the United Nations Sustainable Development Goals 3 and 4, in particular, give priority to social sector development, while Goal 8 is concerned with increasing employment potentials of nations.

One of the most vital drivers of economic growth in Africa's present era is the development of the social sector (Pattayat & Rani, 2017). Evidence shows that social sector development paves way for increases in income and employment opportunities, stimulates technological advancement in an economy and boosts productivity growth. Hence, social sector development helps to reduce poverty and improve the overall standard of living in a country. Without improvements in social sector development, it becomes difficult to achieve higher sustainable economic growth rates thus one can safely say that social sector development is crucial to national development.

The social sector comprises sub-sectors including education, public health and nutrition, as well as other social sector services that can add value to human capital formation and human capital development (Chadha & Chadda, 2019). Development in education, public health and nutrition, tourism, communication and other social services adds value to human capital formation and human capital development. The importance of education – as a component of the social sector, is affirmed in many studies including Mankiw, Romer and Weil (1992), Lucas (1988), Nelson and Phelps (1966), Grant (2017), Chankseliani, Qoraboyev and Gimranova (2020) and UNICEF (2021). These studies assert that education plays a significant role in the innovation process and that accumulation of human capital is necessary for labour productivity to increase and inevitably for higher economic growth rates. Without a strong human capital base, economic progress may not be achieved. A strong human capital base is a prerequisite for social sector development, which is attainable through quality education, an effective health system, social security measures and job opportunities in the organized sector. The development of the social sector expands human capabilities, which is a necessary condition for the economic growth and development targets of developing countries.

Employment, on the other hand, is an engagement in paid work either as an employee or self-employment. Employment secures income and heightens self-worth and self-confidence by fostering the social and economic status of individuals most especially the active working population (United Nations Development Programme – UNDP, 2013). Unemployment occurs if an individual is eligible and is actively searching for work but could not find one. The issue of unemployment is a global reality that has become a hindrance to economic growth. Employment has been identified as a key determinant of the nexus between economic growth and the reduction of poverty (Islam 2004). Even, multiple empirical studies have broken down the vital determinants of poverty reduction in non-fragile countries, and employment is established consistently as a key factor in a range of diverse country contexts (Holmes, McCord, Hagen-Zanker, Bergh & Zanker, 2013; Islam, 2004; Leibbrandt & Woolard 2001). Underutilization of the labour force is as well common in countries with a high unemployment rate (Pettinger, 2019). Social sector development and the achievement of higher rates of national employment have implications for long-run socio-economic development, in which governance could play a significant role.

The establishment of rule of law and contract and agreement enforcement between people, maintenance of law and order, security of lives and property, and quality service delivery are common facts with good governance. With good governance, resources are optimally allocated and utilized efficiently. Governance is considered vital to achieving social sector development and employment. Good governance directly enhances life evaluations since individuals are happier living within the context of good government, or indirectly improves the well-being of people by helping them achieve things that are necessary for well-being (Ott, 2010). It is specifically related to regulatory quality, bureaucratic quality, control of corruption, government effectiveness and rule of law, which has been demonstrated to influence economic well-being both directly and indirectly by creating favourable conditions for human capital development and employment.

Despite attempts by a proliferation of studies to establish such links, the evidence of a connection between good governance, social sector development and employment remains tenuous. Besides, most studies in support of the primacy of governance for social sector development and employment may be contested on conceptual and methodological grounds (Gisselquist, 2012). In the case of the SSA in particular, the implementation of good governance reforms including democracy or decentralization or liberalization is yet to translate into better governance or welfare enhancement in any SSA country. For example, in the SSA, between 2010 and 2019, the change in security and safety, rule of law and justice, accountability and transparency, and anti-corruption was as low as −5.3, +0.8, +0.8 and +1.1, respectively. According to the Ibrahim Index of African Governance Report (2020), most countries including Namibia, Ghana, Malawi, Kenya, Zambia, Nigeria and Mali were showing signs of increasing deterioration. While the democratic experiences of SSA countries have not made positive impressions, the economic liberalization of SSA economies – which has also resulted in the privatization of public enterprises, subsidy removal and monetary austerity – has worsened the level of unemployment and poverty in the region. Unemployment rates were 6.63% in 2020 – a 0.35% increase from 2019, 6.28% in 2019 – a 0.04% increase from 2018, 6.23% in 2018 – a 0.08% decline from 2017 and 6.31% in 2017 – a 0.14% increase from 2016 (International Labour Organization, 2021). Poverty in the region, on the other hand, accounted for two-thirds of the global extreme poor population, with half of the countries having over 35% poverty rates (Schoch & Lakner, 2020). The SSA democracies are placed under the prescription of the International Monetary Fund (IMF), World Bank, etc., and by concentrating on meeting the demands of foreign donors at the expense of the welfare of their people, most democratic leaders in the region have become corrupt and very selfish (Enwere, 2013).

Given the conditions of persistently high unemployment and slow social sector development, as well as the endemic poverty and corruption despite good governance reforms in the SSA, this chapter examines the issue of governance, social sector development and employment in European and SSA countries with the intent of comparing Europe with the SSA countries to ascertain if there is a significant difference in the effect of governance and, therefore, the role of governance upon social sector development and employment. This comparative study is made in a bid to empirically ascertain that the role of governance on social sector development and employment may be higher for more developed countries than for SSA economies because of structural differences and these structural deficits, fully displayed in SSA countries may have nontrivial implications on how these countries pursue good governance reforms. Good governance is not yet applicable to all SSA countries. Therefore, by this comparative study, we provide more evidence that governance plays a sensitive role in social sector development and employment with better dimensions and measurement of good governance. We provide these empirical evidences using the generalized method of moments (GMM) technique. This chapter is relevant to the governments and researchers for social sector development and employment-enhancing policies.

3.2 Literature Review

3.2.1 *Extant Literature*

In the past, the concept of governance connoted the outcome of government activities and majorly applied to political science, anthropology and political phInternational Labour Organizationsophy disciplines. Although this idea is still in existence, presently, there are different conceptualizations of governance in research and various disciplines. Governance is a construct, or in specific terms, the context of the concept which is based on the area of interest. It is for this reason that the concept of governance can be transferred to other disciplines including the social sciences. Even though it is quite flexible and covers several issues, the concept of governance may be ambiguous to some extent though it seems quite easy to comprehend irrespective of the fact that there may be some disagreements among social scientists concerning its meaning. In broad terms, governance has two different meanings. First, governance is a state of being governed. This concept is of political origin and meaning. Second, governance is a process and an act of governing power. This meaning reflects key preconditions for governing, active operators and their basic characteristics. It is more of the action and the influence of the governing system (Vymětal, 2007).

World Bank (2007) define governance as traditions and institutions through which a country exercises its authority. It consists of the selection, monitoring and replacement processes of governments; the government's ability to formulate and implement sound and effective policies; as well as the value for citizens and institutions governing social-economic interactions. The Asian Development Bank (1999) views governance as to how a government exercises its power in the management of economic and social resources of a country for developmental purposes. Governance is also conceptualized by the UNDP (1998) as the exercise of political, economic and administrative authority at every level to manage the affairs of a country as well as the means whereby social cohesion and integration are facilitated by States and through which the well-being of their populace is guaranteed. Governance encompasses all methods employed to distribute power and manage public resources; the organizations that form a government; and the conduct of policies and policymaking. It embraces the processes, mechanisms and institutions, in which people articulate their interests, carry out their legal rights, achieve their obligations and settle their differences (Vymětal, 2007).

Fukuyama (2013) and Iwarimie-Jaja and Lasisi (2019) described governance as a process whereby governments are responsible for providing for the needs of the people. This definition views governance in terms of its responsibility and effective administrative outcome. If the administrative outcome is good, then it is good governance; otherwise, it is bad governance. Some other scholars define governance based on its decision-making process. They include Sharma, Sadana and Harpreet (2013) who defined governance as to how government exercises its authority, control, or power to mobilize social and economic resources for the common interest of the general public. Nkana, Ekpu and Dode (2013) define the concept of governance as the management of the affairs of the State. Onichakwe (2016) sees governance as the decision-making process of the government as well as the process of implementing the decisions.

Some of the elements of (good) governance are political stability, safety and rule of law, bureaucratic accountability, participation and human rights, control of corruption and government effectiveness, among others. The definitions of governance earlier presented are quite narrow. The broad definitions of governance are those that defined governance to include its elements. For example, Sharma, Sadana and Kaur (2013) define governance (especially good) governance to include the implementation of established rule of law, contract enforcement, enforcement of agreements between people, maintenance of law and order, insurance of security, protection of the government faculties, and efficient service delivery and enforcement of appropriate use of government resources.

The social sector is a concept used to capture the education sector, nutrition sector, health sector and other sectors under social and community services. The concept of the social sector has two main views. One of these views is from the human capital development perspective, while the second view takes the approach of human development. The human capital development approach underscores investment in education, health and community services including nutrition as a channel for improving the quality of human capital, which, as defined by Sharma (2014) is the store of knowledge and creative skills embodied in people. Expenditures on education, health, on-the-job training, etc., comprise an investment made by people to develop them and is often referred to as human capital development. An investment in these sectors is stressed as a way to improve labour force productivity and is justified based on better chances of employment with a higher rate of financial return – as is the case of education development or estimates rising from production functions – as in the aspect of health.

An alternative view to the social sector is human development. The concept has been described by the UNDP as the process of broadening the choices of people. The term comprehends empowerment, equity in opportunity and capabilities, sustainability and security (Sharma, 2014). As stated by Sharma (2014), this view of social sector education, health and nutrition, for example, is betokened from their intrinsic value and does not concern their human capabilities enhancing role. Even though the two concepts have differences, they are linked on the basis that human capital development offers the precondition for the development of human resources necessary for employment and economic growth.

The social sector of a country is thus defined as the provision of social security wherein, the concept of social security is adopted in a broader sense. The definition of the social sector cannot be separated from what such the concept intends to achieve. If the purpose of human development is to meet some basic human requirements by enhancing the capabilities of the very poor people for their survival, then the two move towards capability enhancement, through income generation using rural development and employment programmes and government provision of education, health and other social services through government expenditure on education, health and other services cannot be seen to be exclusively mutual. In this chapter, the concept of the social sector includes education, health, nutrition and other social services. It is the improvement in people's welfare in terms of education, health and other social services, which in most cases are measured by government expenditures on education, health, nutrition, etc. Oftentimes, the concept of social security is connected to the rights of people. In this perspective, the provision of minimum income level, education, health and other social services such as nutrition could be considered people's basic rights.

It is also necessary to define social development. Sharma (2014) defines social development as a process of transforming values, institutions and practices through the use of deliberate policy instruments and planning with the engagement of people who are concerned with the aim of improving their standard of living. Social development describes the entire progression of a country, which can only be possible if the needs of individuals are satisfied. It can also be referred to as the development of the quality of life and social welfare of people. The interconnectedness of the two concepts (social development and social sector development) means that disparities in one may result in disparities in the other.

Employment can be described as all jobs (both in the formal or informal sector) or every person who, at a given reference period, were employed, regardless of the status of employment and irrespective of whether the job is a secondary job or the main job. Employment could also be described as all persons involved in one or more work hours in a given reference period, as well as individuals who are absent from work temporarily as a result of sickness, maternity leave or holidays (International Labour Organization, 2021).

The conceptualization and measurement of employment in most cases adequately grasp the reality of unemployment. Employment and unemployment are commonly considered dependent concepts, but not concepts that can be determined. Fleetwood (2001) describes the two concepts as objective states of affairs that are applied with subjective meaning for those passing through these states. International Labour Organization (2021) defines an unemployed person as an individual over age 15 with no work throughout a certain week, or who has already found but will begin in the next two weeks, and who is ready to begin work in the next three months. A common definition of unemployment is the percentage of people in the labour force (labour force is the totality of persons in employment and unemployment) who are not employed. It is also a common measure of employment.

The Keynesian theory of unemployment considers unemployment as an involuntary phenomenon that is cyclical and generated by a deficiency in aggregate demand. Whereas the neo-classical approach posits that employment (unemployment) is exogenous to the rate of growth of output, the Keynesian theory of employment is premised on the fact that the strength of demand determines the extent of resource utilization for every economy. As such, employment is demand-determined and economic growth is an important determinant of employment, such that growing output results in decreases in unemployment as more jobs would be created. Keynes visualized ineffective demand as the prime cause of unemployment. Therefore, to lower unemployment, effective demand has to be raised. That is, countries should pursue economic expansion as a way of reducing unemployment and one of such ways to achieve this is through government expenditure on commodities including social sector goods like education and health, in which good governance plays a pivotal role in its success.

Several recent studies have analyzed the effect of governance on different macroeconomic variables both in developed and developing countries. The study by Mohammadi, Shahnoush and Ronaghi (2016) examines the effects of governance indicators on per capita income, investment and employment in selected MENA countries from 2002 to 2012 using the granger causality test and vector auto-regression test techniques. The study found that governance indicators had a significant positive effect on per capita income, investment and employment. Using a case study of South Asian countries, Shabbir, Kousar, Kousar, Adeel and Jafar (2019) examine the effect of governance on unemployment from 1994 to 2016 using the panel vector error correction technique. The study found a negative and significant effect of governance on human capital and unemployment. The study also found bidirectional causality between governance and the unemployment rate. In a comparison of the European Union countries with the North American countries, Samarasinghe (2018) examines the impact of governance on economic growth from 2002 to 2014. The fixed effects and random effects techniques were employed for data analysis. The study found control of corruption as the most significant determinant of economic growth among political stability and absence of violence/terrorism indicators of governance. Focusing on the Sub-Sahara African countries, Fayissa and Nsiah (2013) examine the impact of governance on economic growth using the fixed and random effects and Arellano–Bond techniques. The study found that good governance contributed to the differences in growth in SSA countries. It was also found that the role of governance in economic growth depends on the level of income of the country. Employing the fixed effects technique, Fawaz, Mnif and Popiashvili (2021) examine the impact of governance on economic growth in low and high-income countries. The study covered the period from 1996 to 2018. The findings showed evidence of the significant impact of governance on economic growth.

3.2.2 Research Gaps

Existing recent studies have analyzed the effect of governance on different macroeconomic variables such as per capita income, investment and employment. Most of these studies (both at country levels and panel studies) have examined the effect of governance on economic growth but despite the large literature on governance, empirical evidence on the effect of governance on social sector development and employment especially in the SSA countries is lacking. Therefore, by providing empirical evidence on it, this chapter adds value to the body of existing knowledge in this area of study.

3.2.3 Objectives of the Study

The specific objectives of this chapter are:

i   To examine the effect of governance on unemployment in SSA and European countries
ii To determine the effect of governance on social sector development in SSA and European countries
iii To ascertain if there is a significant difference in the effects of governance between SSA and European countries.

3.3 Data and Method of Study

This chapter engaged annual data from selected SSA countries and European countries drawn from the World Development Indicators (WDI), Macro Trend database and the United Nations Development Programme composite report. The three top economies (Kenya, Morocco and Côte d'Ivoire) and the three least economies (Somalia, Chad and Sudan) in terms of governance performance according to the Ibrahim Index of African governance were selected to represent the SSA region. The three top economies (Finland, Sweden and Denmark) and the three least economies (Romania, Bulgaria and Greece) in European countries in terms of governance performance were also selected to represent Europe for this study (Ardielli, 2019). The reason for this selection is to include in this study, both the weak and the strong governance-performing economies in each of the two selected regions. The period of study covered 1996 to 2020. The variables engaged by our study are the governance variables (control of corruption, safety and rule of law, political stability and absence of violence/terrorism, and government effectiveness), unemployment rate – a measure for employment and social sector development – proxied by an index of social development (SDI). The other variables are per capita gross domestic product and population growth.

The governance variables and measures used are broad and appropriate. The measures capture the two mean governance structures or dimensions – the political and economic governance dimensions. Control of corruption, political stability and absence of violence/terrorism measures are the political dimensions of governance while safety and rule of law, and government effectiveness measure the economic dimension of governance. Control of corruption captures the government's anti-corruption policies. It includes the prevention of public power by public office holders for private gains, the extent of irregular payments, the level of corruption in administration and cases of corruption in public institutions. Political stability, on the other hand, captures the level of politically inspired violence, terrorism, armed conflicts and social unrest. The rule of law captures the confidence in a country's judicial system, the quality of contract enforcement, property rights, law enforcement against violent and organized crime (the police and the court) and judicial independence. This indicator is a proxy for the entire quality of the legal system of a country. Government effectiveness, for example, captures the level of quality and satisfaction of public services, infrastructure and bureaucracy of government by the general public. This indicator makes a proxy for the government's ability to deliver efficient and effective governmental policies.

In the literature, unemployment rate commonly measures the extent of employment. The SDI is a broad measure of social sector development. The index combines more than 200 indicators from 25 sources to generate a composite index of social sector development (de Haan & Foa, 2014). It is a well-known index in the literature. The control variables such as per capita gross domestic product and population growth are chosen on the basis of the theoretical framework used and economic realities.

The data sources are the WDI, the Macro Trend database and the United Nations Development Programme composite report. The data on the governance variables were sourced from the WDI, while the data on unemployment, per capita GDP and population growth rate were sourced from the Macro Trend database. The data on the SDI, on the other hand, was sourced from the United Nations Development Programme composite report. All results were generated using STATA version 16 econometric package.

To establish the relationship between governance and employment, a dynamic panel unemployment equation is specified. The functional form of the model is specified as:

$$UNEMP_{it} = u\left(CCOR_{it}, SRLAW_{it}, GEFFECT_{it}, PSTAB_{it}, PGDP_{it}, POPG_{it}\right) \quad (3.1)$$

The panel model specification of Equation (3.1) is:

$$UNEMP_{it} = \beta + \beta_x E_{it} + \beta_z W_{it} + \gamma_{it} + \varepsilon_{it} \quad (3.2)$$

where $UNEMP_{it}$ is the unemployment rate and E_{it} is a set of governance variables, which are control of corruption, safety and rule of law, government effectiveness and political stability and absence of violence/terrorism; W_{it} is a set of control variables, which are per capita GDP and population growth rate; γ_{it} is a between-country error term; ε_{it} is a within-country error term; i is observational units and t is time.

To fit a linear model with one dynamic variable $\left(UNEMP_{i,\ t-1}\right)$, we add the dynamic variable:

$$UNEMP_{it} = \beta_0 + \beta_1 UNEMP_{i,\ t-1} + \beta_2 CCOR_{it} + \beta_3 SRLAW_{it} + \beta_4 GEFFECT_{it} \\ + \beta_5 PSTAB_{it} + \beta_6 PGDP_{it} + \beta_7 POPG_{it} + \gamma_{it} + \varepsilon_{it} \qquad (3.3)$$

Equation (3.3) is specified to capture the effect of governance on unemployment. It will be estimated specifically for the SSA countries and European countries, respectively. To estimate the effect of governance on social sector development, on the other hand, the unemployment variable $(UNEMP)$ in Equation (3.3) will be substituted with the SDI and the equation will be estimated again, respectively, for the SSA countries and European countries.

The estimation technique of the equations is the GMM, developed by Arellano and Bover (1995) and Blundell and Bond (1998). This technique is preferable because the presence of the lagged dependent variables (for example, $UNEMP$ in Equation 3.3) at the right-hand side of the regression equations leads to autocorrelation. Also, some of the right-hand side variables could be endogenous. For example, the per capita GDP (PGDP) variable in the models is assumed to be endogenous because causality may run in both directions: from per capita GDP to the SDI and unemployment and vice versa. Time-invariant country characteristics (fixed effects), like that of geography and demographics, may be correlated with the explanatory variables in the respective regression equations. The fixed effects are captured in the error term, which consists of the unobserved country-specific effects $\left(\gamma_{it}\right)$ and the observation-specific errors $\left(\varepsilon_{it}\right)$. Fixed-effects instrumental variables estimation (two-stage least squares or 2SLS) can be used, but the instruments could be weak at the first stage of the 2SLS regressions. With weak instruments, the fixed-effects IV estimators could be biased in the way of the ordinary least square (OLS) estimators. In the GMM framework, the Sargan test of overidentifying restrictions is mostly used to test if the model is overidentified. The null hypothesis is that overidentifying restrictions are valid.

3.4 Results

The variables were tested for unit root using the Im, Persaran and Shin (IPS) unit root test, while Pedroni's test for cointegration was employed to test for the cointegration of the variables. The results are reported in Table 3.1. Panel A of Table 3.1 reports the IPS results, while panel B presents Pedroni's cointegration test results.

Table 3.1 shows that none of the variables was significant at the 5% level for both the SSA countries and the European countries. Therefore, the null hypothesis of all panels containing unit roots is accepted at the level. This warranted differencing the variables once in both regions. At 1st difference,

Table 3.1 Im, Persaran and Shin (IPS) Unit Root Test and Pedroni's Test for Cointegration

Panel A: Im, Pesaran and Shin (IPS) Unit Root Test

For Sub-Saharan African Countries

Variable	ADF – Statistic Level	1st Diff.	Lag	~I(d)
GEFFECT	-0.3247 (0.3727)	-5.2282 (0.0000)*	2	I(1)
SRLAW	-0.3868 (0.3494)	-4.9494 (0.0000)*	2	I(1)
CCOR	-0.0672 (0.5268)	-3.0275 (0.0012)*	2	I(1)
PSTAB	-1.5858 (0.0564)	-2.5589 (0.0053)*	2	I(1)
PGDP	-0.9280 (0.8233)	-2.0796 (0.0402)*	2	I(1)
POPG	-0.9075 (0.1282)	-5.0479 (0.0000)*	2	I(1)
UNEMP	-0.9305 (0.2268)	-2.9966 (0.0014)*	2	I(1)
SDI	-0.9363 (0.1746)	-2.5339 (0.0025)*	2	I(1)

For European Countries

Variable	ADF – Statistic Level	1st Diff.	Lag	~I(d)
GEFFECT	-1.1992 (0.1152)	-5.6913 (0.0000)*	2	I(1)
SRLAW	-1.2043 (0.1142)	-3.3479 (0.0004)*	2	I(1)
CCOR	-0.1358 (0.5540)	-3.6634 (0.0001)*	2	I(1)
PSTAB	-0.8030 (0.1025)	-2.8030 (0.0025)*	2	I(1)
RGDP	-0.1418 (0.1012)	-4.3468 (0.0000)*	2	I(1)
POPG	-1.9560 (0.0452)	-3.1434 (0.0008)*	2	I(1)
UNEMP	-1.3948 (0.0815)	-2.4525 (0.0071)*	2	I(1)
SDI	-0.2054 (0.4186)	-3.3561 (0.0004)*	2	I(1)

1. Im, Pesaran and Shin (IPS) p-values are presented in parenthesis. 2. * denotes significance at 5% and the rejection of the null hypothesis of the panels containing unit roots. 3. Cross-sectional means were removed to help control for possible correlation of panels

Panel B: Pedroni's Test for Cointegration

For Sub-Saharan African Countries

	Test Statistic
Modified Phillips–Perron t	2.9066 (p = 0.0018)
Phillips–Perron t	-1.0388 (p = 0.0195)
Augmented Dickey-Fuller t	-1.7976 (p = 0.0361)

For European Countries

	Test Statistic
Modified Phillips–Perron t	3.1284 (p = 0.0009)
Phillips–Perron t	2.0825 (p = 0.0395)
Augmented Dickey-Fuller t	1.5404 (p = 0.0417)

Source: Authors' computations.

the variables became significant at the 5% level. Thus, the null hypothesis is rejected at 1st difference. This means that all the variables are stationary at 1st difference for both the SSA countries and the European countries.

The modified Phillips–Perron, the Phillips–Perron and the Augmented Dickey–Fuller tests statistics are significant in both regions. This guides us to reject the null hypothesis of no cointegration at the 5% level. This means that all panels are cointegrated. We went further to estimate the panel models using the GMM techniques and the results are reported in Table 3.2.

In Table 3.2, column A reports the GMM results of the effect of governance on unemployment (column A1) and social sector development (column A2) in SSA countries, while column B presents the results of the effects of governance on unemployment (column B1) and social sector development (column B2) in European countries.

In column A1, all the coefficients of governance variables, respectively, showed a negative coefficient. This means that an improvement in those areas of governance leads to a reduction in unemployment. In other words, an improvement in governance in terms of more effective government, appropriate control of corruption, safety and rule of law, political stability and absence of violence/terrorism led to an increase in employment in the SSA countries. Government effectiveness, control of corruption, political stability and absence of violence/terrorism were significant at the 5% level, indicating that the variables were significant determinants of employment in the countries in the region. Safety and rule of law, on the other hand, was not significant. This implies that though, it increased employment, the increase in employment associated with safety and rule of law was not significant. Per capita GDP also, had a negative and significant effect on unemployment, implying that an increase in per capita GDP brings about an increase in employment. Population growth, however, brought about a non-significant increase in unemployment (decrease in employment).

In column A2, the coefficients of governance variables were positive and significant at the 5% level. This means that the variables were significant determinants of social sector development in SSA countries. Good governance through effective government, control of corruption, safety and rule of law, political stability and absence of violence/terrorism significantly stimulated social sector development in SSA countries. An increase in per capita GDP also led to a significant increase in social sector development by 0.02%, while an increase in population growth negatively affected social sector development by 0.01%.

As regards the European countries, the coefficients of governance variables, respectively, in column B1 were negative and significant. This suggests the rejection of the null hypothesis of governance having no significant effect on unemployment in European countries. The governance variables significantly reduced unemployment. It implies that in European countries, employment was significantly determined by the effective government, control of corruption, safety and rule of law, political stability and absence of violence/terrorism. Good governance in these areas significantly increased

Table 3.2 GMM Estimates of the Effects of Governance on Employment and Social Sector Development

	(A) For Sub-Saharan African Countries		(B) For European Countries	
	(A1) Unemployment	(A2) Social Sector Development	(B1) Unemployment	(B2) Social Sector Development
GEFFECT	−0.2708 (z = −2.46) (p = 0.030)	0.0022 (z = 2.46) (p = 0.027)	−0.3787 (z = 2.82) (p = 0.000)	0.0015 (z = 3.72) (p = 0.000)
SRLAW	−0.2267 (z = −1.10) (p = 0.269)	0.0041 (z = 2.80) (p = 0.022)	−0.0262 (z = −2.12) (p = 0.039)	0.0008 (z = 3.41) (p = 0.000)
CCOR	−0.1565 (z = −2.80) (p = 0.023)	0.0043 (z = 3.87) (p = 0.000)	−0.1231 (z = −3.81) (p = 0.000)	0.0004 (z = 2.26) (p = 0.030)
PSTAB	−0.2583 (z = −2.05) (p = 0.041)	0.0021 (z = 3.63) (p = 0.000)	−0.3426 (z = −2.77) (p = 0.006)	0.0003 (z = 0.03) (p = 0.978)
PGDP	−0.0003 (z = −2.25) (p = 0.036)	0.0211 (z = 3.37) (p = 0.001)	−1.5500 (z = −3.33) (p = 0.000)	3.4000 (z = 3.52) (p = 0.000)
POPG	0.0284 (z = 0.26) (p = 0.797)	−0.0068 (z = −2.30) (p = 0.021)	0.3070 (z = 1.30) (p = 0.195)	0.0002 (z = 0.13) (p = 0.895)
Constant	289.6896 (z = 2.02) (p = 0.043)	0.0595 (z = 3.28) (p = 0.001)	1.4183 (z = 2.65) (p = 0.008)	0.0553 (z = 3.38) (p = 0.001)
Wald chi2(8)	496.44 (p = 0.0000)	1895.80 (p = 0.0000)	353.64 (p = 0.0000)	5580.40 (p = 0.0000)
Sargan chi2(118)	12.0972 (p = 0.3099)	119.7166 (p = 0.4901)	120.2839 (p = 0.4755)	118.5992 (p = 0.5190)

Source: Authors' computations.

employment in European countries. Also, an increase in per capita GDP led to an increase in employment, while an increase in population was not significant in reducing employment.

To ascertain if there was a significant difference in the effects of governance between Europe and SSA countries, we compared the absolute z-values of the governance variables for Europe and SSA countries. The absolute z-values of government effectiveness, control of corruption, safety and rule of law, political stability and absence of violence/terrorism for Europe were greater than the z-values of the variables for SSA countries. This shows that the effect of governance on employment and social sector development in European countries was more significant than its effect in SSA countries. All the European countries selected had better governance performance (higher governance values for the indicators selected) than the SSA countries. Therefore, the higher governance effect (z-values) for European countries implies that governance was more effective in determining employment and social sector development in developed countries in terms of good governance than in developing countries.

3.5 Conclusion

This chapter has examined the relationship between governance, social sector development and employment in European and SSA countries, comparing Europe with the SSA countries to ascertain if there was a significant difference in the effect of governance and, therefore, the role of governance upon social sector development and employment. Based on the findings, it is concluded that good governance is crucial to ensuring social sector development, which is also necessary for achieving key macroeconomic goals such as employment. Higher governance performance specifically in government effectiveness, control of corruption, safety and rule of law, political stability and absence of violence/terrorism is associated with higher employment and social sector development, which is the reason for the significant difference in the effect of governance on social sector development and employment between Europe and SSA. Other variables such as per capita GDP and population growth also play diverse roles in affecting employment and social sector development of Europe and SSA countries. SSA countries, in particular, should set good governance as a top priority and set a timeframe and work towards improving the governance performance to achieve the target within the specified timeframe.

References

Ardielli, E. (2019). Use of TOPSIS method for assessing of good governance in European Union countries. *Review of Economic Perspectives*, 19(3), 211–231.

Arellano, M. & Bover, O. (1995), Another look at the instrumental variable estimation of error-components models. *Journal of Econometrics*, 68, 29–51.

Asian Development Bank (1999). Governance: Sound development management.

Blundell, R. & Bond, S. (1998). Initial conditions and moment restrictions in dynamic panel data models. *Journal of Econometrics*, 87, 115–143.

Chadha, V. & Chadda, I. (2019). Social sector development as a catalyst of inclusive growth in India. *Journal of the Gujarat Research Society*, 21(4), 144–149.

Chankseliani, M., Qoraboyev, I. & Gimranova, D. (2020). Higher education contributing to local, national, and global development: new empirical and conceptual insights. *Higher Education*, 81, 109–127.

de Haan, A. & Foa, R. (2014). *Indices of social development and their application to Africa*. United Nations University (UNU)-WIDER Working Paper No. 132. https://www.researchgate.net/publication/336693437_Indices_of_social_development_and_their_application_to_Africa

Enwere, C. (2013). *Impact of the political leadership on industrial development in Nigeria: Issues and challenges of the national economic empowerment and development strategy*. Available at: https://www.researchgate.net/publication/320288525_Impact_of_the_Political_Leadership_on_Industrial_Development_in_Nigeria_Issues_and_Challenges_of_the_National_Economic_Empowerment_and_Development_Strategy

Fawaz, F., Mnif, A. & Popiashvili, A. (2021). Impact of governance on economic growth in developing countries: A case of HIDC vs. LIDC. *Journal of Social Science and Economic Development*, 23, 44–58.

Fayissa, B. & Nsiah, C. (2013). Impact of governance on economic growth in Africa. *The Journal of Developing Areas*, 47(1), 162–178.

Fleetwood, S. (2001). Conceptualizing unemployment in a period of atypical employment: A critical realist perspective. *Review of Social Economy*, 59(1), 45–69.

Fukuyama, F. (2013). *What is governance?* Centre for Global Development Working Paper No. 314.

Gisselquist, R. M. (2012). *Good governance as a concept, and why this matters for development policy*. United Nations University – Wider Working Paper No. 30.

Grant, C. (2017). *The contribution of education to economic growth*. Knowledge, Evidence and Learning for Development Helpdesk Report. Available at: https://assets.publishing.service.gov.uk/media/5b9b87f340f0b67896977bae/K4D_HDR_The_Contribution_of_Education_to_Economic_Growth_Final.pdf

Holmes, R., McCord, A., Hagen-Zanker, J., Bergh, G. & Zanker, F. (2013). *What is the evidence on the impact of employment creation on stability and poverty reduction in fragile states: A systematic review*. Available at: https://assets.publishing.service.gov.uk/media/57a08a15e5274a31e00003fa/What_is_the_evidence_on_the_impact_of_employment_creation_on_stability_and_poverty_reduction_in_fragile_states.pdf

Ibrahim Index of African Governance Report (2020). *2020 Ibrahim Index of African Governance – Index Report*. Mo Ibrahim Foundation. Available at: https://mo.ibrahim.foundation/sites/default/files/2020-11/2020-index-report.pdf

International Labour Organisation – INTERNATIONAL LABOUR ORGANIZATION (2021). *Employment*. Available at: https://www.insee.fr/en/metadonnees/definition/c1159

International Labour Organization (2021). *Unemployment, total (% of the total labour force) (Modeled INTERNATIONAL LABOUR ORGANIZATION estimate) – Sub-Saharan Africa*. Available at: https://data.worldbank.org/indicator/SL.UEM.TOTL.ZS?locations=ZG

Islam, R. (2004). *The nexus of economic growth, employment and poverty reduction: An empirical analysis*. Issues in Employment and Poverty Discussion Paper,

No. 14. Geneva: International Labour Organization, Recovery and Reconstruction Department.

Iwarimie-Jaja, D. & Lasisi, R. (2019). Good governance, social order and development in Nigeria. *Port Harcourt Journal of Social Sciences*, 8(1), 295–313.

Leibbrandt, M. & Woolard, I. (2001). Household incomes, poverty and inequality in a multivariate framework. In H. Bhorat, M. Leibbrandt, M. Maziya, S. van der Berg, & I. Woolard (Eds) *Fighting Poverty: Labour Markets and Inequality in South Africa. Cape Town*, South Africa: UCT Press.

Lucas, R. (1988). On the mechanics of economic development. *Journal of Monetary Economics*, 22(1), 3–42.

Mankiw, G. N., Romer, D. & Weil, D. (1992). A contribution to the empirics of economic growth. *Quarterly Journal of Economics*, 107(2), 407–437.

Mohammadi, H., Shahnoush, N. & Ronaghi, M. (2016). The effects of governance indicators on per capita income, investment and employment in selected Mena countries. *Iran Economic Review*, 21(2), 211–229.

Nelson, R. & Phelps, E. (1966). Investment in humans, technological diffusion and economic growth. *American Economic Review*, 5(2), 69–75.

Nkana, N. S., Ekpu, F. S. & Dode, R. O. (2013). *Citizenship and Peace Studies*. Uyo: CHF.

Onichakwe, C. C. (2016). The role of good governance and development administration in national development. *International Journal of Development and Management Review*, 11, 176–186.

Ott, J. (2010). Good governance and happiness in nations: Technical quality precedes democracy and quality beats size. *Journal of Happiness Studies*, 11(3), 353–368.

Pattayat, S. S. & Rani, P. (2017). Social sector development and economic growth in Haryana. *Journal of Economics and Economic Education Research*, 18(3), 1–13.

Pettinger, T. (2019). *Economic costs of unemployment*. Available at: https://www.economicshelp.org/macroeconomics/unemployment/costs/

Samarasinghe, T. (2018). *Impact of governance on economic growth*. Munich Personal RePEc Archive Working Paper No. 89834.

Schoch, M. & Lakner, C. (2020). *African countries show mixed progress towards poverty reduction and half of them have an extreme poverty rate above 35%*. Available at: https://blogs.worldbank.org/opendata/african-countries-show-mixed-progress-towards-poverty-reduction-and-half-them-have-extreme

Shabbir, A., Kousar, S., Kousar, F., Adeel, A. & Jafar, R. A. (2019). Investigating the effect of governance on unemployment: A case of South Asian countries. *International Journal of Management and Economics*, 55(2), 160–181.

Sharma, D. A. (2014). Understanding the social sector, economic growth, social development and economic development: Interrelationship and linkages. *Economic Affairs*, 59(4), 585–590.

Sharma, M. P., Sadana, B. L. & Kaur, H. (2013). *Public Administration, in Theory, and Practice*. Kitab Mahal: Marg Allahabad.

UNDP (1998). *Governance: Experiences and lessons learned*. Lessons Learned Series No. 1. Available at: http://magnet.undp.org/docs/gov/Lessons1.htm

UNICEF (2021). *Education Sector Analysis Methodological Guidelines Volume III*. Available at: https://www.unicef.org/media/101366/file/Education%20Sector%20Analysis%20-%20Volume3.pdf

United Nations Development Programme (2013). *Social protection, growth and employment: Evidence from India, Kenya, Malawi, Mexico and Tajikistan.*
Vymĕtal, P. (2007). *Governance: Defining the concept.* Available at: https://www.researchgate.net/publication/40345960_Governance_defining_the_concept
World Bank (2007). *World Development Report: The State in Changing World.* Washington D.C.: World Bank.

4 Effectiveness of Good Governance on Human Development
Empirical Evidence from Selected Countries in the World

Kishor Naskar, Sourav Kumar Das and Tonmoy Chatterjee

4.1 Introduction

Economists have often blamed the mishandling of resource optimization as a major cause of the poor status of wellbeing in labour-rich countries. As the main moto of a developing economy is to enhance the level of wellbeing of its people, concentration on resource handling is encouraged (Pradhan & Sanyal, 2011). Traditional literature claims that improvement in wellbeing is possible only through better economic growth and development (Ahamed & Saleem, 2014). In fact, per capita gross domestic product (GDP) has been categorically employed in order to describe the wellbeing of the people. However, in the recent past, such a simplistic approach to look at the wellbeing issue has been questioned, as mainstream economic measures may not be able to capture the wellbeing of people by ignoring multidimensional aspects like economic, social and cultural (Despotis, 2005; Pradhan, 2007). It is to be noted that later, the focus has been shifted from the growth aspect to the multidimensionality of human development in order to show the significance of social activities in the process of development (Clarke et al., 2006; Clarke & Islam, 2004; Daly, 1996; Dodds, 1997; Doyal and Gough, 1991; McGillivray, 1991; Nussbaum, 2000; Stiglitz, 2002).

However, the effectiveness of human development in order to reveal society from a multidimensional angle may depend upon a proper policy implementation and substantial set up in all the dimensions simultaneously. To maintain such simultaneity, the state should intervene with effective governance (Anand & Ravallion, 1993; Fukuda-Parr, 2003). In fact, quality governance has a crucial function in several associated fields for instance health, environment protection, infrastructure, economic stability, creation of a good business environment education, legal system, etc. All such elements are the basic requirement for the development process of a country and fulfilment of these can influence human development (Boeninger, 1992; Brautigam, 1991; Landell-Mills & Serageldin, 1991). Governance has a significant effect on sustained economic growth, development as well as human welfare, at least in the very long run (Kaufmann & Kraay, 2002; Kaufmann, Kraay & Mastruzzi, 2010; Pradhan & Sanyal, 2011; Sebudubudu, 2010; Turner, 2011).

DOI: 10.4324/9781003245797-5

From such a brief introduction, we can accumulate enough information by which we can argue that human development and governance are associated with each other. More precisely, the effectiveness of good governance on human development is remaining at the centre of our research. Under such a backdrop, we employ a panel data set up to endorse the just mentioned motivation behind the present chapter.

The rest of the chapter is organized in the following manner. Sections 4.2 and 3.3 provide the concept of good governance with a literature review and describe data and methodology, respectively. Section 3.4 discusses the results of the empirical exercise, and conclusions are made in Section 3.5.

4.2 Literature Review

The term "Good Governance" has been extensively used in every spare of administration during the last three decades. This concept incorporates a variety of principles and is described in a number of important documents with international scope (Klimovský, 2010). However, good governance is not legislatively defined at the national or international level. A comprehensive look at the issue of good governance is available in the "Council of Europe (COE) Recommendation on good administration" from 2007; see Council of Europe (2007) and its supplement.

It is a difficult transition which can affect people and groups engaged in power conflicts at the economic and political levels (CIPE, 2002, p. 9). Experiencing globalization process, we can observe that good governance as the prerequisite of perfection and effective policy intervention is one of the factors of this phenomenon of generalizing good practices. Girishankar (2001) defined governance as the power to run economic, social and political institutions and mentioned those dimensions of this power which were (a) the process of selecting government, accountability, monitoring and replacement of government, (b) efficient management of resources, formulation and implementation of sound policies by government and (c) respect of social and economic institutions.

Rothstein and Teorell (2008) make a similar distinction between two dimensions of good governance, namely (1) elements that concern (citizen's) access to authority of a state or nation, which would include democratic accountability and (2) elements that concern the exercise of authority, thus referring to the implementation side.

Khan (2007) examined theoretically the impact of governance on economic development. There are two points of view regarding governance, one is about the state capacities that are necessary for speeding up the development process and the other is about the importance of governance factors relative to other economic variables associated with development.

Chaudhry et al. (2009) analyzed various factors that impact good governance in Pakistan. They have taken the macroeconomic variables and by using time series data from 1972 to 2007 explored their relationship using the Ordinary Least Squares (OLS) regression technique. Good governance provides an environment favourable for investment no matter international or in local markets, people increasing their education and skill which can give them higher income and thus contribute towards better economic and social indicators.

Torres and Anderson (2004) declared that a state with poor governance is a fragile state. They provided a complete overview of the fragile states. Severe problems are attached to the fragile states, such as poverty, violations of human rights, conflict issues, unstable state policy and regional security threats. The situations of fragility could also be observed by considering the social environment of the country as well. In such a situation, the effective utilization and mobilization of domestic as well as international resources become difficult.

Fayissa and Nsiah (2010) tested the significance of governance for economic growth in African economies. They used panel data from 28 African countries from 1995 to 2005. There is a positive significant relationship between good governance and economic growth.

Haq and Zia (2009) developed a link between the quality of governance and pro-poor growth in Pakistan for the period from 1996 to 2005. Pro-poor growth is measured by three variables: income inequality, poverty (percentage of the population below the poverty line) and growth. Two variables; voice and accountability and political instability were used to measure political governance. Government effectiveness and regulatory quality were used to measure economic governance, rule of law and control of corruption were used to measure institutional governance. The results showed that both indicators of political governance were significantly and inversely related to poverty, one economic governance indicator, that is, regulatory quality had a negative and significant impact on poverty and, finally, institutional governance that is rule of law was also inversely related to poverty.

Turner (2011) examined that sustainable development impact positively on the governance of developing countries if spending on the poor ensures equality as it gives importance to the poorest citizens of the society with the data on sub-Saharan African countries from 1996 to 2009. It considers them in decision-making process. As a result, government consumption expenditure, control of corruption and government effectiveness improve and play a major role in bringing sustainable growth and development. He concluded that sustainable growth and development can be achieved through working for the poor, making them self-sufficient and thus helping them to participate in decision-making. It will improve the governance of the countries as a result.

Rodrik (2000) argues that democracies rather than autocracies generate more predictable long-term growth rates and generate greater stability in the short term, absorb negative shocks more effectively and result in a less skewed distribution of income.

From the above literature review, we can say that institutions can be thought of as the "set of rules" that determine the behaviour of individuals within a society. Governance can be seen as the outcome of the effectiveness of a society's institutions. If the institutions are appropriate and effective, the outcome should be good governance (Duncan, 2003). If governance is an outcome of the appropriateness and effectiveness of a country's institutions (formal and informal), governance indicators can be seen as indicators of the quality of a country's institutions. Besley and Burgess (2003) argue that greater emphasis on institutional reforms to expand household opportunities, improve the business environment and enhance the accountability of elected officials are important in reducing poverty and achieving higher growth levels. Hence, poor governance caused and reinforced poverty and also made to improve the living standard of the poor. This study tries to find the relationship between good governance and human development.

4.3 Methodology and Materials

4.3.1 Sources of Data

To measure the quality of governance this study uses the six Worldwide Governance Indicators (WGIs) developed and maintained by the World Bank. We label these WGIs as WGI1, WGI2, WGI3, WGI4, WGI5 and WGI6. Based on the World Bank's definitions, we provide a brief description of each of the WGIs. WGI1 (control of corruption) indicates the extent to which public power is used for private gain and the extent to which public power is controlled by private interests. WGI2 (government effectiveness) measures the quality of the public or civil service and the degree to which it is independent of the political process. It also includes the quality of policy formulation and the government's commitment to its implementation. WGI3 (political stability and absence of violence/terrorism) identifies the extent to which a government may be overthrown by unconstitutional or violent means. WGI4 (regulatory quality) captures the extent to which a government develops and implements sound policies for the regulation and development of the private sector. WGI5 (rule of law) measures the extent to which people have confidence in and abide by the laws of the land, including civil and business laws and the possibility of crime and violence. WGI6 (voice and accountability) indicates the extent to which people are able to freely participate in social media, etc.

The data on governance indicators are taken from the World Bank's project of WGI; under this project, Kaufmann et al. (1999) develop the six indicators to measure governance. Data on Human Development Index (HDI), for 164 countries for the duration 2002–2019, are taken from United Nations Development Programme (UNDP). Human development is not a local issue; rather, in general, it is treated as a global phenomenon. In order to describe a status quo of a nation from the perspective of economic and social development, human development plays a crucial role. Hence, we use an almost global panel consisting of 164 nations to critically explore the behavioural pattern of human development and causation with other factors by means of spatial and time heterogeneity techniques. Therefore, the use of large samples like ours always help policy- and law-makers to find the threshold marking of human development and, thereby, can implement new policy and realignment of the existing policy measures. Linear Regression Analysis has been used to fulfil the objectives. Principal Component Analysis (PCA) has been used to estimate the major components that are responsible for the nexus between governance and the HDI.

4.3.2 Constructing Human Development Index

HDI as an indicator of development was developed by the UNDP (Human Development Report, 1990 & 2020). The HDI is a composite index of three social indicators: life expectancy, adult literacy and years of schooling. It also takes into account real GDP per capita. Thus, the HDI is a composite index of achievements in three fundamental dimensions: living a long and healthy life, being educated and having a decent standard of living.

The HDI value of a country is calculated by taking three indicators: 1. Longevity, as measured by life expectancy at birth. 2. Educational attainment, as measured by a combination of adult literacy (two-thirds weight) and combined primary, secondary and tertiary enrolment ratio (one-third weight). 3. Decent standard of living, as measured by real GDP per capita based on purchasing power parity in terms of dollar (PPP$).

Before the HDI is calculated, an index is created for each of these dimensions: Life Expectancy Index, Education Index and GDP Index. To calculate these indices, minimum and maximum values or goalposts are chosen for each indicator as shown in Table 4.1.

Performance in each dimension is expressed as a value between 0 and 1 by applying the following formula. The HDI is then calculated as a simple average of the three dimension indices.

$$HDI = \left(\text{Life Expectancy Index} + \text{Educational attainment Index} + \text{Real GDP per capita Index}\right) / 3$$

The HDI value for each country indicates the distance it has travelled towards the maximum possible value of 1 and how far it has to go to attain certain defined goals: an average life span of 85 years, access to education

Table 4.1 Indicators of HDI

Indicator	Minimum Value	Maximum Value
(i) Life expectancy at birth	25	85
(ii) Adult-literacy rate	0%	100%
(iii) Combined gross enrolment ratio	0%	100%
(iv) Real GDP per capita (PPP*S)	$100	$40000

Source: UNDP, www.undp.org.

for all and GDP per capita. The HDI ranks countries in relation to each other. A country's HDI rank is within the world distribution, that is, it is based on its HDI value in relation to each developed and developing country for which the particular country has travelled from the minimum HDI value of 0 towards the maximum HDI value of 1. Countries with an HDI value below 0.5 are considered to have a low level of human development, those between 0.5 and 0.8, a medium level, and those above 0.8, a high level. In the HDI, countries are also ranked by their GDP per capita.

4.3.3 Constructing Governance Index

The WGI are a long-standing research project to develop cross-country indicators of governance. The WGI consist of six composite indicators of broad dimensions of governance covering over 163 countries since 2002: Voice and Accountability, Political Stability and Absence of Violence/Terrorism, Government Effectiveness, Regulatory Quality, Rule of Law and Control of Corruption. These indicators are based on several hundred variables obtained from 31 different data sources, capturing governance perceptions as reported by survey respondents, non-governmental organizations, commercial business information providers and public sector organizations worldwide.

- Voice and Accountability (VA) – capturing perceptions of the extent to which a country's citizens are able to participate in selecting their government, as well as freedom of expression, freedom of association and a free media.
- Political Stability and Absence of Violence/Terrorism (PV) – capturing perceptions of the likelihood that the government will be destabilized or overthrown by unconstitutional or, violent means, including politically motivated violence and terrorism.
- Government Effectiveness (GE) – capturing perceptions of the quality of public services, the quality of the civil service and the degree of its independence from political pressures, the quality of policy formulation and implementation and the credibility of the government's commitment to such policies.
- Regulatory Quality (RQ) – capturing perceptions of the ability of the government to formulate and implement sound policies and regulations that permit and promote private sector development.
- Rule of Law (RL) – capturing perceptions of the extent to which agents have confidence in and abide by the rules of society and, in particular, the quality of contract enforcement, property rights, the police and the courts, as well as the likelihood of crime and violence.
- Control of Corruption (CC) – capturing perceptions of the extent to which public power is exercised for private gain, including both petty and grand forms of corruption, as well as "capture" of the state by elites and private interests.

4.4 Functional Relationship between Worldwide Governance Indicators and Human Development Index

Good governance should be conceptualized as a goal and as a process that accelerates growth, equity and human development potential for the people and the society. Worldwide good governance indicators have been accepted for six broad indices classified as voice and accountability, rule of law, government effectiveness, political stability, regulatory framework and corruption.

Voice and accountability capture the participation of the public in the voting process, freedom of press and media, freedom from control, civil liberties and freedom of choices coupled with control and participatory institutional policy-making (Kaufmann, Kraay & Mastruzzi, 2009). People are happier when they feel that they are free to make key life decisions and that this impact is above and beyond the effects of better health and higher incomes that greater freedom may enable them to achieve. Wellbeing is slightly higher where civil rights are greater and where press freedom is greater. Freedom of choice needs to be sufficient, but there can be too much of a good thing – when choices and brands multiply, making decisions is harder and post-decision regret is more likely (Iyengar & Lepper, 2000).

Citizens with a voice in policy-making and the governance of institutions could impact human development in several ways. Assuming that people are the best judges of their needs and preferences, allowing the citizen to have a bigger say in the direction of government should create a government that better suits their needs. In contrast, policies made through procedures that exclude the public could alienate the public and reduce wellbeing, even if the outcomes are fair and desirable (Frey & Stutzer, 2000).

The aggregate indicator "rule of law" depends on judicial independence, courts' scrutiny of law, judicial control on governance and judicial review. Fairness and the rule of law are closely related. Trust and the rule of law are substitutes. With respect to trust, there is less ambiguity: people are happier living where trust levels are high. Across communities and countries, trust and trustworthiness go hand in hand (Knack, 2001). It is said that laws are there but there are applied only in favour of privilege people or class (Levithan, 2001). The environment of inappropriate and non-observance of the rule of law can outweigh the basic rights of the poor, which is an important aspect of good governance (Mollah, 2003). To establish rule of law transparency is a prerequisite condition.

The aggregate indicator "government effectiveness" indicates the provision of providing quality civic services, free from political interference, formulation of policies with effective implementation and reliability and responsiveness to such policies. The administration can merely take free and fair decisions. The indicator "political stability" takes into account politically motivated violence including terrorism. Corruption is another aspect of fairness. Subjective wellbeing is significantly lower where there is more corruption (Kaufmann et al., 2008). It is possible that improving the inclusiveness of government decreases corruption if citizens who are directly involved are better able to discover and stop improper behaviour. For sustainable development, government functionaries should not act as "rent-seekers" (World Bank, 1996).

With the help of a diagram (Figure 4.1, we explain the functional relationships among the indicators of good governance and human development.

The six factors are mutually related to each other to make success the effectiveness of other indicators. Figure 4.1 explains the effectiveness of the governance indicators upon overall development. Voice and accountability are the prerequisites to establishing the rule of law, and the rule of law is very much essential for the government effectiveness. Government effectiveness determines the regulatory quality. Along with the above four factors, political stability and control of corruption influence the decision-making environment which affects the country's socioeconomic environment for effective activities of socio-economic institutions and policy choices for better use of natural resources to influence the decisions of different economic agents, such as private investors. The decision-making environment also influences the decisions of the different actors involved in implementing policies and programs. Thus influencing the effectiveness of policy interventions, it creates a productive environment within the society. Both the political stability and rule of law indices examine crime levels, vulnerability to coups, ethnic and religious tensions, protection of property rights, corruption and quality of the bureaucracy. The governance indicators constituting the decision-making environment may also influence the political processes. For example, if the poor lack confidence in the state's ability to meet their

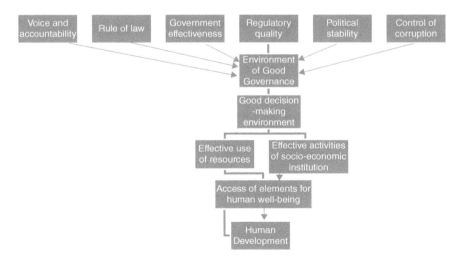

Figure 4.1 Functional Relationship between Good Governance and HDI.
Source: Compiled by the authors.

needs, they may refrain from engaging in the political process (Moore and Putzel 1999). The socioeconomic system captures some of the initial conditions that are important with regard to stimulating growth and determining the poor's access to growth opportunities.

The socioeconomic system influences growth and poverty outcomes directly as well as indirectly via the political system and the decision-making environment. Good governance encourages productive investment (Campos et al. 1999; Dahlström et al. 2012) and a good economic power structure promoting the optimization of resource allocation (Zhang and Yu 2009). A country's natural resources play an important role in growth and poverty outcomes. The improved political stability and government effectiveness result in improved productivity and increased output via good management of natural resources. Economic growth creates more jobs and thus improves political stability and increases productivity to further enhance economic growth. With increased output and government effectiveness, the corruption index would decrease, leading to improved reserves, which would result in investment growth and hence increased productivity and output. With increased output, the productive environment improves and then the investment gets a boost that results in further production growth.

Economic management is an essential responsibility of government and can be considered from the comparative advantage perspective as proposed by Krueger (1990): Government is a non-market organization and, generally, it must do things on a large scale. It follows that activities such as the maintenance of law and order (especially enforcement of contracts), provision of information and provision of basic services which are inherently large scale in scope (roads and communications) are those in which the government is at no disadvantage in providing services on a large scale and where private agents may face a disadvantage in attempting to do so.

The rule of law forbidding the negative effect of market subjects and government entities, and encouraging the positive effect of them ensures the fair distribution of goods and services produced by the national citizen and get access to all the basic facilities for human wellbeing. Thus protecting private property rights and intellectual property rights and supporting investment and innovation (North 1990) via good governance can enhance the betterment of life and ensure human development.

4.5 Results and Discussions

The empirical results are analyzed in this section. From the correlation matrix given in Table 4.2, we can see that all the variables are strongly correlated with each other. So, we cannot consider the entire variable simultaneously in our analysis. To consider the importance of the variable, we used PCA to form our governance index (GVI). This section presents and discusses the empirical results of this analysis.

Table 4.2 Correlation Matrix

	GE	PV	RQ	RL	CC	VA
GE	1					
PV	0.7436	1				
RQ	0.9399	0.7198	1			
RL	0.9579	0.7776	0.938	1		
CC	0.9424	0.7612	0.8994	0.9564	1	
VA	0.7805	0.659	0.8142	0.8133	0.7871	1

Source: Authors' calculation.

Table 4.3 Principal Components Analysis

Number of obs =2934 Number of comp. = 6
Trace = 6 Rotation: (unrotated = principal) Rho = 1.0000

Component	Eigenvalue	Difference	Proportion	Cumulative
Comp1	5.18137	4.8162	0.8636	0.8636
Comp2	0.365174	0.085523	0.0609	0.9244
Comp3	0.279651	0.182536	0.0466	0.971
Comp4	0.097115	0.05446	0.0162	0.9872
Comp5	0.042655	0.008619	0.0071	0.9943
Comp6	0.0340352		0.0057	1.0000

Source: Authors' calculation.

By using the PCA, we are able to extract much of the information in all the indicators, while at the same time, avoiding the potential multicollinearity problem of including more than one proxy in a given equation. The Eigenvalues given in Table 4.3 is greater than 1 for the first component whereas the value is less than 1 for other components, which indicates that the first principal component is valid for selection. The first component also explains 86% of the standardized variance. Hence, the first principal component is a more relevant measure of the GVI, as it explains the variations of the dependent variable better than any other linear combination of explanatory variables. Therefore, only information related to the first principal component is considered to form a composite indicator.

Figure 4.2 validates the results of Table 4.3 and the first component will be selected only.

The Table 4.4 gives us the initial picture of the loadings of the variables onto the factors. We can see that all variables appear to load onto factor 1 to a reasonable extent. The first principal component is moderately correlated with six of the original variables. The first principal component increases with increasing all of the six variables.

For each country in the analysis here, the factor scores are obtained by the corresponding factor score coefficients. Thus, a composite GVI is obtained.

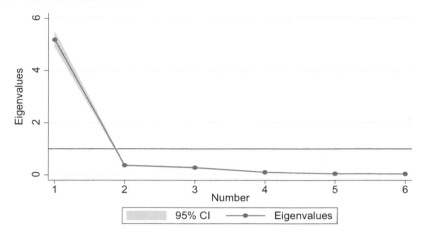

Figure 4.2 Screenplot of Eigenvalues after PCA.
Source: Drawn by the authors.

Table 4.4 Principal Components (Eigenvectors)

Variable	Comp1	Comp2	Comp3	Comp4	Comp5	Comp6	Unexplained
GE	0.4246	−0.1295	−0.3288	0.0599	0.8199	0.1379	0
PV	0.3651	0.9025	0.1977	0.1032	0.0175	0.0463	0
RQ	0.4202	−0.2244	−0.1508	0.7293	−0.4058	0.2319	0
RL	0.4304	−0.0694	−0.1969	−0.1274	−0.1599	−0.854	0
CC	0.4229	−0.0553	−0.2589	−0.6539	−0.3581	0.4419	0
VA	0.3819	−0.3324	0.851	−0.1	0.0949	0.0204	0

Source: Authors' calculation.

In order to find the effect of GVI on the HDI across the world panel regression for countries has been attempted by regressing HDI for the period of 2002 to 2019.

Panel data regression model can be defined as:

$$(HDI)_{it} = \alpha_0 + \alpha_1 (GVI)_{it} + \varepsilon_{it} \quad (4.1)$$

The dependent variable used in Equation (4.1) refers to the HDI. The independent variable is the GVI. We also consider ε_{it} as the error term distributed normally with mean 0 and variance 1 (Table 4.5).

In order to select the appropriate model, the Hausman test is carried out. It is found that for the estimation of HDI, both Fixed Effect Model (FEM)

Table 4.5 Regression Result of Effect on Human Development

HDI	Fixed Effect Model			Random Effect Model		
	Coefficient	t statistic	Prob. value	Coefficient	z statistic	Prob. value
_cons	.695713	1203.91	0.000	.6962967	89.21	0.000
GVI	.0402454	10.10	0.000	.058507	15.97	0.000
	Number of obs = 2934			Number of obs = 2934		
	R-sq with in = 0.6041			R-sq with in = 0.652		
	R-sq between = 0.6319			R-sq between = 0.6712		
	R-sq overall = 0.6042			R-sq overall = 0.6148		
	F(1,2770) = 102.10			Wald chi2(3) = 254.92 (0.0000)		

Source: Authors' calculation.

and Random Effect Model (REM) are statistically significant. The statistical significance of the Housman test [Wald chi2 (3) = 254.92 (0.0000)] suggests for choice of the FEM over REM. Hence, the regression results of the FEM are used for statistical inference and further analysis of the individual coefficients. GVI is positively and significantly related to HDI. From the panel data estimation, it is observed that a 10% rise in GVI leads to 0.4% rise in HDI.

4.6 Conclusion

This study has analyzed the indirect effect of HDI through Qualitative improvement in a country. The chapter also tries to find if good governance is an important factor through which human development can be enhanced across the world. This implies that good governance can be thought of as the policy variables through which high human wellbeing and human development can be ensured to some extent. On the other hand, to ensure good governance, the determinants of good governance have to enhance. Our findings coincide with the similar results of Hartati et al. (2018), Dijkstra (2018) and Davis (2016). Good university governance has a positive effect on the quality of human capital development. The effective distribution of aid will depend on good governance and it also helps the governance to become more effective. Improvements in political governance, economic governance and institutional governance are essential for effective policy intervention which leads to sustainable human development. So, without good governance, it is impossible to achieve the developmental goal as well as human wellbeing.

References

Ahamed, Z & Saleem, A. (2014). Impact of Governance on Human Development. *Pakistan Journal of Commerce and Social Sciences*, 8 (3), 612–628.

Anand, S. & Ravallion, M. (1993). Human Development in Poor Countries: On the Role of Private Incomes and Public Services. *Journal of Economic Perspectives*, 7 (1), 135–150.

Besley, T. & Burgess, R. (2003). Halving Global Poverty. *Journal of Economic Perspectives*, 17 (3), 3–22. https://pubs.aeaweb.org/doi/pdfplus/10.1257/089533003769204335

Boeninger, E. (1992). Governance and Development: Issues and Constraints, *Proceeding of the World Bank Annual Conference on Development Economics*, Washington D. C: The World Bank.

Brautigam, D. (1991). Governance and Economy: A Review, *World Bank Policy Research Working Paper, No. 815*, Washington D. C., World Bank.

Campos, J. Edgardo, Lien, Donald & Pradhan, Sanjay. (1999). The Impact of Corruption on Investment: Predictability Matters. *World Development*, 27, 1059–67. http://www.sciencedirect.com/science/article/pii/S0305-750X(99)00040-6. Accessed on 20. 12. 2021.

Chaudhry, I., Malik, S., Khurram, K. & Rasool, S. (2009). Factors affecting good governance in Pakistan: An Empirical Analysis. *European Journal of Scientific Research*, 35 (3), 337–346.

CIPE. (2002). Instituting corporate governance in developing, emerging and transitional economies, Center for International Private Enterprise, http://www.cipe.org

Clarke, M. & Islam, S. (2004). *Economic Growth and Social Wellbeing: Operationalizing Normative Social Choice Theory*. Amsterdam: North Holland.

Clarke, M., Islam, S. M. N. & Paech, S. (2006). Measuring Australia's Wellbeing Using Hierarchical Needs. *Journal of Socio-Economics*, 35, 933–945.

Council of Europe. (2007). Recommendation CM/Rec(2007)7 of the Committee of Ministers to member states on good administration. [online]. 2015 [cit. 2019-02-22] Available at: https://wcd.coe.int/ViewDoc.jsp?id=1155877

Dahlström, C., Victor L. & Jan T. (2012). The Merit of Meritocratization: Politics, Bureaucracy, and the Institutional Deterrents of Corruption. *Political Research Quarterly*, 65, 656–68.

Daly, H. (1996). *Beyond Growth*. Boston: Beacon Press.

Davis, J. T. (2016). Good governance as a foundation for sustainable human development in sub-Saharan Africa, Third World Quarterly, Routledge, Taylor & Francis Group. http://dx.doi.org/10.1080/01436597.2016.1191340

Despotis, D. K. (2005). Measuring Human Development via Data Envelopment Analysis: The Case of Asia and the Pacific. *OMEGA*, 33 (5), 385–390.

Dijkstra, G. (2018). *Aid and Good Governance: Examining Aggregate Unintended Effects of Aid, Evaluation and Program Planning*, Elsevier, 68, 225–232. Accessed on 8. 9. 2020. https://www.sciencedirect.com/science/article/pii/S0149718917302975

Dodds, S. (1997). Economic Growth and Human Wellbeing. In Diesendorf, M. & Hamilton, C. (eds.), *Human Ecology and Human Economy*. Sydney: Allen and Unwin.

Doyal, L. & Gough, I. (1991). *A Theory of Need*. London: Macmillan.

Duncan, R. C. (2003). Governance and growth, *paper presented to the Symposium on Governance held at the University of the South Pacific*, Suva.

Fayissa, B. & Nsiah, C. (2010). The impact of governance on economic growth: Further evidence for Africa. *Middle Tennessee State University, Department of Economics and Finance, No. 201012*. http://capone.mtsu.edu/berc/working/Governance_WPS_2010_12.pdf

Frey, B. S. & Stutzer, A. (2000). Happiness, economy and institutions. *Economic Journal*, 110 (466), 918–938. http://papers.ssrn.com/sol3/papers.cfm?abstract_id=203211

Fukuda-Parr, S. (2003). Rescuing the Human Development Concept from the HDI: Reflections on a New Agenda, In Fukuda-Parr, S. & Shiva Kumar, A. K. (Eds.), *Readings in Human Development*. UK: Oxford University Press.

Girishankar, N. (2001). Evaluating Public Sector Reform Guidelines for Assessing Country-Level impact of Structural Reform and Capacity Building in the Public Sector, *Operations Evaluation Department Partnerships & Knowledge Programs (OEDPK)*, The World Bank, Washington. https://ieg.worldbankgroup.org/sites/default/files/Data/reports/public_sector_reform.pdf

Haq, R. & Zia, U. (2009). Governance and Pro-poor Growth: Evidence from Pakistan. *The Pakistan Development Review*, 45 (4), 761–776. https://www.pide.org.pk/pdf/PDR/2006/Volume4/761-776.pdf. Accessed on 22. 12. 2021.

Hartati, N, Hadiwidjaja, R. D. & Muktiyanto, A. (2018). The Influence of Good University Governance on Human Capital. *Accounting and Finance Review*, 3 (1), 1–8.

Human Development Report (1990). Concept and Measurement of Human Development. https://hdr.undp.org/content/human-development-report-1990

Human Development Report (2020). Human Development Indices and Indicators, assessed on 20/1/2021, HDRO (Human Development Report Office).

Iyengar, S. & Lepper, R. (2000). When Choice is Demotivating: Can One Desire Too Much of a Good Thing? *Journal of Personality and Social Psychology*, 79 (6), 995–1006. http://www.columbia.edu/~ss957/articles/Choice_is_Demotivating.pdf

Kaufmann, D. & Kraay, A. (2002). Growth without Governance, *World Bank Policy Research Working Paper*, No. 2928.

Kaufmann, D., Kraay, A. & Mastruzzi, M. (2009). Governance matters VIII: Aggregate and individual governance indicators, 1996-2008. *World Bank Policy Research Working Paper No. 4978*. http://ssrn.com/abstract=1424591

Kaufmann, D., Kraay, A. & Mastruzzi, M. (2010). *The Worldwide Governance Indicators Methodology and Analytical Issues*, The World Bank Development Research Group Macroeconomics and Growth Team, Policy Research Working Paper 5430, September, 2010.

Kaufmann, D., Montiorol-Garriga, J. & Recanatini, F. (2008). How does bribery affect public service delivery? Micro evidence from service users and public officials in Peru, World Bank Policy Research Working Paper No. 4492, http://papers.ssrn.com/sol3/papers.cfm?abstract_id=1088550

Kaufmann, Daniel, Kraay, Aart and Zoido-Lobatón, Pablo (1999). Aggregating Governance Indicators. World Bank Policy Research Working Paper No. 2195, Washington, D.C.

Khan, M. H. (2007). Economic Growth and Development since the 1960s, *DESA Working Paper No. 54 ST/ESA/2007/DWP/54*, https://www.un.org/esa/desa/papers/2007/wp54_2007.pdf

Klimovský, D. (2010). Genéza koncepcie good governance a jej kritické prehodnotenie v teoretickej perspektive [The Genesis of the Concept of Good Governance and the Critical Review of Theoretical Perspective]. *Ekonomický časopis*, 58 (2), 188–205. https://www.researchgate.net/publication/289802060_Genesis_of_Good_Governance_Concept_and_Critical_Overview_on_It_in_Theoretical_Perspective

Knack, S. (2001). Trust, Associational Life and Economic Performance In Helliwell, J. & Bonikowska, A. (eds.), *The Contribution of Human and Social Capital to Sustained Economic Growth and Well-Being*. Ottawa and Paris: HRSDC and OECD, 172–202. https://www.researchgate.net/search.SearchPublications.html?query=the+contribution+of+human+and+social+capital+to+sustained+economic+growth+and+well-being

Krueger, Anne O. (1990). Government Failures in Development, No 3340, NBER Working Papers from National Bureau of Economic Research, Inc as. *Journal of Economic Perspectives*, 4 (3), 9–23. http://www.nber.org/papers/w3340.pdf

Landell-Mills, P. & Serageldin, I. (1991). Governance and the Development Process. *World Bank Finance and Development*, 28 (3), 14–17.

Levithan, T. (2001). *Reforming Governance in Bangladesh*, Unknown publishing information, 11–19.

McGillivray, M. (1991). The Human Development Index: Yet another Redundant Composite Development Indicator? *World Development*, 19, 1461–1468.

Mollah, M. A. H. (2003). *Good Governance in Bangladesh: Role of Parliament*. http://unpan1.un.orgintradocgroupspublicdocuments/UNPANUNPAN014209.pdf

Moore, M. & Putzel, J. (1999). Thinking Strategically about Politics and Poverty. IDS Working Paper 101, https://www.ids.ac.uk/download.php?file=files/Wp101.pdf

North, D. (1990). *Institutions, Institutional Change and Economic Performance*. New York: Cambridge University.

Nussbaum, M. (2000). *Women and Human Needs*. Oxford: Oxford University Press.

Pradhan, R. P. (2007). India's Human Development and Social Sector Expenditure in the Globalization Regime. *Man and Development*, 29 (1), 17–38.

Pradhan, R. P. & Sanyal, G. S. (2011). Good Governance and Human Development: Evidence from Indian States. *Journal of Social and Development Science*, 1 (2), 1–8.

Recommendation CM/Rec (2007). 7 of the Committee of Ministers to member states on good administration. Adopted by the Committee of Ministers on 20 June 2007 at the 999bis meeting of the Ministers' Deputies. https://rm.coe.int/cmrec-2007-7-of-the-cm-to-ms-on-good-administration/16809f007c

Rodrik, D. (2000). Institutions for High-quality Growth: What They are and How to Acquire Them, *NBER working paper series, Working Paper 7540*, National Bureau of Economic Research, 1050 Massachusetts Avenue Cambridge, MA 02138. https://www.nber.org/system/files/working_papers/w7540/w7540.pdf

Rothstein, B. & Teorell, J. (2008). What Is Quality of Government? A Theory of Impartial Government Institutions. *Governance: An International Journal of Policy, Administration, and Institutions*, 21 (2), 165–190. https://doi.org/10.1111/j.1468-0491.2008.00391.x. Accessed on 16. 12. 2021.

Sebudubudu, David (2010). The impact of good governance on development and poverty in Africa: Botswana - A relatively successful African initiative. African Journal of Political Science and International Relations, 4 (7), 249–262. http://www.academicjournals.org/ajpsir

Stiglitz, J. E. (2002). Employment, Social Justice and Societal Wellbeing. *International Labour Review*, 141 (1–2), 9–29.

Torres, M. M. & Anderson, M. (2004). Fragile states: defining difficult environments for poverty reduction. *PRDE Working Paper*, https://reliefweb.int/sites/reliefweb.int/files/resources/F222CC56A426F832C125757F00359321-DFID_aug04.pdf

Turner, K. (2011). The Importance of Good Governance in Achieving Economic Growth for Developing Nations: An Analysis of Sub-Saharan Africa. *Bryant Economic Research Paper*, 4 (4).

World Bank (1996). *Bangladesh Government That Works: Reforming the Public Sector*. Dhaka, Bangladesh, Washington, D.C: World Bank Group. http://documents.worldbank.org/curated/en/556251468741620360/Bangladesh-Government-that-works-reforming-the-public-sector

Zhang, Yishan & Yu, Weisheng. (2009). Economic Power Structure and Optimal Allocation of Productive Factors. *Economic Research Journal*, 6, 65–72.

5 Linkages between Social Sector Spending, Governance and Economic Growth
Case Study of India and China

Rajib Bhattacharyya

Introduction

Throughout the entire history of development, including those in modern times, the prime focus is on "what determines or propels faster economic growth", rather than what enables qualitatively better and sustainable good life. The Human Development Index (HDI) states that there are three dimensions of a good life: (a) a long and healthy life (health dimension), (b) Enhancement of knowledge (education dimension) and (c) having a decent standard of living (standard of living dimension is measured by gross national income per capita). But the question that has the crux of the debate is whether investment in the social sector (particularly in health and education) enhances economic growth or not. There has also been a trade-off between military or defense expenditure and social spending in the context of countries achieving a faster rate of economic growth. One school of thought is of the opinion that increase in military expenditure ensures stable and secured government which attracts investment, both domestic and foreign, which propels economic growth and translates into development at a later stage. But the other school believes that economic development can be best achieved by spending more on the improvement of the social sector and practising good governance as it helps to reduce corruption and enhance productivity.

The literature on the governance of public policy in the social sector can be broadly divided into two approaches: (a) the income-centred approach or human capital/resource development approach and (b) the human development approach of the United Nations Development Programme (UNDP). According to the former approach, public investment in social sectors, like health and education will contribute to the enhancement of human capital, skill formation and knowledge development and thereby increasing productivity and higher returns which stimulates economic growth. Thus, according to this approach, the justification of the role of public policy in the social sector is accepted on the ground that human capital has a positive spill-over effect on economic growth as well as development. A totally different view of development has been spelt out by the UNDP in their Human Development Report in 1990, in line with the ideas of Prof. Sen (1984, 1985).

DOI: 10.4324/9781003245797-6

This view was more concerned with a qualitatively good life and does not attach too much importance to per capita income alone. The inclusion of per capita income in HDI is justified on the ground that besides contributing directly to human development, it enables one to exercise choice with respect to the other means of human development such as education and healthcare. In this approach, private income may not always result in the attainment of human development. Private activities and market signals often fall short when it comes to the widespread and equal provision of certain services like basic health and education. This is where public provisioning of social services as an instrument of human development has a larger role to play.

> The importance of good and effective governance has gained importance over the years as a fundamental tool for the proper allocation and distribution of public resources in order to achieve a desirable outcome by means of monitoring through public institutions.
>
> Good governance is epitomized by predictable, open, and enlightened policy making (that is, transparent processes); a bureaucracy imbued with a professional ethos; an executive arm of government accountable for its actions; and a strong civil society participating in public affairs; and all behaving under the rule of law.
>
> World Bank (2007)

It has often been argued that many countries of the world are lagging behind in good governance – often resulting in government failures. In fact, institutional inefficiencies (such as corruption, leakages, frauds, etc.) and poor targeting are supposed to be major reasons for the ineffective implementation of public policy. Poor budget management has frequently been cited as one of the main reasons why governments in developing countries find it difficult to translate public spending into effective services (World Bank, 2003). In fact, the issue of "poor governance" is linked directly with a nation's political environment and incentives of the government to rectify its problems (Keefer, 2004). India is still following the mixed nature of the economic system but China is following a new set-up known as market socialism.

Governance consists of the traditions and institutions by which authority in a country is exercised. This includes the process by which governments are selected, monitored and replaced; the capacity of the government to effectively formulate and implement sound policies; and the respect of citizens and the state for the institutions that govern economic and social interactions among them. The Worldwide Governance Indicators (WGI) report on six broad dimensions of governance for over 200 countries and territories over the period 1996–2019: (a) Voice and Accountability; (b) Political Stability and Absence of Violence; (c) Government Effectiveness; (d) Regulatory Quality; (e) Rule of Law; (f) Control of Corruption.

The Corruption Perception Index (CPI), 2020, published by Transparency International (TI), has ranked 180 countries and territories by their perceived levels of public sector corruption according to experts and business people, using a scale of 0–100, where 0 is highly corrupt and 100 is very clean. Like in previous years, more than two-thirds of countries score below 50 on this year's CPI, with an average score of just 43. The data shows that despite some progress, most countries still fail to tackle corruption effectively. This again emphasizes the need for effective and good governance to reduce corruptive practices. The top six cleaner countries in respect of CPI (2020) are Denmark, New Zealand, Finland, Singapore, Sweden and Switzerland with their scores above 85 (much higher than average). Corruption shifts public spending away from essential public services. Countries with higher levels of corruption, regardless of economic development, tend to spend less on health. Among the two Asian Tigers and the fastest-growing nations, China's rank is 78 while India has slipped back six places to secure 86th among 180 countries.

Of late, the two giants of Asia, India and China, with their domestic markets providing vast scope for diversified industrialization and trade, are classified by international agencies as emerging markets with the potential for rapid economic growth. Both economies possess the capacity to become the "power houses" of the global economy. There are many similarities between the two economies such as the vast pool of employable labour and the abundance of natural resource endowments. Both India and China are home to the world's largest pools of the skilled workforce and are expected to be the engines of global economic growth in the present century. If we compare the GDP growth rates of these two countries (Figure 5.1), we will see that from 2000 to 2013 China was much above

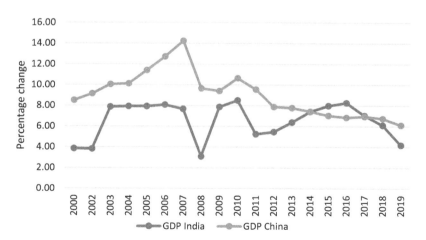

Figure 5.1 GDP growth rates in India and China.

Source: Author's construction based on the World Development Indicator (2020).

Link between Social Sector Spending, Governance and Growth 77

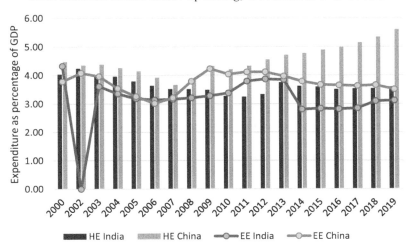

Figure 5.2 Comparison of Health and Educational Expenditure in India and China.
Source: Author's construction based on the World Development Indicator (2020).

India though, over time, the gap was narrowing down. In 2015, India surpassed the growth of China but, again in 2018, it is the other way around.

If we compare the expenditure of the two countries in their respective social sector, mainly health and education (Figure 5.2), we will observe that in health expenditure (as a percentage of GDP) China is way ahead of India (particularly since 2009, when the gap started to increase between the two nations). But in the case of educational expenditure, the gap has narrowed over time (in 2019, it was the minimum).

Literature Survey

Many researchers have attempted to explore the interrelationship between social sector spending (mostly in the health and education sectors) and its impact on economic growth.

Baldacci et al. (2004), in their paper, tried to explore both the direct and indirect linkages between social spending, human capital and growth in 120 developing countries for the period 1975–2000 using panel data. The paper establishes a positive and significant relationship between education and health spending and economic growth through the accumulation of education and health capital. The study also arrives at a conclusion that improving governance can also be helpful in moving towards achieving Millennium Development Goals (MDGs). Barro (1991), in his study, found a positive but insignificant relationship between public investment and economic growth in 98 developed and developing economies over the 1960–1985 period. Gangal and Gupta (2013), in their study, attempted to examine the impact of public expenditure on economic growth. The study reveals that there is linear stationarity in both the variables that indicates the long-run equilibrium and there is a positive impact of Total public expenditure on economic growth. There is a unidirectional relationship, i.e., from total public expenditure to GDP found by Granger causality Test. Goswami and Bezbaruah (2011) and Prabhu (2005) present a detailed analysis of public expenditure on social sectors in India during the post-reform period with an eye on its contribution to the process of human development in the country. Cooray (2009) tried to examine the role of the government in economic growth by extending the neoclassical production function to incorporate two dimensions of the government – the size and the quality dimensions across 71 countries. The results indicate that both the size and quality of the government are important for economic growth. His work also emphasized that investing in the capacity for enhanced governance is a priority for the improved growth performance of the countries examined. Dev and Mooij (2002a, 2002b, 2004 and 2015) and Mooij and Dev (2004) elaborately analyze patterns in social sector expenditures, particularly on health and education in both the centres and across the states of India. The trends are examined at three levels: (a) combined Centre and States, (b) Centre and (c) States. The expenditures refer to both plan and non-plan. Harbison and Hanushek (1992) examined 12 studies on developing countries that look at the association between public education spending and educational outcomes. Six of these studies report a statistically significant positive relationship between the two; others found no evidence of any measurable impact of spending on outcomes. Hanushek (1995), Mingat and Tan (1992, 1998) and Wolf (2004) also find that there is little if any relationship between public education spending and educational outcomes. Using a sample of 70 countries, Gupta et al. (1999) note that the relationship between public spending and the health status of the poor is stronger in low-income countries than in higher-income countries. Xu (2010) in his paper examines the history of educational expenditure as a proportion of GDP and also highlights the current situation and comparison in China. Li (2011, 2017) shows that educational expenditure is an important indicator to measure the level of education development and overall growth of a nation. Based on the data from 2006 to 2014, the paper (2011) analyzes the educational expenditure and fiscal educational expenditure in the aspects of total amount and growth rate. OECD (2020), in their updates on social expenditure, has stated that over the past decade public social expenditure has declined in OECD countries in 2019 and they have released a new Social Expenditure Database (SOCX) that includes detailed social expenditure programme data for 1980–2017/19 for 37 OECD countries.

A huge body of literature has developed on the relationship between a variety of governance indicators and development outcomes. The majority of these studies show that improved governance leads to better development outcomes. These studies have analyzed the effects of corruption and institutions on, among other variables, economic growth, public investment, foreign direct investment and social infrastructure. Kaufmann et al. (1999), Kaufman et al. (2004) and Kaufmann et al. (2006) show that governance indicators (including voice and accountability, political stability and violence, government effectiveness, regulatory burden, rule of law and graft) have a strong direct negative impact on infant mortality. World Bank (2007a and b) depicts the changes occurring across the world in a decade with respect to measuring the quality of governance and asserts that governance does matter in the Report World Wide Governance Indicators (1996–2006).

Objective of the Study and Methodology

The present study wants to establish the linkages between social sector spending (measured by the percentage of GDP spent on health and education), governance (measured by Worldwide Global Governance indicators) and economic growth (measured by the percentage of annual GDP growth) with reference to two fastest-growing emerging nations China and India. It is based on the secondary time series data available from the World Development Indicator (WDI) (2018–2019), The Worldwide Governance Indicator (2020) of the World Bank Group (2020), and CPI developed by Transparency International (2020). The study also attempts to examine both the long-run and short-run relationship between Health Expenditure (HE), Educational Expenditure (EE), WGI and economic growth (changes in GDP). Secondary time-series data from WDI and the Statistical Year Book (2019) have been used to examine the relationship between health and education expenditure, governance and GDP for the period 1990–2019. The reason for taking these two countries is that India and China are considered to be the fastest-growing economies in the years to come.

Here, the Autoregressive distributed lag approach (ARDL) and Error Correction Model (ECM) technique have been applied to examine the long- and short-run causality among the variables. Before starting any time series analysis, the ADF unit root test is performed. Having determined that all series are integrated of order one I (1), we proceed with the testing of co-integration between the variables, based on the ARDL framework. We have an unrestricted ARDL model with no trends with 2 lags and estimated it. Then, we check Residual Diagnostics (Serial correlation) using the LM test. Then, a stability analysis check is performed using the CUSUM Test and, finally, in order to find whether there exists a long-run association between the variables, the Wald test is performed.

Empirical Analysis

Before starting any time series analysis, the ADF unit root test is performed to check whether the series is stationary. The results of the ADF unit root tests are shown in Table 5.1.

Table 5.1 Results of Unit Test (ADF)

	Variable	t-Statistic	Probability	Critical value	Series Type
CHINA	GDP	−3.120247	0.0384	−3.737853*	NS
	D(GDP)	−4.041560	0.0052	−2.998064**	S
	DE	−2.788202	0.0749	−2.991878**	NS
	D(DE)	−4.243362	0.0033	−2.998064**	S
	HE	−1.520509	0.5019	−3.029970**	NS
	D(HE)	−3.513133	0.0200	−3.04391**	S
	EE	−3.572113	0.0159	−3.788030*	NS
	D(EE)	−4.765278	0.0010	−2.998064**	S
	WGI	−1.331640	0.5912	−3.857386*	NS
	D(WGI)	−4.437558	0.0034	−3.886751*	S
INDIA	GDP	−3.706832	0.0107	−3.737853*	NS
	D(GDP)	−5.052606	0.0006	−3.004861**	S
	DE	−3.187197	0.0340	−3.752946*	NS
	D(DE)	−4.249305	0.0034	−2.998064**	S
	HE	−1.703735	0.4136	−3.029970**	NS
	D(HE)	−6.239701	0.0001	−3.052169**	S
	EE	−2.074966	0.2557	−3.012363**	NS
	D(EE)	−5.386976	0.0014	−3.632896	S
	WGI	−0.594723	0.8488	−3.857386*	NS
	D(WGI)	−4.799339	0.0017	−3.886751*	S

Notes: [(*), (**) and (***) are significant at 1%, 5% and 10%, respectively.]
Source: Author's calculations.

Clearly, the ADF test statistic indicates that GDP, Health Expenditure (HE), Educational Expenditure (EE) and Governance (WGI) series in selected Asian countries (China and India) are stationary after first differencing (I(1)). Having determined that all series are integrated of order one I(1), we proceed with the testing of co-integration between the variables, based on the ARDL framework. Pesaran et al. (2001) suggested the ARDL to test for co-integration as an alternative to the co-integration model for Engle-Granger (1989). The ARDL-ECM model has been developed to check both long-run and short-run relationships between GDP, Health Expenditure (HE), Educational Expenditure (EE) and Governance (WGI). In general, the ARDL restricted error correction model (RECM) is as follows:

$$\Delta GDP_t = \alpha + \sum \alpha 1 \Delta GDP_{t-1} + \sum \alpha 2 \Delta LWGI_{t-1} + \sum \alpha 3 \Delta LHE_{t-1} + \sum \alpha 4 \Delta LEE_{t-1} + \delta 1 GDP_{t-1} + \delta 2 LWGI_{t-1} + \delta 3 LHE_{t-1} + \delta 4 LEE_{t-1} + \gamma 1 ecm_{t-1}$$

But here we first take an unrestricted ARDL model with no trends with 2 lags and estimate the following equation:

$$d(gdp) = c + \alpha 0 d\big(gdp(-1)\big) + \alpha 1\, d\big(gdp(-2)\big) + \delta 0\, d\big(he(-1)\big) \quad (5.1)$$
$$+ \delta 1\, d\big(he(-2)\big) + \gamma 0 d\big(ee(-1)\big) + \gamma 1\, d\big(ee(-2)\big)$$
$$+ \beta_1 d\big(wgi(-1)\big) + \beta_2 d\big(wgi(-2)\big) + \mu gdp(-1)$$
$$+ \phi he(-1) \sigma ee(-1) + \theta wgi(-1)$$

where D (GDP) is the dependent variable and GDP, HE, EE and WGI with 1 and 2 lags are taken as independent variables.

Then, we check Residual Diagnostics (Serial correlation) using the LM test. Then, a stability analysis check is performed using CUSUM Test and, finally, in order to find whether there exists a long-run association between the variables, the Wald test is performed. For checking short-run relationship, we have incorporated the error term [ECT(-1)] from our basic long-run model and again estimated our model with 2 lags. The error term indicates the speed of adjustment towards long-run equilibrium. Again, serial correlation is tested for short-run model using the LM test. Then, long-run causality is checked for each of the three independent variables – Health Expenditure (HE), Educational Expenditure (EE) and Governance (WGI) using the Wald test. These have been done separately for the two countries China and India (Table 5.2).

Stability Analysis (Results of CUSUM Test)

The results of the stability analysis of the econometric exercise as given above are given in Figures 5.3 and 5.4.

For both Figures 5.3 and 5.4, the dashed line lies between the two dotted lines, signifying a stable situation.

Checking Long-Run Association between Variables

Here the objective is to determine whether there exists any long-run association between GDP, HE EE and WGI. This has been tested through the

Table 5.2 Results for Serial Correlation (LM Test) and Stability Analysis (CUSUM Test)

Country	Test Result (Breusch–Godfrey Serial Correlation LM Test)				CUSUM Test
China	F-statistic	1.829242	Prob. F(2,1)	0.4633	Stable (Figure 5.3)
	Obs*R-squared	12.56541	Prob. Chi-Square(2)	0.0019	
India	F-statistic	45.34214	Prob. F(2,1)	0.1044	Stable (Figure 5.4)
	Obs*R-squared	13.84730	Prob. Chi-Square(2)	0.0610	

Source: Author's calculations.

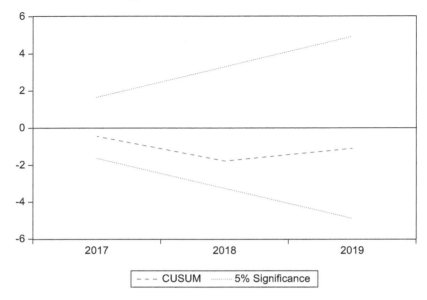

Figure 5.3 Stability test results for China.
Source: Author's drawing.

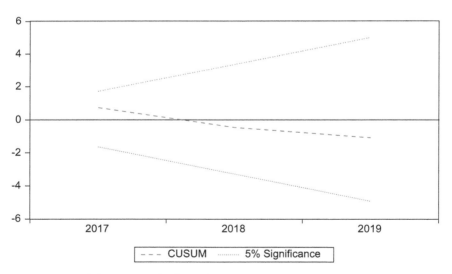

Figure 5.4 Stability test results for India.
Source: Author's drawing.

Wald test. The *F* test is used to determine whether the long-run relationship exists between the variables by testing the significance of the lagged levels of the variables. When the long-run relationship exists, the *F* test will show which variable should be normalized. The null hypothesis of no co-integration amongst the variables in the Equation (5.1), i.e., coefficients of GDP(-1), HE(-1), EE(-1) and WGI(-1) are all zeros. The results of the Wald test are given in Table 5.3.

Table 5.3 shows that there is a long-run association between GDP, HE, EE and the level of Governance (using WGI) in the case of both India and China.

Short-Run Associations between Variables

In the short run, we have incorporated the error term ECT(-1) as one independent variable and again checked for serial correlation using the LM test. Here, it is ensured that there is no serial correlation and further stability has

Table 5.3 Long-Run Association between Variables (Wald Test)

Country	Test Result for Wald Test				Interpretation
China	Test Statistic	Value	df	Probability	F-Stat 11.14 > upper Bound 4.85. GDP, HE, EE and WGI have long-run association.
	F-statistic	11.14113	(4, 3)	0.0381	
	Chi-square	44.56454	4	0.0000	
	Null Hypothesis: C(10) = C(11) = C(12) = C(13) = 0				
	Null Hypothesis Summary:				
	Normalized Restriction (= 0)		Value	Std. Err.	
	C(10)		-1.576053	0.686735	
	C(11)		-13.17922	3.852626	
	C(12)		-5.422317	1.516929	
	C(13)		32.99340	13.09645	
India	Test Statistic	Value	df	Probability	F-Stat 5.35 > upper Bound 4.85. GDP, HE, EE and WGI have long-run association.
	F-statistic	5.350009	(4, 3)	0.0998	
	Chi-square	21.40003	4	0.0003	
	Null Hypothesis: C(8) = C(9) = C(10) = C(11) = 0				
	Null Hypothesis Summary:				
	Normalized Restriction (= 0)	Value		Std. Err.	
	C(8)	-2.196503		0.507337	
	C(9)	1.324583		5.648085	
	C(10)	-4.441575		4.422483	
	C(11)	-23.10445		21.73830	

Notes: The notations are of usual meanings and are derived from the software.
Source: Author's calculations.

been checked using the CUSUM test. Finally, the Wald test has been applied to check whether there exists short-run causality.

In both cases, the ECT(-1) is negative and statistically significant and the speed of adjustment towards long-run equilibrium is 90% and 89% for China and India, respectively.

From Table 5.4, it is clear that except in the case of China (where EE with lag 1 and 2 causes a change in GDP in the short run) and India (where WGI with lag 1 and 2 causes a change in GDP in the short run) there is no short-run causality in case of any other country and any other variable.

Major Findings and Conclusions

The analysis clearly demonstrates a long-run association between annual percentage change in GDP, health expenditure as a percentage of GDP (HE), educational expenditure as a percentage of GDP (EE) and world governance indicators (WGI) in both the Asian countries viz. India and China. The

Table 5.4 Short-Run Causality (Wald Test)

Country	Probability	Null Hypothesis	Interpretation
China Prob. Chi-Square(2)= 0.0944 No serial Correlation (LM Test Result)	0.0868 > 0.05	C(4) = C(5) = 0	Accept Null – HE(-1) and HE(-2) cannot cause change in GDP. There is no short-run causality running from HE to GDP
	0.0076 < 0.05	C(6) = C(7) = 0	Reject Null – EE(-1) and EE(-2) can cause change in GDP. There is short-run causality running from EE to GDP.
	0.6334 > 0.05	C(8) = C(9) = 0	Accept Null – WGI(-1) and WGI(-2) cannot cause change in GDP. There is no short-run causality running from WGI to GDP
India Prob. Chi-Square(2)= 0.9529 No serial Correlation (LM Test Result)	0.2067 > 0.05	C(4) = C(5) = 0	Accept Null – HE(-1) and HE(-2) cannot cause change in GDP. There is no short-run causality running from HE to GDP.
	0.1592 > 0.05	C(6) = C(7) = 0	Accept Null – EE(-1) and EE(-2) cannot cause change in GDP. There is no short-run causality running from EE to GDP
	0.0172 < 0.05	C(8) = C(9) = 0	Reject Null – WGI(-1) and WGI(-2) cant cause change in GDP. There is short-run causality running from WGI to GDP

Notes: The notations are of usual meanings and are derived from the software.
Source: Author's calculations.

bound testing ADRL model also confirms that there is no serial correlation (in terms of the LM test) and that the relationship is stable (in terms of the CUSUM test). The analysis also reveals that except in the case of China (where EE with lag 1 and 2 causes a change in GDP in the short run) and India (where WGI with lag 1 and 2 causes a change in GDP in the short run), there is no short-run causality in case of any other country and any other variable. But as per The Corruption Perceptions Index (CPI), 2020, published by Transparency International, these two countries are lagging far behind the top nations in terms of perceived levels of public sector corruption and this indicates the poor governance in these nations. The corruption rank of India averaged 75.84 from 1995 until 2019, reaching an all-time high of 95 in 2011 and a record low of 35 in 1995. China's rank is 78 while India has slipped back six places to secure 86th among 180 countries. So, not only social sector expenditures (particularly in health and education) in these two countries are below the world average, but poor governance has also been responsible for the decline in growth in these two countries in recent times. Hence, in policy terms, expenditure on the social front needs to be increased along with good governance for higher and sustainable growth in these two nations.

Although the growth rates of these two countries are much better compared to the high-income countries on average, when compared with social sector investment and level of governance, their performances are not satisfactory and are much below the world average. The influence of bureaucratic (or "state") capacity and corruption on development is the fundamental root cause of poor governance in these two nations, despite their differences in the natures of the economies. The effect of political variables like bureaucratic efficiency and integrity, extent of democracy and credibility of the government emerge as the prime factors that need more attention. Looking from the angle of long-run policy, one clearly finds that these two Asian Giants, viz. India and China, need to focus and devote more investment towards the development of their social sectors, mainly health and education.

Appendix 5A

India

Table A1 Regression

Dependent Variable: D(GDP)
Method: Least Squares
Date: 08/18/21 Time: 17:19
Sample (adjusted): 2006 2019
Included observations: 14 after adjustments

Variable	Coefficient	Std. Error	t-Statistic	Prob.
C	18.54820	17.91611	1.035281	0.3767
D(GDP(-1))	0.999584	0.402680	2.482325	0.0891
D(HE(-1))	-0.701114	4.480032	-0.156498	0.8856
D(HE(-2))	-9.013758	6.805178	-1.324544	0.2772
D(EE(-1))	0.238638	5.251918	0.045438	0.9666
D(EE(-2))	2.679591	2.589979	1.034600	0.3769
D(WGI(-1))	41.11892	15.99435	2.570840	0.0824
GDP(-1)	-2.196503	0.507337	-4.329475	0.0227
HE(-1)	1.324583	5.648085	0.234519	0.8297
EE(-1)	-4.441575	4.422483	-1.004317	0.3892
WGI(-1)	-23.10445	21.73830	-1.062846	0.3658
R-squared	0.915805	Mean-dependent var		-0.267388
Adjusted R-squared	0.635155	SD-dependent var		2.190131
S.E. of regression	1.322891	Akaike info criterion		3.428499
Sum squared resid	5.250121	Schwarz criterion		3.930616
Log likelihood	-12.99950	Hannan–Quinn criter.		3.382019
F-statistic	3.263161	Durbin–Watson stat		3.270257
Prob(F-statistic)	0.179746			

Table A2 LM Test

Breusch–Godfrey Serial Correlation LM Test:

F-statistic	45.34214	Prob. F(2,1)	0.1044
Obs*R-squared	13.84730	Prob. Chi-Square(2)	0.0610

Test Equation:
Dependent Variable: RESID
Method: Least Squares
Date: 08/18/21 Time: 17:12
Sample: 2006 2019
Included observations: 14
Presample missing value lagged residuals set to zero.

Variable	Coefficient	Std. Error	t-Statistic	Prob.
C	10.66163	3.502504	3.044001	0.2021
D(GDP(-1))	-0.151539	0.098042	-1.545656	0.3656
D(HE(-1))	2.343388	0.853474	2.745707	0.2224
D(HE(-2))	-2.250360	1.433654	-1.569668	0.3611
D(EE(-1))	-1.147951	1.202210	-0.954867	0.5147
D(EE(-2))	-0.159240	0.469324	-0.339297	0.7918
D(WGI(-1))	-0.733872	3.237350	-0.226689	0.8581
GDP(-1)	0.298705	0.097379	3.067445	0.2006
HE(-1)	-3.312207	1.121101	-2.954424	0.2078
EE(-1)	-0.384120	0.832733	-0.461276	0.7249
WGI(-1)	-0.899997	4.205220	-0.214019	0.8658
RESID(-1)	-1.760264	0.210811	-8.349951	0.0759
RESID(-2)	-1.053469	0.366480	-2.874564	0.2131

R-squared	0.989093	Mean-dependent var	1.06E-15
Adjusted R-squared	0.858209	SD-dependent var	0.635496
S.E. of regression	0.239297	Akaike info criterion	-0.804137
Sum squared resid	0.057263	Schwarz criterion	-0.210727
Log likelihood	18.62896	Hannan–Quinn criter.	-0.859068
F-statistic	7.557024	Durbin–Watson stat	2.223199
Prob(F-statistic)	0.277641		

Table A3 Incorporating the Error Correction Term

Dependent Variable: D(GDP)
Method: Least Squares
Date: 08/19/21 Time: 13:29
Sample (adjusted): 2006 2019
Included observations: 14 after adjustments

Variable	Coefficient	Std. Error	t-Statistic	Prob.
C	-0.548204	0.407059	-1.346745	0.2493
D(GDP(-1))	1.412426	0.633909	2.228119	0.0898
D(GDP(-2))	0.364904	0.407984	0.894409	0.4217
D(HE(-1))	-0.566790	3.141435	-0.180424	0.8656
D(HE(-2))	-11.08983	6.536867	-1.696506	0.1650
D(EE(-1))	2.563839	2.953726	0.868001	0.4344
D(EE(-2))	5.066566	2.708585	1.870558	0.1347
D(WGI(-1))	41.40172	14.73516	2.809723	0.0483
D(WGI(-2))	7.911470	12.09829	0.653933	0.5488
ECT1(-1)	-0.896030	0.956904	-3.026459	0.0389

R-squared	0.892998	Mean-dependent var	-0.267388
Adjusted R-squared	0.652244	SD-dependent var	2.190131
S.E. of regression	1.291538	Akaike info criterion	3.525353
Sum squared resid	6.672282	Schwarz criterion	3.981823
Log likelihood	-14.67747	Hannan–Quinn criter.	3.483099
F-statistic	3.709174	Durbin–Watson stat	1.798374
Prob(F-statistic)	0.109710		

China

Table A4 Regression

Dependent Variable: D(GDP)
Method: Least Squares
Date: 08/19/21 Time: 12:32
Sample (adjusted): 2004 2019
Included observations: 16 after adjustments

Variable	Coefficient	Std. Error	t-Statistic	Prob.
C	109.5447	26.63432	4.112916	0.0260
D(GDP(-1))	0.376774	0.805257	0.467892	0.6718
D(GDP(-2))	0.112246	0.704651	0.159293	0.8836
D(HE(-1))	19.81581	7.271079	2.725291	0.0722

D(HE(-2))	1.833970	2.683936	0.683314	0.5435
D(EE(-1))	-10.07446	1.712102	-5.884267	0.0098
D(EE(-2))	0.262483	1.356406	0.193514	0.8589
D(WGI(-1))	-30.10626	9.381988	-3.208942	0.0490
D(WGI(-2))	-23.35826	9.578734	-2.438554	0.0926
GDP(-1)	-1.576053	0.686735	-2.294995	0.1055
HE(-1)	-13.17922	3.852626	-3.420839	0.0418
EE(-1)	-5.422317	1.516929	-3.574535	0.0374
WGI(-1)	32.99340	13.09645	2.519263	0.0862
R-squared	0.977976	Mean-dependent var		-0.245350
Adjusted R-squared	0.889881	SD-dependent var		1.462461
S.E. of regression	0.485305	Akaike info criterion		1.342946
Sum squared resid	0.706563	Schwarz criterion		1.970674
Log likelihood	2.256435	Hannan–Quinn criter.		1.375090
F-statistic	11.10139	Durbin–Watson stat		3.294244
Prob(F-statistic)	0.035885			

Table A5 LM Test

Test Equation:
Dependent Variable: RESID
Method: Least Squares
Date: 08/19/21 Time: 12:34
Sample: 2004 2019
Included observations: 16
Presample missing value lagged residuals set to zero.

Variable	Coefficient	Std. Error	t-Statistic	Prob.
C	9.701816	23.15036	0.419078	0.7474
D(GDP(-1))	-0.370740	0.920205	-0.402888	0.7562
D(GDP(-2))	-0.538183	0.771206	-0.697846	0.6121
D(HE(-1))	-5.421663	6.884936	-0.787467	0.5753
D(HE(-2))	-1.810419	2.405045	-0.752759	0.5892
D(EE(-1))	-0.639803	1.718216	-0.372365	0.7731
D(EE(-2))	-0.581813	1.623393	-0.358393	0.7809
D(WGI(-1))	-10.36690	14.58403	-0.710839	0.6066
D(WGI(-2))	-7.905000	16.91909	-0.467224	0.7217
GDP(-1)	-0.134899	0.581365	-0.232039	0.8548
HE(-1)	-1.177094	3.181920	-0.369932	0.7744
EE(-1)	1.008729	1.326900	0.760215	0.5862
WGI(-1)	12.55209	18.13315	0.692218	0.6145
RESID(-1)	-1.562061	0.972189	-1.606746	0.3544
RESID(-2)	-1.118593	1.701799	-0.657300	0.6298
R-squared	0.785338	Mean-dependent var		1.34E-14
Adjusted R-squared	-2.219932	SD-dependent var		0.217035
S.E. of regression	0.389451	Akaike info criterion		0.054256
Sum squared resid	0.151672	Schwarz criterion		0.778557
Log likelihood	14.56596	Hannan–Quinn criter.		0.091346
F-statistic	0.261320	Durbin–Watson stat		2.715719
Prob(F-statistic)	0.929305			

Table A6 Incorporating the Error Correction Term

Dependent Variable: D(GDP)
Method: Least Squares
Date: 08/19/21 Time: 13:05
Sample (adjusted): 2005 2019
Included observations: 15 after adjustments

Variable	Coefficient	Std. Error	t-Statistic	Prob.
C	−0.126170	0.423790	−0.297718	0.7779
D(GDP(-1))	−0.054088	0.575973	−0.093907	0.9288
D(GDP(-2))	−0.421423	0.596197	−0.706852	0.5112
D(HE(-1))	4.583883	6.420584	0.713935	0.5072
D(HE(-2))	−11.47806	5.248571	−2.186892	0.0804
D(EE(-1))	−9.880187	3.474906	−2.843296	0.0361
D(EE(-2))	6.189005	3.822232	1.619213	0.1663
D(WGI(-1))	−4.460145	10.78010	−0.413739	0.6962
D(WGI(-2))	8.538391	10.19800	0.837261	0.4406
ECT(-1)	−0.907342	1.612274	−1.183014	0.0200
R-squared	0.754715	Mean-dependent var		−0.266748
Adjusted R-squared	0.313201	SD-dependent var		1.511196
S.E. of regression	1.252378	Akaike info criterion		3.522687
Sum squared resid	7.842257	Schwarz criterion		3.994720
Log likelihood	−16.42015	Hannan–Quinn criter.		3.517659
F-statistic	1.709382	Durbin–Watson stat		2.037173
Prob(F-statistic)	0.287897			

References

Baldacci, E., Clements, B. Gupta, S. & Cui, Q. (2004). Social Spending, Human Capital, and Growth in Developing Countries: Implications for Achieving the MDGs, IMF Working Paper, WP/04/217.

Barro, R. (1991). Economic Growth in a Cross Section of Countries. *Quarterly Journal of Economics*, 106, 407–443.

Cooray, A. (2009). Government expenditure, Governance and Economic Growth. *Comparative Economic Studies*, 51 (3), 401–418.

Dev, S.M., & Mooij, J. (2002a). Social Sector Expenditures in the 1990s. An Analysis of Central and State Budgets. *Economic and Political Weekly*, 37 (9), 853–866.

——— (2002b). Social Sector Expenditures and Budgeting: An Analysis of Patterns and the Budget making process in India in the 1990s, Working paper no. 43, Hyderabad: Centre for Economic and Social Studies.

——— (2015). Patterns of Social Sector Expenditures: Pre and Post-reform Period. Available at https://www.researchgate.net/publication/241849710_Patterns_of_Social_Sector_Expenditures_Pre_and_Post-reform_period

Gangal, V.N.L. & Gupta, H. (2013). Public Expenditure and Economic Growth: A Case Study of India, *Global Journal of Management and Business Studies*, 3(2), 191–196. Available at: http://www.ripublication.com/gjmbs.htm

Goswami, B., & Bezbaruah, M.P. (2011). Social Sector Expenditures and Their Impact on Human Development: The Indian Experience, *Indian Journal of Human Development*, 5(2) 365–385.

Gupta, S., Verhoeven, M., & Tiongson, T. (1999). Does higher government spending buy better results in education and health care? Working Paper 99/21. International Monetary Fund, Washington, DC.

Hanushek, E. (1995). Interpreting Recent Research on Schooling in Developing Countries. *The World Bank Research Observer*, 10(2), 227–246.

Harbison, R., & Hanushek, E. (1992). *Educational Performance of the Poor: Lessons from Rural Northeast Brazil*. Oxford: Oxford University Press.

Kaufman, D., Kraay, A., & Mastruzzi, M. (2004). Governance matters III: governance indicators for 1996, 1998, 2000, and 2002. *World Bank Economic Review*, 18, 253–287.

Kaufmann, D., Kraay, A., & Mastruzzi, M. (2006). Governance Matters V: Governance Indicators for 1996–2005, World Bank Policy Research Working Paper 4012.

Kaufmann, D., Kraay, A., & Zoido-Lobaton, P. (1999). *Governance Matters*. Washington, D.C.: World Bank, Development Economics Research Group.

Keefer, P (2004). A Review of the Political Economy of Governance: From Property Rights to Voice, World Bank Policy Research Working Paper 3315.

Li, Y, (2011). An Empirical Study on the Relationship between Public Education Expenditure and Economic Growth in China - Based on the Perspective of Financial Educational Expenditure. *Shanxi Finance & Taxation College*, 06, 3–6.

——— (2017). The Analysis of Educational Expenditure of China, 3rd International Conference on Management Science and Innovative Education, ISBN: 978-1-60595-488-2.

Mingat, A., & Tan, J. (1992). *Education in Asia: A Comparative Study of Cost and Financing*. Washington, D.C.: World Bank, Human Development Department, Education Group.

——— (1998). The Mechanics of Progress in Education: Evidence from Cross-country Data. Policy Research Working Paper 2015. Human Development Department, Education Group, World Bank, Washington, D.C.

Mooij, J & Dev, S.M. (2004). Social Sector Priorities: An Analysis of Budgets and Expenditures in India in the 1990s. *Development Policy Review*, 22(1), 97–120.

OECD (2020). Social Expenditure (SOCX) Update. Available at: http://www.oecd.org/social/expenditure.htm

Prabhu, K.S. (2005). Social Sectors and Economic Development. In R.K. Sen (ed.), *Social Sector Development in India*. New Delhi: Deep and Deep Publications, pp. 3–25.

Sen, A.K. (1984). The Living Standard, *Oxford Economic Papers*, 36(Supplement), 74–90.

——— (1985). *Commodities and Capabilities*. North-Holland, Amsterdam: Oxford India paper back. ISBN-13: 978-0195650389 and ISBN-10: 9780195650389

Statistical Year Book, 2019, The Republic of China.

The Corruption Perceptions Index (CPI), 2020, Transparency International.

The Worldwide Governance Indicator, 2020 Update. Available at: www.govindicators.org

Wolf, A. (2004). *Does Education Matter?* London: Penguin Books Ltd.

World Bank group (2020). World Development Indicator. https://databank.worldbank.org/source/world-development-indicators

World Bank (2003). Making services work for poor people. World development report 2003. World Bank, Washington, D.C.

―――― (2007a). *Strengthening World Bank Group Engagement on Governance and Anticorruption*. Washington, D.C.: World Bank.

―――― (2007b). *A Decade of Measuring the quality of Governance-Governance Matters: World Wide Governance Indicators (1996 to 2006)*. Washington, D.C.: World Bank.

Xu, J. (2010). Educational Expenditure as the Proportion of GDP: History, Current Situation and Comparison, China Education Society Education Economics Branch.

6 Governance, Social Sector Spending and Sustainable Growth in Selected African Countries

Ebikabowei Biedomo Aduku, Richardson Kojo Edeme and Ogochukwu Christiana Anyanwu

6.1 Introduction

In recent decades, developing countries of Africa have experienced high growth rates, even more than some developed countries. However, such growth has not translated to a better quality of life. Kraay (2004) and Baqir (2020) stipulates that the growth rates reported by developing countries of Africa are not inclusive and pro-poor. It is anticipated that the growth experienced would have a trickle-down effect on welfare, especially for the most venerable in the society with the ultimate goal of reducing poverty and inequality (World Bank, 2021).

Economic growth is the process whereby an economy increases its production and consumption over some time, usually a year. Economic growth is sustainable when the rate of economic growth is maintained without causing other major economic problems, particularly for the future generation (Mensah & Casadevail, 2019). Sustainable economic growth creates economic progress, generates decent jobs in the economy and enhances the standard of living of the people. Basiago (1999), Bourguignon (2003), Godinot (2012) and Brand and Monje Barón (2012) aver that sustainable growth is a stimulus to technological advancement and it can generate opportunities for economic wellbeing such as ameliorations in education and health, among others. The government is anticipated to come up with frameworks that instigate sustainable economic growth that engender inequality and poverty reduction through the conduct of expenditure in the social sectors.

The social sector has been identified as a sector with the potential to drive growth. The success story of Asian economies epitomizes the social sector-led growth model. This mantra saw the nations looking for wider alternative to income and output mainly from the social sector. Although much of the argument of developing country's economic transformation has focused on a shift from agriculture to manufacturing, they have failed to recognize and appreciate the role the social sector can play. Rodrik (2015) clearly notes that the social sector is considered important for the overall economic performance of African economies and the welfare of its citizens. Besides, a more productive social sector also strengthens the performance of other

DOI: 10.4324/9781003245797-7

sectors of the economy (Simoes et al. 2014). The knowledge-intensive business social sector literature shows that the sector influences the innovative capacity of other sectors and hence the growth potential of the economy. The social sector contributes significantly to GDP and provides input for the rest of the economy, hence largely affecting the overall performance of the economy. Education and health services contribute largely to human development which is a part of the institutional framework required to supporting a healthy market economy and achieving social development objectives. This has guided the suggestions that investment in the social sector could be a progressive course towards sustainable growth and an engine of economic transformation (Kaasa, 2016). To stimulate the social sector, expenditure is oftenhandled by the government. Social sector spending is crucial because it is likely relatively to benefit the poor more than the rich and because, defensibly, it improves the human capital in the economy, which can have direct sustainable growth effects and indirect spillover advantages on the rest of the economy. The endogenous growth theory also gives priority to social sector policy, which focuses largely on human capital – education and health enhancement. However, the ability of countries to create an enabling environment where the lives of individuals and properties are secured and civil society can flourish; the government has to efficiently and transparently carry out its responsibilities that could play a major role in determining the success of sustainable economic growth (Olaniyan, 2017). These assumptions led to the interest of policymakers and researchers in the role of governance in sustainable economic growth in recent years, especially in developing countries that are scrupulously pursuing good governance.

Some pundits have argued that since the major output of the social sector comes from a public expenditure pattern, there is a need for countries to have an appropriate level of good governance. Governance is the way and manner in which power is exercised in the distribution and management of a country's resources to spur growth and development. The World Bank (2011) aver that sustainable development can only be achieved if there is the existence of a predictable framework of rules and institutions in the conduct of government business. The essence, therefore, is that good governance exclusively concerns the manner in which economic and social resources are distributed for the fundamental objective of sustainable poverty reduction. Governance means leadership style and how a country through a panoply of regulatory quality, bureaucratic quality and control of corruption, government effectiveness and rule of law manages human and material resources to achieve growth (World Bank 2011). In recent years, governance has gained recognition as an important concept in developed and developing countries. Thus, most countries, especially developing countries, are working towards establishing good governance to achieve sustainable economic growth. Good governance could play a key role in ensuring prudence in social sector spending – education and health, which are seen as sectors necessary for the attainment of sustainable growth. Godinot

(2010) categorized three distinctive forms of governance to include the form of political regime, the process by which power is exercised in the management of economic and social resources and the capacity of the government to design, formulate and implement policies and discharge functions. Contributing further, the International Development Association (IDA) (2020) underscores the importance of governance as necessary in choosing the size of the resources needed to accentuate growth in an economy. It was emphasized that sound policies, effective partnerships and systematic inclusion of the poor, affected groups and women in the development process are critical in sustainable poverty reduction. The Asian Development Bank defined good governance as the way power is exercised in the management of economic and social resources in a country. Going by this, good governance is perceived to be synonymous with accountability, participation, predictability and transparency. In achieving developmental goals, these elements as inter-woven, mutually supportive and stimulates each other. In this sense, good governance has been recognized as central in creating and sustaining enabling environment for sound development policies. Iheonu, Ihedimma and Onwuanaku (2017) and United Nations (2021) further emphasize that good governance is translated into accountability, transparency, combating corruption, participation and legal and judicial reform. In a document titled *Governance for Sustainable Development*, The United Nations Development Programme (UNDP) (1997) defines governance as the exercise of economic, political and administrative power in the management of the affairs of the country at all levels. While economic governance entails the decision-making process that affects economic activities and its connections with other economies, political governance is the process of decision-making to formulate policy. Administrative governance deals with the system of policy implementation. In line with the three dimensions, good governance, therefore, defines the process and structures that stimulate political and socio-economic relationships. As embedded, the essential features of good governance include participation, rule of law, transparency, equity, responsiveness, consensus orientation, effectiveness and efficiency, accountability and strategic vision.

From the preceding discussion, it is clear that governance can play a great role in the conduct of expenditure and attainment of sustainable growth and can be invoked in the assessment process and taken into account in allocating resources to different sectors in the overall development of the economy. While little research exists on the determinants of government spending in these sectors, a common view is that good governance could encourage more participation of the less privileged in the political process, leading to results that are beneficial to the poor. One such result is the number of government supports or resources allocated to the provision of education and health. In the practice of good governance where the rule of law is honoured and there is a free expression of political voice and encourages the poor to take part in the political process could likely deliver more effectively to the people in form of greater spending on education and health.

This could lead to a positive sustainable growth effect as a result of human capital externalities. Social sector spending can be crucial for sustainable growth and sustainable growth manifests in social sector spending. Good governance will play a key role in ensuring prudent social sector spending, which is necessary for sustainable growth. There is, however, very little empirical evidence on the relationship between governance, social sector spending and sustainable growth, especially in the African region.

The main objective of this chapter is to examine the role of governance and social sector spending on sustainable growth in the context of education and health expenditure in relation to control of corruption, government effectiveness and rule of law. The main finding indicates that governance promotes sustainable growth. Among the components of governance, control of corruption is the most effective in stimulating growth. Other findings are that social sector spending had no significant effect on sustainable growth. Control of corruption and government spending on education had a complementary effect on sustainable growth. Government effectiveness, rule of law and government expenditure on education play complementary roles in accentuating sustainable growth. Control of corruption, government effectiveness and rule of law and government health spending had substitution effects on sustainable growth. Policymakers will find this chapter relevant based on formulating sustainable growth-enhancing policies.

6.2 Review of Literature

Sustainable economic growth is perceived as a growth process whereby there is no diminution of economic activities over time and, there is no reduction in economic welfare as a result of mismanagement of economic resources or a fall in production and consumption activities. It is an economic condition such that the per capita income of a country demonstrates a tendency to expand over a period of time; nevertheless, the process could have spasmodic periods of declination and stagnation similar to that caused by the business cycle. That is, sustainable economic growth is an economic growth process – an increase in per capita material output such that the economic welfare does not display a likelihood of decline over time (Roy, 2019). Sustainable economic growth differs from sustainable development. Following Giraldo (2019), sustainable development refers to every form of growth in preserving the needs of the current generation without compromising future generations. Sustainable development also refers to maintaining a balance between natural resource usage and the proper functioning of the natural system. In developing countries, especially countries in the African region, growth seems not to have been sustainable as most of the economies frequently experience a diminishment of economic activities with increasing unemployment rates and environmental degradation. This is mostly linked to corruption and other governance issues.

World Bank (2021) defined governance as the traditions and institutions through which a country exercised authority. It comprises the process through which governments are formed, supervised and replaced; the ability of the government to efficaciously formulated and implement good policies; and the value of people and the state for the institutions that oversee and control economic and social interactions within the economy. A policy output and outcomes concerning the definition of governance are also posited by the Mo Ibrahim Foundation (2017). Accordingly, governance is defined as the government's provision of socio-economic and political public goods and services delivered to the citizens. To Udah and Ayara (2014), governance is the ability of the government to organize economic policies that will smoothen market interactions such that it will generate higher payoffs and sustainable growth rates. It is the style of leadership in a country as well as the manner a country organizes human and material resources. Though different authors may view the concept from different perspectives, common among the definitions is the fact that all the definitions give cognizance to social sector policy, which largely concerns government spending on human capital – education and health enhancement, among others. The occurrence of sustainable growth is dependent on the way resources are allocated (making governance a significant factor) over a period of time and across economic activities. Evaluating the impact of institutional quality on efficient investment for economic growth in the Italian regions, Arbolino and Boffardi (2017) sort to ascertain the return on investment from structural funds while putting into account the institutional quality and spending ability. A two-way fixed effect panel regression model was employed to achieve the objective of the study. It was reported that in general, cohesion investment and institution are positively related to growth. Mtiraoui (2015) researched on the direct and indirect effects of corruption and institutional quality on economic growth in the Middle East and North African region. The dataset covered 100 countries in the Middle East and and North Africa (MENA) region over the period 1998–2006. The dynamic panel data was used to estimate the model. Results reveal that quality of governance positive has a positive and significant impact on economic growth for the whole sample, though not on a country-specific basis. When estimated individually, some countries show a negative and insignificant relationship between governance quality and economic growth. In a related study, Nawaz, Iqbal and Khan (2014) examined the influence of institutions on economic growth in selected Asian economies applying both panel and generalized method of moments (GMM) estimation techniques. It was found that institutions indeed are important in determining the long-run growth.

Dias and Tebaldi (2012) postulate that strong institutions accelerate human and physical capital accumulation, which in turn accelerate economic growth. Providing empirical evidence, the relationship between institutions, human capital and growth was examined using cross-country panel data from 1965 to 2005. It was reported that structural and political institution has a diverse effect on economic performance. While structural institutions affect long-term economic performance, political institution was found to be uncorrelated with productivity and long-term growth. Bergougui, Sami and Talbi (2017) examined the impact of natural resources, institutional quality and economic development in oil-rich countries for the period 1996–2015. It was found that countries that possess natural resources with high-quality institutions experienced economic development while most of the Arab oil-rich countries have inadequate institutional frameworks to insulate the economy from resource curse. Louis, Arpit and Stephen (2015) studied the effect of institutions on economic development using data from 48 African countries. The finding indicates that institutions can be considered a powerful factor in explaining the differences in development.

According to Mahendra Dev and Mooij (2010) and Okoye, Omankhanlen, Okoh, Urhie and Ahmed (2019), expenditure on the social sector is handled by the government on social services and rural development. Social services include education and health, while rural development encompasses anti-poverty programmes. Social sector spending is government spending for human capital development such as education development, health development and other social services development. Osuji and Nwani (2020) examined the effectiveness of the government expenditure in tracking social, economic and environmental sustainable development goals (SDGs). The study used quarterly data from 2000 to 2018, while vector autoregression and impulse response estimation techniques were employed. It was found that government expenditure reduces poverty only in the short run. Government expenditure had a negative effect on the SDG of rapid economic growth in the long run, but improves SDG of quality education both in the short run and the long run, through improvement in school enrolment. Noja, Cristea, Thalassinos and Kadłubek (2021) examined the cumulative effects of good public governance dimensions on economic welfare and poverty lessening. The results showed that general government expenditure increases welfare, but environmental support did not generate the same positive effects. Using the descriptive technique, Raghupathi and Raghupathi (2020) examined the impact of public health expenditure on economic performance in the United States and found that healthcare expenditure had a positive impact on economic performance. Using time-series data from 1980 to 2015, Shafuda and De (2020) examined the impact of government spending on human development indicators such as healthcare outcomes, education achievements and national income in Namibia. The Vector Auto-Regressive (VAR) and Error Correction Model (ECM) techniques were employed. Findings indicate that government spending on education had a positive and significant impact on literacy rate, net primary, gross tertiary enrolment and national income. Liao, Du, Wang and Yu (2019) investigated the impact of investment in education on sustainable economic growth in China. The study used Panel data of 21 cities in Guangdong province covering the period 2000–2016. Investment in education was found to have a positive impact on sustainable economic growth.

However, the level of impact varies across different regions. Oserei and Uddin (2019) examined the impact of government expenditure on primary health care on real national output in Nigeria using the Ordinary Least Square (OLS) technique. The findings reveal a positive impact of government spending on health on gross domestic output. In Iran, Tabar, Yaser and Badooei (2016) investigated the relationship between government educational expenditure, total government expenditure and real GDP from 1981 to 2012 using the Auto-Regressive Distributive Lag (ARDL) technique. It was found that in the long run, real GDP and the labour force had a positive impact on total government expenditure. However, in the short run, the capital stock had a negative impact on total government expenditure. Basu, Calamitsis and Ghura (2000) and World Bank (2022) allude that the overall economic performance of African countries can be greatly improved through good governance.

From the literature review, this chapter contributes to existing literature apparently on two fronts. First, it undertakes an encompassing cross-country panel study of selected developing countries in Africa where there is a handful of studies. Second, it focuses on education, health and other social service segments in relation to control of corruption, government effectiveness and rule of law. The basic characteristics of spending in these sectors compared to transfers is that they are more pro-poor and have probable positive spillover effects on economic growth. More importantly, this chapter also examined the complementarity or otherwise of the effect of governance and social sector spending on sustainable growth, which has been ignored by previous studies.

6.3 Data and Methodology

Data for this study is annual series involving selected African countries drawn from the World Bank's World Development Indicators (2022) and the African Development Bank Data Base (2022). The study period covers 1981–2021. The largest economies in each of the five sub-regions in Africa are selected. The selected countries are Egypt (North Africa), Nigeria (West Africa), Kenya (East Africa), South Africa (South Africa) and the Democratic Republic of Congo (Central Africa). These countries are also selected on the basis that they have made attempts at democratic changes to provide good governance and political and economic sustainability. Variables of interest are sustainable economic growth (measured by GDP per head as a ratio of the percentage unemployment and as a ratio of carbon dioxide emissions per head), social sector spending (measured by government expenditure on education and health), governance (measured by control of corruption, government effectiveness and rule of law). National savings rate and population growth rate are added as control variables.

This study is anchored on the Augmented Solow human-capital-growth framework. In the original version of the thesis, human capital is not explicitly incorporated into the growth process. Human capital was

Governance, Social Sector Spending and Sustainable Growth 99

incorporated into the original Solow growth theory by Mankiw, Romer and Weil (1992). Non-homogeneity of labour in the production process within an economy or across different economies because different countries or countries within a region could have different levels of education and skills was the basis for justification for the inclusion of human capital in the theory. A major assumption of the theory is that human capital development enhances output growth. In line with Eigbiremolen and Anaduaka (2014) and Oluwatobi and Ogunrinola (2011), the relationship can be specified as:

$$Y = AK^\alpha (hL)^\beta \qquad (6.1)$$

where

Y = Output
K = physical stock of capital
h = human capital development
L = labour
A = total factor productivity
α = capital input elasticity with respect to output
β = labour input elasticity with respect to the output

Total factor productivity (A) in Equation (6.1) is influenced by past physical capital investments, specified as;

$$A = DOINV = DOINV^\theta \qquad (6.2)$$

where DOINV is a domestic investment, proxied by gross fixed capital formation. Substituting Equation (6.2) into (6.1) and representing output (Y) with sustainable economic growth (SUSG – to be measured by GDP per head as a ratio of the percentage unemployment and as a ratio of carbon dioxide emissions per head), the capital stock (K) with national savings rate (NSR), human capital development (h) with government expenditures on education (GXEDU) and health (GXHELT) and labour (L) with population growth rate (POPG) yields:

$$SUSG = DOINV^\theta, NSR^\alpha, (GXEDU^\varphi, GXHELT^\beta) POPG^\psi \qquad (6.3)$$

We augment governance variables (control of corruption – CONCOR, government effectiveness – GEFFECT and rule of law – RLAW) into Equation (6.3) and take the logs of the variables to arrive at Equation (6.4):

$$SUSG = \theta In DOINV + \alpha NSR + \varphi In GXEDU + \beta In GXHELT \\ + \psi POPG + bCONCOR + \delta GEFFECT + \vartheta RLAW \qquad (6.4)$$

To fit a linear panel model with a dynamic variable, we add the dynamic variable and re-specify Equation (6.4) as:

$$\begin{aligned}SUSG_{it} = &\ \gamma + \rho SUSG_{it-1} + \theta InDOINV_{it} + \alpha NSR_{it} + \varphi InGXEDU_{it} \\ &+ \beta InGXHELT_{it} + \psi POPG_{it} + bCONCOR_{it} + \delta GEFFECT_{it} \\ &+ \vartheta RLAW_{it} + \gamma_{it} + e_{1it}\end{aligned} \quad (6.5)$$

Equation (6.5) is specified to examine the effect of the explanatory variables on sustainable growth, SUSG, NSR, POPG, CONCOR, GEFFECT and RLAW are not logged because the variables are in rate. γ_{it} is a between-country error term, while e_{it} is a within-country error term. On the other hand, i represents observational units and t is time.

In addition, for robustness check and in order to determine if the effect of social sector spending is significantly dependent on governance, we interact the governance variables with the social sector variables. The equation for the empirical estimation is specified as follows:

$$\begin{aligned}SUSG_{it} = &\ h_0 + h_1 SUSG_{it-1} + h_2 GXEDU_{it} + h_3 GXHELT_{it} + h_4 CONCOR_{it} \\ &+ h_5 GEFFECT_{it} + h_6 RLAW_{it} + h_7 CONCOR\_GXEDU_{it} \\ &+ h_8 CONCOR\_GXHELT_{it} + h_9 GEFFECT\_GXEDU_{it} \\ &+ h_{10} GEFFECT\_GXHELT_{it} + h_{11} RLAW\_GXEDU_{it} \\ &+ h_{12} RLAW\_GXHELT_{it} + \gamma_{2it} + e_{2it}\end{aligned} \quad (6.6)$$

Equations (6.5) and (6.6) were estimated using the GMM estimator because the lagged dependent variable, $SUSGROW_{t-1}$ in the equations can result in autocorrelation. Also, some variables such as the governance variables and sustainable growth may be endogenous and causality may run in both directions. Although the two-stage least squares (2SLS) instrumental variables (IV) estimation can be used in the estimation of such an equation, the instruments might be weak at the first stage of the 2SLS regressions. With weak instruments, the fixed-effects IV estimators may be biased in the way of the OLS estimators. GMM estimator will be more appropriate for the equations for estimation. Two forms of GMM are the first-differenced GMM – developed by Arellano and Bond (1991) and the system GMM estimator – developed by Arellano and Bover (1995) and Blundell and Bond (1998). The first-difference GMM uses first-differenced variables with appropriate lagged levels as instruments, while the system GMM estimator uses variables in their level form with lagged differences as instruments. Independent variables such as $SUSGROW_{t-1}$ is highly persistent and, lagged levels could be very weak instruments for first differenced equations. Thus, the system GMM estimator is preferred to the first-differenced GMM estimator.

Governance, Social Sector Spending and Sustainable Growth 101

6.4 Results and Discussion

6.4.1 Unit Root and Cointegration Tests

The variables were subjected to a stationarity test using the Breitung and the Im, Pesaran and Shin (IPS) unit root tests. Pedroni's test for cointegration was also conducted on the variables in the model. Table 6.1 reports the unit root and the cointegration tests results.

As shown in panel A, none of the p-values of the variables is significant at the level in both tests. Therefore, the null hypothesis that the panels contain unit roots is accepted at the 5% level. Since there is the unit root at the level form of the variables, 1st difference of the variables became necessary. Thus, the variables were differenced once and the tests were further carried out. At 1st difference, both tests showed significant p-values, indicating the rejection of the null hypothesis. From the result, it was observed that all the variables are all stationary at order 1. This justifies the conduct of the Pedroni's cointegration test and the result presented in panel B of Table 6.1. The p-values of the test are significant at the 5% level, which means that the variables are cointegrated. We went further to estimate Equation (6.4) using the system GMM technique and the result are reported in Table 6.2.

6.4.2 Effect of Governance and Social Sector Spending on Sustainable Growth

Equation (6.5) was estimated using GMM to determine the effect of governance and social sector spending on sustainable growth. Table 6.2 reports the results of the estimates. In Table 6.2, two specifications are presented based on two measures of sustainable growth. In column (1), GDP per head as a ratio of carbon dioxide emissions per head is used to measure sustainable growth. In column (2), GDP per head as a ratio of the percentage unemployment is used to measure sustainable growth. The reason for the change was to ensure the robustness of the findings and provide extra proof of the impact of the independent variables on sustainable growth. Rule of law, government effectiveness and control of corruption have negative coefficients of –4.8500, –1.4300 and –5.7300 with z-values of –0.29, –1.04 and –8.57, respectively, in column (1). The insignificant rule of law and government effectiveness coefficients means that the variables have no significant effect on GDP per head as a ratio of carbon dioxide emissions per head in column (1). The significant control of corruption coefficient, on the other hand, means rejecting the null hypothesis that the variable has no significant effect on GDP per head as a ratio of carbon dioxide emissions per head. An improvement in governance in terms of rule of law and government effectiveness results in an insignificant sustainable growth in terms of an insignificant reduction in GDP per head as a ratio of carbon dioxide emissions per head. However, an improvement in the control of corruption brings about significant sustainable growth in terms of the significant

Table 6.1 Results of Breitung and Im, Pesaran and Shin (IPS) unit root test and Pedroni's test for cointegration

Panel A: Breitung and Im, Pesaran and Shin (IPS) Unit Root Test Results

Variable	Breitung unit root Test Result		Im, Pesaran and Shin (IPS) Test Result		~I(d)
	Level	1st Difference	Level	1st Difference	
SUSGROW_CO2	-1.8987 (0.0688)	-2.8069* (0.0025)	-0.9933 (0.1603)	-5.0796* (0.0000)	I(1)
SUSGROW_PU	-1.2966 (0.0608)	-1.6598* (0.0085)	0.2433 (0.5961)	-3.6376* (0.0001)	I(1)
NSR	-0.4668 (0.3203)	-2.1092* (0.0037)	-1.4168 (0.0783)	-2.5863* (-5.1604)	I(1)
GXEDU	-0.2624 (0.3965)	-3.5031* (0.0002)	-0.0075 (0.5030)	-5.2575* (0.0000)	I(1)
GXHELT	-1.1539 (0.1243)	-5.0614* (0.0000)	-0.7939 (0.7864)	-2.8716* (0.0020)	I(1)
POPG	-1.9439 (0.9740)	-2.1491* (0.0158)	-1.4242 (0.2110)	-2.6213* (0.0044)	I(1)
DOINV	-1.2270 (0.1130)	-3.5962* (0.0002)	-1.1871 (0.2027)	-4.7607* (0.0000)	I(1)
CONCOR	-2.3561 (0.0092)	-3.4183* (0.0181)	-1.2403 (0.1016)	-6.3580* (0.0000)	1(1)
GEFFECT	-1.3289 (0.2104)	-3.3688* (0.0055)	-1.8346 (0.1263)	-6.6995* (0.0000)	1(1)
RLAW	-1.5049 (0.1061)	-4.1045* (0.0000)	-1.0741 (0.1105)	-5.8663* (0.0000)	1(1)

(1) The Breitung and the IPS p-values are presented in parenthesis. * denotes significance at 5% and rejection of the null hypothesis that the panels contain unit roots.

Panel B: Result of Pedroni's Test for Cointegration

	Statistic	p-value
Modified Phillips–Perron t	1.5415	0.0016
Phillips–Perron t	-1.1403	0.0271
Augmented Dickey–Fuller t	-1.4688	0.0409

The model underlying the reported statistics includes panel-specific means and panel-specific AR parameters and does not include a time trend. Bartlett kernel with 2 lags was used, as selected by the Newey–West methods, to adjust for serial correlation.

Source: Computation by the authors.

Table 6.2 Estimated results of the effect of governance and social sector spending on sustainable growth

Variables	(1) GDP per head as a ratio of carbon dioxide emissions per head	(2) GDP per head as a ratio of the percentage unemployment
RLAW	−1.4300 (z = −0.29) (p = 0.773)	6.4100 (z = 4.58) (p = 0.000)
GEFFECT	−4.8500 (z = 1.04) (p = 0.296)	−4.9500 (z = −0.35) (p = 0.724)
CONCOR	−5.7300 (z = −8.57) (p = 0.000)	−1.3300 (z = −6.72) (p = 0.000)
GXEDU	−8.1700 (z = 0.68) (p = 0.499)	−2.0100 (z = −0.63) (p = 0.530)
GXHELT	−5.74 (z = 0.93) (p = 0.352)	−1.0900 (z = 0.60) (p = 0.545)
DOINV	1.6900 (z = 7.95) (p = 0.000)	−7.48 (z = −9.74) (p = 0.000)
NSR	−6.37 (z = −2.33) (p = 0.020)	−8.07 (z = −0.72) (p = 0.471)
POPG	1.9000 (z = 0.56) (p = 0.577)	1.17 (z = 1.15) (p = 0.249)
SUSG_CO2; SUSG_PU	9.2200 (z = 0.33) (p = 0.741)	0.8988 (z = 31.61) (p = 0.000)
Wald chi2(9)	87.46 (p= 0.0000)	71.95 (0.0000)
Sargan Test	2449.724 (p = 0.0000)	2953.223 (p = 0.0000)

Source: Computation by the authors.

reduction in GDP per head as a ratio of carbon dioxide emissions per head. In column (2), similar to column (1), control of corruption significantly reduces the GDP per head as a ratio of the percentage unemployment by 1.33%, while government effectiveness has a negative and insignificant effect on GDP per head as a ratio of the percentage unemployment by 4.95%. Rule of law, however, has a positive and significant effect on GDP per head as a ratio of the percentage of unemployment. Our result is in line with Arbolino and Boffardi (2017) in which they find that quality institution is good for growth. Furthermore, our results are also consistent with the findings of Mtiraoui (2015), Nawaz, Iqbal and Khan (2014).

Government expenditures on education and health have a negative and insignificant effect on GDP per head as a ratio of carbon dioxide emissions per head in column (1) and GDP per head as a ratio of the percentage unemployment in column (2). The negative and insignificant effect of government education and health expenditure is suggestive that social sector spending has not adequately contributed to sustainable growth. This contradicts the findings of Liao et al. (2019) that education positively contributed to economic growth in the case of China.

Moreover, we found that domestic investment has a positive and significant effect on GDP per head as a ratio of carbon dioxide emissions per head in column (1). But the effect on GDP per head as a ratio of the percentage unemployment is negative and significant in column (2). This means that domestic investment increases GDP per head as a ratio of carbon dioxide emissions per head but significantly reduces the GDP per head as a ratio of the percentage unemployment. The national savings rate has a negative effect in both columns (1) and (2). Surprisingly, population growth has a positive effect on both GDP per head as a ratio of carbon dioxide emissions per head and the GDP per head as a ratio of the percentage unemployment as in columns (1) and (2), though not statistically significant. As portrayed, an increase in population growth increases the GDP per head as a ratio of carbon dioxide emissions per head and the GDP per head as a ratio of the percentage unemployment by 1.90 per cent point and 1.17 per cent point, respectively. The result confirms the harmful effect of population growth on the attainment of sustainable growth. As argued by Edeme and Thank God (2022), rising population growth is harmful to growth, especially in the absence of good governance.

We further investigated if governance and social sector spending have a complementary or substitution effect on sustainable growth. To do this, we interacted the governance with the social sector and estimated a dynamic model using GMM (see Equation 6.5). The estimates are reported in Table 6.3. To determine the nature of the interaction effect, that is, if the interaction variables have a substitution effect or a complementary effect, we compare the signs and significance of the interaction coefficients with the coefficients for government spending on education and health, respectively.

Concerning the interaction effect of governance variables on sustainable growth, we observe that control of corruption and government spending on education have positive effects in both columns (1) and (2) – significant only in column (2). But the coefficient for control of corruption is negative. Since control of corruption is negative and the interaction term is positive, it indicates that the control of corruption and government spending on education has a complementary effect on sustainable growth. The interaction term for control of corruption and government spending on health is negative and significant in columns (1) and (2) compared to the negative coefficient for control of corruption means that control of corruption and government spending on health has a substitution effect on sustainable growth. Similarly, the interaction terms for government effectiveness and education, and rule of law and education, respectively, are positive and significant in both columns (1) and (2). The negative coefficients for government effectiveness and rule of law is suggestive that government effectiveness and rule of law, respectively, and government expenditure on education are complementary. Hence, good governance cannot be ignored to stimulate social sector spending in order to generate adequate growth. However, the interaction of government effectiveness and government spending on health,

Table 6.3 Estimated results of the interaction effects of governance and social sector spending on sustainable growth

Variables	(1) GDP per head as a ratio of carbon dioxide emissions per head	(2) GDP per head as a ratio of the percentage unemployment
RLAW	−1.7700	−1.9400
	(z = −1.45) (p = 0.148)	(z = −6.95) (p = 0.000)
GEFFECT	−8.0300	−4.3300
	(z = −5.28) (p = 0.000)	(z = 1.50) (p = 0.134)
CONCOR	−7.7500	−5.5000
	(z = −0.46) (p = 0.648)	(z = −1.85) (p = 0.064)
GXEDU	1.6400	3.7100
	(z = 4.42) (p = 0.000)	(z = 5.17) (p = 0.000)
GXHELT	2.5800	4.2100
	(z = 1.64) (p = 0.101)	(z = 1.39) (p = 0.165)
CONCOR_GXEDU	2.7500	7.8200
	(z = 1.48) (p = 0.138)	(z = 2.03) (p = 0.042)
CONCOR_GXHELT	−1.5000	−2.6900
	(z = −3.45) (p = 0.001)	(z = −3.17) (p = 0.002)
GEFFECT_GXEDU	1.3600	8.8000
	(z = 7.29) (p = 0.000)	(z = 2.68) (p = 0.007)
GEFFECT_GXHELT	−1.6600	−4.2900
	(z = −0.40) (p = 0.687)	(z = −5.00) (p = 0.000)
RLAW_GXEDU	2.0100	1.2700
	(z = 2.82) (p = 0.003)	(z = 5.37) (p = 0.000)
RLAW_GXHELT	−7.3500	4.2500
	(z = −2.48) (p = 0.013)	(z = 6.77) (p = 0.000)
Wald chi2(9)	165.98 (p= 0.0000)	829.57 (0.0000)
Sargan Test	4417.185 (p = 0.0000)	6732.505 (p = 0.0000)

Source: Computation by the authors.

and rule of law and health spending have negative coefficients, indicating that government effectiveness and rule of law, respectively, and government health spending have substitution effects on sustainable growth. These results are not only highly significant but of economic importance. For instance, an increase in social sector spending and control of corruption by one standard deviation increases economic growth by 8.80 per cent point. In this case, stronger country governance makes social sector spending more productive. Therefore, our results imply that countries with high social sector spending should focus on enhancing their country governance in order to accentuate sustainable growth.

6.5 Conclusion

We have demonstrated in this chapter the effects of good governance in achieving very heterogeneous sustainable growth goals in African countries.

The endogenous growth theory also gives priority to social sector policy, which focuses largely on human capital such as education and health enhancement. Therefore, social sector spending was also considered in this chapter as immanence in the sustainable growth process. The empirical evidence indicates that governance promotes sustainable growth. Among the components of governance, control of corruption is the most effective for sustainable growth; it had a significant effect on the two indicators of sustainable growth. Similarly, social sector spending does not significantly promote sustainable growth. But, the negative effect of government expenditure on education and health on the indicators of sustainable growth means that with appropriate measures, social sector spending tends to bring about significant sustainable growth. Control of corruption and government spending on education has a complementary effect on sustainable growth. Also, government effectiveness, rule of law and government expenditure on education are complementary. However, control of corruption, government effectiveness and rule of law, respectively, and government health spending has substitution effect on sustainable growth.

The policy direction is that the pursuit of good governance coupled with an increase in social sector spending is imperative in the attainment of sustainable growth. It will be more appropriate if it is complemented with the effective control of corruption and rule of law, especially if the intention is on education development for sustainable growth.

References

African Development Bank Data Base (2022). Social Economic Indicator. Retrieved from https://dataportal.opendataforafrica.org/bbkawjf/afdb-socio-economic-database

Arbolino, R. & Boffardi, R. (2017). The impact of institutional quality and efficient cohesion investments on economic growth evidence from Italian regions. *Sustainability*, 9(8), 14–32.

Arellano, M. & Bond, S. (1991). Some tests of specification for panel data: Monte Carlo evidence and an application to employment equations. *The Review of Economic Studies*, 58(2), 277–297.

Arellano, M. & Bover, O. (1995). Another look at the instrumental variable estimation of error-components models. *Journal of Econometrics*, 68(1), 29–51. https://doi.org/10.1016/0304-4076(94)01642-D

Austin, G. (2015). Is Africa too late for late development: gerschenkr on South of the Sahara. World Economic History Congress, In: Andersson, M & Axelsson, T. (Eds.). *Diverse development paths and structural transformation in the escape from poverty*. London: Oxford University Press.

Baqir, R. (2020). Social sector spending in a panel of countries, International Monetary Fund (IMF) Working Paper No. 135, International Monetary Fund.

Basiago, A. D. (1999). Economic, social and environmental sustainability in development theory and urban planning practice, *The Environmentalist*, 19(5), 145–161.

Basu, A., Calamitsis, E. A. & Ghura, D. (2000). Promoting growth in Sub-Saharan African, learning what works, Economic Issues, No. 23.

Bergougui, B., Sami, L. & Talbi, B. (2017). Natural resources, institutional quality and economic development in oil-rich countries: The case of Arab countries. *Les Cahiers du MECAS*, 13(2), 6–15.

Blundell, R., & Bond, S. (1998). Initial conditions and moment restrictions in dynamic panel data models. *Journal of Econometrics*, 87(1), 115–143.

Bourguignon, F. (2003). The growth elasticity of poverty reduction; Explaining heterogeneity across countries and time periods. In: T. Eicher & S. Turnovsky (Eds.). *Inequality and Growth: Theory and Policy Implications*. Cambridge, MA: MIT Press.

Brand, A. & Monje Barón, B. (2012). *Extreme poverty is violence, breaking the silence, searching for peace*, Vauréal, France: International Movement ATD Fourth World.

Dias, J. & Tebaldi, E. (2012). Institutions, human capital, and growth: the long-run institutional mechanism. *Structural Change and Economic Dynamics*, 23(3), 300–312. https://doi.org/10.1016/j.strueco.2012.04.003

Edeme, R. K. & ThankGod, E. E. (2022). Interactive effect of population growth and institutional quality on environmental sustainability in West African region. In: Chakraborty, C. & Pal, D. (Eds.). *Environmental sustainability, growth trajectory and gender: Contemporary issues of developing economies*, Bingley: Emerald Publishing Limited, pp. 37–49. https://doi.org/10.1108/978-1-80262-153-220221004

Eigbiremolen, G. O. & Anaduaka, U. S. (2014). Human capital development and economic growth: The Nigeria experience, *International Journal of Academic Research in Business and Social Sciences*, 4(4), 25–35.

Giraldo, A. (2019). Sustainability and 5 examples of economic growth. Retrieved from: https://ideasforus.org/sustainability-and-5-examples-of-how-it-helps-economic-growth/

Godinot, X. (2010). *Extreme poverty and world governance*. Paris: Forum for a new World Governance.

Godinot, X. (2012). *Eradicating extreme poverty: democracy, globalization and human rights*. London: Pluto Press.

Iheonu, C., Ihedimma, G. & Onwuanaku, C (2017). Institutional quality and economic performance in West Africa. MPRA Paper No. 82212. Retrieved 16 January 2022 from: https://mpra.ub.uni-muenchen.de/82212/

International Development Association (IDA) (2020). Governance. Retrieved from https://www.worldbank.org/en/topic/governance/overview#1

Kaasa, A. (2016). Social capital, institutional quality and productivity: evidence from European regions. *Economics & Sociology*, 9(4), 11.

Kraay, A (2004). When is growth pro-poor? cross-country evidence. IMF Working Paper 4–47, International Monetary Fund, Washington, DC.

Liao, L., Du, M., Wang, B. & Yu, Y. (2019). The impact of educational investment on sustainable economic growth in Guangdong, China: A cointegration and causality analysis. *Sustainability*, 11, 749–766. Retrieved from: https://doi.org/10.3390/su11030766

Louis, C., Arpit, P. & Stephen, S. (2015). *Institutions and the economic development of Africa*. Manuscript, Atalanta: Georgia Institute of Technology.

Mahendra Dev, D. & Mooij, J (2010). Social Sector Expenditures in the 1990s: Analysis of central and state budgets, *Economic and Political Weekly*, 37(9), 853–886. https://doi.org/10.2307/4411812

Mankiw, N. G., Romer, D. & Weil, D. N. (1992). A contribution to the empirics of economic growth, *The Quarterly Journal of Economics*, 107(2), 407–437.

Mensah, J. & Casadevail, S. R. (2019). Sustainable development: Meaning, history, principles, pillars and implications for human action: Literature Review, *Cogent Social Science*, 5(1), 1–9. https://doi.org/10.1080/2331186.2019.165353

Mo Ibrahim Foundation (2017). Ibrahim Index of African governance Index Report.

Mtiraoui, A. (2015). Control of corruption, action of public power, human capital and economic development: Application two sectors of education and health in the MENA region.

Nawaz, S., Iqbal, N. & Khan, M. A. (2014). The impact of institutional quality on economic growth: Panel evidence. *The Pakistan Development Review*, 53(1), 15–31.

Noja, G. G., Cristea, M., Thalassinos, E. & Kadłubek, M. (2021). Inter-linkages between government resources management, environmental support, and good public governance. *Advanced Insights from the European Union. Resources*, 10(41), 1–23.

Okoye, L. U., Omankhanlen, E. A., Okoh, A. E., Urhie, A. & Ahmed, A. (2019). Government expenditure and economic growth: The case of Nigeria. *Proceedings of SOCIOINT 2019-6th International Conference on Education, Social Sciences and Humanities*, 1184–1194, Istanbul.

Olaniyan, R. O. (2017). Governance in Africa challenges and prospects. Retrieved from: http://www.institut-gouvernance.org/en/chapitrage/fiche-chapitrage-64.html

Oluwatobi, S. O. & Ogunrinola, A. I. (2011). Government expenditure on human capital development: Implications for economic growth in Nigeria. *Journal of Sustainable Development*, 4(3). 72–80. https://doi.org/10.5539/jsd.v4n3p72

Oserei, K. & Uddin, G. (2019). The myth and reality of government expenditure on primary health care in Nigeria: Way forward to inclusive growth. MPRA Paper No. 99094. Retrieved from: https://mpra.ub.uni-muenchen.de/99094/

Osuji, E. & Nwani, S. E. (2020). Achieving sustainable development goals: Does government expenditure framework matter? *International Journal of Management, Economics and Social Sciences (IJMESS)*, 9(3), 131–160.

Raghupathi, V. & Raghupathi, W. (2020). Healthcare expenditure and economic performance: Insights from the United States data front. *Public Health*. Retrieved from: https://doi.org/10.3389/fpubh.2020.00156

Rodrik, D. (2015). *The political economy of liberal democracy* (No. w21540). National Bureau of Economic Research.

Roy, S. (2019). Sustainable growth. *Fundamental Economics*, II, 1–10. Retrieved from: https://www.eolss.net/sample-chapters/c04/e6-28b-05-01.pdf

Shafuda, C. P. P. & De, U. K. (2020). Government expenditure on human capital and growth in Namibia: A time series analysis. *Economic Structures*, 9(21), 20–40.

Simoes, M. C., Duarte, A. & Andrade, J. S. (2014). Assessing the impact of the welfare state on economic growth: A survey of recent developments. *Contemporary Trends and Prospects of Economic Recovery*, 13(1), 13–38.

Tabar, F. J., Yaser, Z. N. & Badooei, S. (2016). The impact of educational expenditures of government on the economic growth of Iran. Retrieved from: https://doi.org/10.17230/ad-minister.30.11

Udah, E. B. & Ayara, N. (2014). Institutions, governance structure and economic performance nexus in Nigeria. *Journal of Economics and Sustainable Development*, 5(3), 8–16.

United Nation Development Programme (UNDP) (1997). Governance indicators: A users' guide. Retrieved from: https://www.un.org/ruleoflaw/files/Governance%20Indicators_A%20Users%20Guide.pdf

United Nations (2021). World economic situation and prospects. Retrieved from https://www.un.org/development/desa/dpad/wp-content/uploads/sites/45/WESP2021_CH3_AFR.pdf

World Bank (2011). World Development Report: Conflict, Security and Development, The World Bank, Washington DC.

World Bank (2021). Worldwide governance indicators. Retrieved from: https://info.worldbank.org/governance/wgi/

World Bank (2022). World Development Indicators. World Bank, Retrieved from https://databank.worldbank.org/source/africa-development-indicators

7 Is Fiscal Decentralization a means to Poverty and Inequality Reduction?
An India–China Comparative Study

Sovik Mukherjee

7.1 Background

Countries in recent times are targeting fiscal decentralization as a means for improving the autonomy at the local levels of governance by delegating some of the centralized responsibilities to get better expected economic and social benefits. Fiscal decentralization goals are being targeted at improving the financial and administrative autonomy at the local levels of governance by devolving some of the centralized responsibilities. This can solve not only the problem of allocative and technical efficiency but also information efficiency, tailor-made to suit the needs of the local governments. As a result, information can be used without any sort of delay, without waiting for permission from central agencies. Even Max Weber (1947), the famous German sociologist, has argued in favor of locally operated and locally accountable institutions. Based on this powerful idea, policymakers have vouched for decentralization in terms of fiscal allocations, autonomously driven local governance, key issues in stakeholders' perception, and service delivery (Panda & Thakur, 2016).

Incidentally, countries across the globe have had wide-ranging experiences; India and China are no exception. But in this chapter, I focus only on the India–China comparative. Why India and China? There are dozens of studies in the economics literature across the globe that talk about the effects of fiscal decentralization on economic growth (Barro, 1990; Davoodi & Zou, 1998; Zhang & Zou, 1998; Akai & Sakata, 2002; Martinez-Vazquez & Mcnab, 2003; Thornton, 2007; Baskaran & Feld, 2013, to name a few) but, interestingly, the potential effects of decentralization, especially, fiscal decentralization on poverty and income inequality have not been extensively discussed, to date. Herein, the contribution of the chapter lies in analyzing the tri-variate nexus of fiscal decentralization, poverty, and inequality in China and India. As newly emerging economic powers on the global stage, China and India are the subjects of great interest, especially considering their remarkable record of economic growth in recent years (Desai, 2005). In terms of sectoral growth pattern, China is particularly good in manufacturing, while India is better in services.

DOI: 10.4324/9781003245797-8

However, China is giving India a tough competition with reference to the service sector (Khanna, 2007). Out of the many, two other reasons that have primarily led to this comparative study are—first, both China and India have introduced economic reforms in a sequential manner over a period contrary to the "big-bang" approach of reforms adopted in many countries of the former USSR, Eastern Europe, among others (Bardhan, 2006). Second, both central governments have been constitutionally devolving more and more "power, resources and responsibility" (Jin, 2009) for service delivery to the sub-national governments. Yet, the majority of the provinces and municipalities in China are a part of the centralized system and does not enjoy a high level of political autonomy[1]. Despite these remarkable similarities, one needs to note that there are three interesting contrasts between the two countries, as well. From a demographic angle, China is the world's largest country in terms of population, while India is the world's largest democratic republic. From the cultural side, India is ethnically diverse, while China's population is relatively homogeneous in comparison to India. From a political perspective, China has a one-party system in place, whereas India, the largest populous democracy in the world, has multi-party competitive elections.

Irrespective of these points of similarity and dissimilarity between India and China, the cause of concern is that the poor in both countries, especially in India, are not fully sharing the benefits of rapid economic growth. While in India, the poverty headcount ratio at $1.90 a day (2011 PPP$) stands at 21.2% and the GINI index at 35.7% in 2011, China's poverty headcount ratio stands at 0.7% and the GINI index at 38.6% in 2015. In view of these comparisons, this comparative analysis sheds light on the performance of the decentralization policies that India and China have taken up and how effective are these in terms of their effects on poverty reduction and inequality position. The belief is that the results of this study might as well provide very useful lessons to other developing countries considering or are currently in pursuit of reforming their fiscal system.

In this chapter, the focus is only on fiscal decentralization and not on other decentralization forms like political and administrative. I distinguish between the direct and indirect effects on poverty and income inequalities. Direct effects are classified as those in which poverty or income inequalities are altered because of changes in the process of fiscal decentralization and its consequential impact on the behavior of economic agents through changes in the composition of public expenditure, tax, share of central revenue, etc. Herein, the direct effects are captured by the modified fiscal decentralization index (MFDI) based on the four ratios, namely i) Expenditure Ratio (ER); ii) Revenue Autonomy (RA); iii) Transfer Dependency Ratio (TD); iv) Debt Autonomy (DA) as suggested by the World Bank (see Section 2 for details). On the other hand, the indirect effects are channelized through a number of socio-economic factors like the size of the government (SZG), logarithm of per capita GDP (LGDP), adult

Fiscal Decentralization a means to Poverty & Inequality Reduction? 113

literacy rate (ALR), mortality rate, ethnic/religious fragmentation (ERF), share of urban population (SUP), trade openness ratio (TOR), and index of democracy that are likely to have an impact on the fiscal decentralization process and also on the levels of poverty and inequality reduction.

Both theoretical and empirical studies have tried to look at the concepts of fiscal decentralization and poverty (see Ahmad & Brosio, 2009; Bird & Rodriguez, 1999; Francis & James, 2003) or for that matter fiscal decentralization and inequality (see Zhang, 2006; Bonet, 2006; Sacchi & Salotti, 2014, among others) separately. Up until now, we have little understanding of what may be the impact of fiscal decentralization on poverty alleviation and inequality in the income distribution in a simultaneous setting. Why do we consider this model in a simultaneous setting? For conceptual understanding, there is a rich literature that has been focusing on the effects of fiscal decentralization on poverty and inequality, primarily, through redistributive regional transfers targeted at primary health and basic education for bringing about an increase in employment and hence pulling people out of the poverty line or correcting the inequality underlying in the income distribution. Going by the famous argument of Oates (Oates, 1993), "If policies regarding infrastructure and human capital are formulated with consideration of regional or local conditions, then they are likely to be more effective in encouraging economic development than centrally determined policies that ignore these geographical differences."

However, if we consider a general setting like ours, the final effects on poverty and inequalities are not very clearly specified in the literature and would depend on the quality of the reforms and the policy targets the sub-national governments would have under the decentralized scenarios. Hence, the motivation for doing this research.

In this chapter, I try to decipher the tri-variate nexus between poverty, inequality, and fiscal decentralization for India and China considering necessary controls, as discussed, by using GMM Kernel estimations based on the Epanechnikov Kernel function as discussed in Section 3. Also, the data is at the first difference level to rule out the possibilities of country-related effects like political ideology. The primary questions this research venture addresses are as follows:

1 Is the existence of the relationship between fiscal decentralization reforms, poverty reduction, and income inequality reduction feasible and significant for India and China? (Given we have in place controls for political, social-economic, and demographic dimensions of a country)
2 Under what condition(s), if any, can we say that fiscal decentralization impacts on poverty and inequality reduction will be counter-productive?
3 To what extent is fiscal decentralization effective in combating social tension arising out of absolute (poverty) and relative (income inequality) deprivations?

114 *Sovik Mukherjee*

To sum up our results briefly, the derivations we get are consistent with the theoretical literature and arguments as already discussed. Interestingly, contrary to what Sepulveda and Martinez-Vazquez (2011) have derived from a panel dataset of Latin American and African economies that fiscal decentralization increases poverty levels. I, in this chapter, derive similar results with reference to the impact of fiscal decentralization on poverty levels. But when it comes to inequality in the income distribution, we have contradictory results. The positively significant coefficient of the fiscal decentralization parameter indicates that fiscal decentralization worsens inequality in the distribution of income. But the negative sign in the interactive term between fiscal decentralization and the SZG sector predicts that approximately for a sufficiently larger government size, i.e., around 20.7% of GDP for India and 18.3% for China, fiscal decentralization reduces inequalities in the income distribution[2].

The chapter is organized as follows. Section 2 presents the motivation from the theoretical models and the methodology in terms of the definition, scope, and the indices used in the process of calculation. In line with the conceptual framework proposed in Section 3, the empirical model is developed in Section 4. Section 5 concludes.

7.2 Methodology

Coming to the methodology part, to understand the concept of fiscal decentralization[3], the study makes use of the World Bank's four ratios[4] for p states in country i to build the MFDI. The ratios are, namely

1 **Expenditure Ratio (ER)**: "The expenditure ratio measures the share of spending taking place at the sub-national level (integrated across all the states using all of the resources available, except borrowing) relative to the total expenditure of the general government (using all resources available)":

$$ER_i = \frac{\sum_{j=1}^{p}(Subnational\ own\ revenues + Grants)_j}{Total\ General\ Government\ revenue} \quad (7.1)$$

As World Bank puts it, "a high ratio signals high decentralization of tasks (spending in the different policy areas and collecting revenues), but not necessarily of decision powers, at the sub-national level."

2 **Revenue Autonomy (RA)**: "The revenue autonomy indicator measures how much of the total resources available to the sub-national (local and state, if it exists at all) authorities (integrated across all the states) (excluding borrowing) is actually raised locally."

Fiscal Decentralization a means to Poverty & Inequality Reduction?

$$RA_i = \frac{\sum_{j=1}^{p}(Subnational\ own\ revenues)_j}{\sum_{j=1}^{p}(Subnational\ own\ revenues + Grants)_j} \qquad (7.2)$$

Again, a high revenue autonomy ratio points to high decentralization.

3 **Transfer Dependency Ratio (TD):** "The transfer dependency ratio is the percentage of the actual total sub-national expenditure covered by transfers from the central government (grants)."

$$TD_i = \frac{\sum_{j=1}^{p} Grants_j}{\sum_{j=1}^{p}(Subnational\_expenditure)_j} \qquad (7.3)$$

As World Bank puts it,

this ratio measures the degree of dependency of the sub-national level on resources distributed from the central level. In contrast to the revenue autonomy indicator, it tends to be low (though not necessarily) in countries with a high degree of fiscal decentralization. The indicator of is approximately a complement to 1 of the revenue autonomy.

So, to ensure that it is in line with the other three indices, i.e., a higher value means higher fiscal decentralization, we take the reciprocal of this index.

4 **Debt Autonomy (DA):** This has been formulated as

$$DA_i = \frac{\sum_{j=1}^{p} D_j}{\sum_{j=1}^{p} E_j} \qquad (7.4)$$

where E is the total expenditure of the regional governments and D is the total regional government debt (including borrowings from international organizations). The total has been calculated by summing up over all the states/provinces.

Since all the features are equally important in determining the degree of fiscal decentralization, the author has given all of them equal weights in this analysis. In a four-dimensional space, the four-dimension indices can be expressed, with "0" being the least value and "1" being the ideal value. The inverse of the weighted Euclidean distance from the ideal point of (1,1,1.1) is used in the MFDI. Thus, the MFDI calculation for country i is given by

$$MFDI_i = 1 - \sqrt{\frac{\left[(1-ER_i)^2 + (1-RA_i)^2 + (1-TD_i)^2 + (1-DA_i)^2\right]}{4}} \quad (7.5)$$

The numerator of the term within the square root gives the Euclidean distance of country i from the ideal point (1,1,1,1). The inverse distance has been calculated to show that the higher the value of MFDI, the better will be the extent of fiscal decentralization and the higher will be the position of the state concerned among other states. As proposed in the paper by Nathan et al. (2008), the MFDI developed in this chapter satisfies the properties of "NAMPUS i.e., normalization, anonymity, monotonicity, proximity, uniformity and signaling." The idea of using a Euclidean distance framework is to relax the assumption of substitutability among the indices, i.e., performing well in terms of one index does not make up for the poor performance in terms of the other. Coming to the interpretability of MFDI, a value of MFDI = 1 means a country has achieved a condition of perfect decentralization, i.e., sub-national governments do not face any intervention from the central government—a rare possibility. However, if the value lies somewhere between 0.5 and 1, a situation of relative fiscal decentralization, i.e., some degree of fiscal decentralization. Similarly, when MFDI lies between 0 and 0.5, it is a case of relative fiscal centralization and MFDI = 0 represents perfect fiscal centralization.

Coming to the measurement of poverty and inequality, we make use of the poverty headcount ratio for the concerned years. Also, as a measure of income inequality for the concerned years for both India and China, we use the Generalized Entropy (GE) index given by

$$GE(2) = \frac{1}{2N} \sum_{i=1}^{N} \left[\left(\frac{y_i}{\bar{y}}\right)^2 - 1\right] \quad (7.6)$$

where N is the number of cases (e.g., households or families), y_i is the income for case i, and $\alpha = 2$ is the weight assigned to the distances between incomes on different parts of the income distribution. The Generalized Entropy measure calculation involves a lot of intricate details. Data accessibility becomes a significant restriction. An estimate of the ratio between the ith class's income and the average income is required by the formal definition. Unfortunately, this data is not accessible, so I, following the methodology I developed in one of my earlier papers (Mukherjee & Karmakar, 2019), have modified the GE(2) index and used the ratios of first to fifth decile income and fifth to ninth decile income in this study instead of the original ratio. Here, the fifth decile kind of acts as the mean decile. The data has been accessed from the OECD database (www.stats.oecd.org/Index.aspx). A measure from the GE class is sensitive to the lower end of the distribution for smaller weight values. As this chapter deals with countries like India and China, the focus remains more on the lower tail of the distribution and as a result, $\alpha = 2$ is taken into consideration.

7.3 The Empirical Model and Variables' Descriptions

Next, the author moves on to the development of the empirical model and the dataset used in this context. Decentralization, inequality, and poverty reduction may be correlated in some form, but theoretically, there is no precise functional form that exists. The hypothesized empirical model for country i (i = India, China) is defined as

$$Pov = f(MFDI, Govt.\_size, Controls) \, \& $$
$$Ineq = f(MFDI, Govt.\_size, Controls) \qquad (7.7)$$

The assumption of the relationship being linear is therefore under question. To date, there is no such paper which talks about a possible non-linear relationship among the key focus variables. The SZG is an important factor in this regard (for China, Government expenditure as a percentage of GDP has been used as a proxy). A relatively large public sector will have a greater capacity of being able to implement a considerable number of welfare programs, leading to greater impacts on poverty and income distribution.

Talking about the control variables, first, we have the LGDP. Countries with greater per capita GDP are expected to have more capacity to reduce poverty and hence a negative coefficient. The ALR takes care of education control and, generally, better literacy rates imply better-paid jobs and lower poverty rates (Dreze & Sen, 1989). The mortality rate (MR) has been used as a proxy for the health infrastructure. The demographic profile is being captured through the share of the population living in the urban areas and is an index of ERF. The share of urban population (SUP) usually enjoys higher income per capita and so a higher share of urban populace should be consistent with poverty reduction. Ethnic fractionalization contributes to the nation's cultural diversity and may have an impact on the political system, institutional structure, and general attitudes about poverty and inequality. Finally, the index of democracy (ID) and TOR serve as the control for the political aspects of the story and to what extent are their controls on foreign capitals, respectively. The TOR is defined as the (Exports + Imports) / GDP. The concept of democracy index on a scale of 0–10 highlights the structural dynamics of the political system and to what extent the government can implement the reforms arising out of the fiscal decentralization pertaining to poverty reduction and income inequality. Subsequently, as an add-on, we carry out the same exercise for India and China but with poverty-based social tension (PBST) and inequality-based social tension (IBST) as dependent variables in place of poverty headcount ratio and Gini coefficient. Here, the forms of social tension indices considered are as follows.

For IBST, the measure is μG, where G is the Gini coefficient or Lorenz ratio. For poverty-gap-based social tension, we consider $\frac{z\theta_1}{\mu_1}$, where z is the poverty line, θ_1 is the poverty gap, and μ is the per capita income level (Kakwani & Son, 2016).

In this chapter, I try to decipher the tri-variate nexus between poverty, inequality, and fiscal decentralization for India and China taking into account necessary controls as discussed by using the Epanechnikov Kernel function under GMM Kernel estimations. The Leave-One-Out error loss function (Looloss) concept must be explained in detail before moving on to the explanation of the Kernel regression results. The difference that results from leaving out a value, such as the ith one, is the loss function governing the Leave-One-Out (LOO) error. This loss function must be minimized for a specific value of λ, the regularization parameter that determines the variation between the model fit and the observed values—fundamentally similar to the minimization of the error in the case of ordinary least square (OLS) (Mukherjee & Karmakar, 2018). It should be noted that to accommodate unbalanced datasets, conceptually we simply use zeros as instruments and residuals for time periods that are missing in the panel dataset. Also, the data is at the first difference level to rule out the possibilities of country-specific effects like political ideology. The novelty of this framework is that it can be extended to many countries not only in South Asia but across the globe to examine the robustness and generality of the results—an exercise that will be a part of the future scope.

The data from 2006 to 2019 has been compiled from various sources. For India, I have compiled it from the CENSUS data, the Planning Commission Databook (2014), the NITI Aayog database, and the World Bank database (especially, World Developmental Indicators). For China, the dataset has been compiled from the OECD database, www.stats.gov.cn, the CEIC database, the Population CENSUS of the People's Republic of China, and the World Bank database (World Developmental Indicators). It should be noted that I have compiled the data for the index of democracy for both the countries from the Economist Intelligence Unit database.

And, for ethnic/religious[5] polarization, I adopt the index formula in Sengupta and Mukherjee (2018) as

$$RQ = 1 - \sum_{i=1}^{m}\left(\frac{0.5 - \pi_i}{0.5}\right)^2 \pi_i, \text{for m such groups} \qquad (7.8)$$

where $\pi_i = \frac{n_i}{N}$ and n_i is the size of the ith group and N is the total population. Contrary to the use of unrealistic proxies like log of population as measures of fiscal decentralization (Sepulveda & Martinez-Vazquez, 2011), this chapter makes use of a proper well-defined index of fiscal decentralization, MFDI, as already discussed.

7.4 Results and Discussion

As discussed, there are many direct and indirect effects working on poverty and income equality reduction that has been controlled for in the presence of fiscal decentralization. The chapter has checked for possible endogeneity through a linear GMM estimation of the proposed relationships described in Section 3 and found that the extent of correlation of the independent variables with the error term is very negligible before moving on to the Kernel estimation.

As expected, the MFDI has been effective in reducing poverty levels in both India and China. This is followed by the coefficient of the SZG which turns out to be positive. This is indicative of the fact that gains from government expenditure have not reached the poor. The coefficient on LGDP has turned out to be negative, i.e., a capacity to reduce the headcount ratio. So are the results of ALR and MR. The greater number of schooling years along with greater survival rates is indicative of better-paid jobs and greater productivity rates among the poor, hence lowering the poverty levels. The SUP for both the countries shows a negative sign implying that people living in the urban areas enjoy a higher per capita income, hence associated with a reduction in poverty levels. The ERF helps to take care of the cultural and religious diversity in both the countries. The strength of the association is stronger for India as compared to China. This is because the Chinese ethnic groups are relatively homogeneous as compared to the Indian case and in India, religious polarization fuels the poverty levels by creating riots or other forms of religious tension thereby hampering the benefits of development to reach the poor. The TOR has not been significant in reducing poverty levels in this case. One reason for this might be the presence of the ID in the model itself which indirectly takes care of the fact that to what extent government is in a position to enact and implement policies within the institutional framework by allowing foreign capital in boosting up the development process to impact poverty and inequality reduction. This is again consistent with the results that obtained for both the countries; India being the largest electoral democracy sets policies which are pro-poor on account of vote bank politics while for China, the impact on poverty reduction is comparatively less may be on account of being under a one-party rule. The p-values of the coefficients indicate the significance of all the explanatory variables except TOR for both the countries and ERF for China (Table 7.1).

With inequality, the model has almost similar results (Table 7.2). The only difference is the role played by the SZG in reducing levels of income inequality and the related tension. The negative and the significant coefficient that are derived for the interaction term between SZG and MFDI indicates the worsening effect of decentralization decreases with the government size

Table 7.1 Impact on Poverty (India and China)

Model 1: Dependent variable is poverty headcount ratio

Looloss: 108.3811 – Iteration = 1; Looloss: 104.8647 – Iteration = 2;
Looloss: 101.6262 – Iteration = 3; Looloss: 98.96312 – Iteration = 4;
Looloss: 96.97307 – Iteration = 5; Looloss: 95.62673 – Iteration = 6;
Looloss: 94.85052 – Iteration = 7;
Lambda = 0.9855
R-square = 0.5538

	India		China	
Variables	Coefficient	$P > |t|$	Coefficient	$P > |t|$
MFDI	−0.171	0.00*	−0.197	0.00*
SZG	1.556	0.00*	2.638	0.00*
LGDP	−10.23	0.00*	−8.234	0.00*
ALR	−3.441	0.00*	−5.441	0.00*
MR	−2.221	0.00*	−3.221	0.00*
ERF	0.015	0.00*	0.001	0.00
SUP	−1.287	0.00*	−2.776	0.00*
TOR	0.462	0.00	0.213	0.00
ID	−0.018	0.00*	−0.004	0.00*

Model 2: Dependent variable is poverty-based social tension

Looloss: 107.1144 – Iteration = 1; Looloss: 100.8647 – Iteration = 2;
Looloss: 101.6226 – Iteration = 3; Looloss: 97.31265 – Iteration = 4;
Looloss: 95.97311 – Iteration = 5; Looloss: 93.66735 – Iteration = 6;
Looloss: 92.85052 – Iteration = 7;
Lambda = 0.8955
R-square = 0.6338

	India		China	
Variables	Coefficient	$P > |t|$	Coefficient	$P > |t|$
MFDI	−0.241	0.00*	−0.256	0.00*
SZG	1.112	0.00*	1.922	0.00*
LGDP	−13.33	0.00*	−10.11	0.00*
ALR	−3.421	0.00*	−4.221	0.00*
MR	−2.003	0.00*	−2.997	0.00*
ERF	0.021	0.00*	0.011	0.00
SUP	−2.001	0.00*	−2.665	0.00*
TOR	0.335	0.00	0.213	0.00
ID	−0.116	0.00*	−0.090	0.00*

* denotes significance at 5% level.
Source: Author's own computations in Stata 12.

Fiscal Decentralization a means to Poverty & Inequality Reduction? 121

Table 7.2 Impact on Income Inequality

Model 1: Dependent variable is GINI coefficient

Looloss: 108.3811 – Iteration = 1; Looloss: 104.8647 – Iteration = 2;
Looloss: 101.6262 – Iteration = 3; Looloss: 98.96312 – Iteration = 4;
Looloss: 96.97307 – Iteration = 5; Looloss: 94.26731 – Iteration = 6;
Looloss: 93.5152 – Iteration = 7;
Lambda = 0.9055
R-square = 0.6122

	India		China	
Variables	Coefficient	$P>\|t\|$	Coefficient	$P>\|t\|$
MFDI	0.233	0.00*	0.216	0.00*
SZG	0.199	0.00*	0.378	0.00*
LGDP	−30.23	0.00*	−40.234	0.00*
ALR	−3.441	0.00*	−5.441	0.00*
MR	−3.221	0.00*	−3.110	0.00*
ERF	0.161	0.00*	0.012	0.00
SUP	−0.669	0.00*	−0.854	0.00*
TOR	−0.019	0.00	−0.023	0.00
ID	−0.023	0.00*	−0.018	0.00*

Model 2: Dependent variable is inequality-based social tension

Looloss: 107.1144 – Iteration = 1; Looloss: 100.8647 – Iteration = 2;
Looloss: 101.6226 – Iteration = 3; Looloss: 97.31265 – Iteration = 4;
Looloss: 95.97311 – Iteration = 5; Looloss: 93.66735 – Iteration = 6;
Looloss: 92.85052 – Iteration = 7;
Lambda = 0.8955
R-square = 0.6338

	India		China	
Variables	Coefficient	$P>\|t\|$	Coefficient	$P>\|t\|$
MFDI	0.237	0.00*	0.219	0.00*
SZG	0.194	0.00*	0.397	0.00*
LGDP	−30.23	0.00*	−40.234	0.00*
ALR	−3.133	0.00*	−4.441	0.00*
MR	−3.313	0.00*	−3.110	0.00*
ERF	0.151	0.00*	0.005	0.00
SUP	−0.671	0.00*	−0.877	0.00*
TOR	−0.021	0.00	−0.028	0.00
ID	−0.024	0.00*	−0.019	0.00*

* denotes significance at 5% level.
Source: Author's own computations in Stata 12.

and after the government reaches a sufficiently large size, fiscal decentralization actually works to reduce inequalities. This is true because a larger government size implies a larger share of the Central Budget can be used for implementing redistributive programs at the sub-national level. This is consistent with the fact that the coefficient of ID is also negative for both the countries under the cases of both poverty and inequality reduction.

7.5 Concluding Remarks

To sum up the results briefly, the derivations obtained are consistent with the theoretical literature and arguments as already discussed. Interestingly, this is contrary to what Sepulveda and Martinez-Vazquez (2011) have derived from a panel dataset of Latin American and African economies that fiscal decentralization increases poverty levels; we, in this chapter, derive consistent results taking necessary care for the controls and the results are statistically significant. But when it comes to inequality in income distribution, we have contradictory results. The positively significant coefficient of the fiscal decentralization parameter indicates that fiscal decentralization worsens inequality in the distribution of income. But the negative sign in the interactive term between fiscal decentralization and the SZG sector predicts that approximately for a sufficiently larger government size, i.e., around 20.7% of GDP for India and 18.3% for China, fiscal decentralization reduces inequalities in the income distribution[6]. This happens because central government budgets under such conditions are substantially large enough to delegate redistributive policies for pro-poor growth at the sub-national level.

For specific answers to the research questions raised, we see that the existence of the relationship between fiscal decentralization reforms, poverty reduction, and income inequality reduction is very much significant for India and China (with controls over political, social-economic, and demographic dimensions of a country). The strength of the impact of the fiscal decentralization parameter is more for China under poverty reduction while it is more for India when inequality is targeted. As it has already been pointed out, fiscal decentralization has a positive impact on poverty reduction but the impact on income inequality might be counter-productive for small SZG (in terms of government expenditure), i.e., below 21% for India and 18% for China, respectively. An interesting result stems from the impact of the fiscal decentralization exercise on combating PBST and IBST. A 1 percentage point increase in MFDI leads to a fall in PBST of a magnitude of 0.24 percentage point for India and 0.26 percentage point for China. But for IBST, the model predicts that India is more sensitive as a 1 percentage point increase in MFDI is effective in combating social tension arising out of relative income inequality deprivations to the extent of 0.24 percentage point for India and 0.22 for China. All the results discussed above imply the importance of growth along with job creation so that both income and employment grow simultaneously with required redistributive effects at the sub-national level and those of poverty alleviation. These clearly point to the important role that programs like Mahatma Gandhi National Rural Employment Guarantee Act can play to achieve such objectives which are fundamental for social sustainability at the sub-national level. The focus on education and, especially, the literacy rate needs to be given high priority for attaining a crime-free-sustainable society. The infrastructure for health including the budgetary spending for strengthening the health infrastructure becomes crucial. Finally, the social harmony among castes and religious groups is of crucial importance, more in the case of India, and fiscal transfers from the Central Government to the sub-national segments can be effective in reducing the incidents of social tension arising out of poverty (absolute deprivations) or income inequality (relative deprivations) across states in India.

Nonparametric methods are not immune to the problem of endogeneity. In addition to following the methodology used in the paper on estimating a linear GMM to examine the extent of possible endogeneity, it would be a good exercise to extend this model after controlling for possible endogeneity by using a control function approach (see Lee (2007)) in the Epanechnikov Kernel function itself like what we have in the parametric literature (Chen & Qiu, 2016). The results can then be compared.

Within the principles of cooperative federalism, the results of the model clearly stress the role of fiscal decentralization to become an instrument of poverty alleviation. In line with the framework of Oates (1993, 1999), the chapter gets theoretically consistent results contrary to the predictions in Ladd and Doolittle (1982) and some recent results derived in Sepulveda and Martinez-Vazquez (2011). While redistribution is primarily a central government function, there can be significant gains by involving the sub-national governments in the task of poverty alleviation[7] (Oates, 1972) for both India and China. Moving on to the inequality results, interestingly, the SZG does matter for both countries in how effective fiscal decentralization can become in reducing income inequality in contrast to the recent results proposed by Rao (2016) that fiscal decentralization is inequality reducing. Policymakers should make a cost–benefit analysis before implementing fiscal decentralization and be ready to understand the impacts of different controls and their related puzzles as and when they crop up.

Notes

1 https://hbr.org/2007/12/china-india-the-power-of-two
2 This is very close to the data that we have for India and China for 2013–2014, standing at 21.4% and 14.32%, respectively.
3 Following the empirical literature, the index of fiscal decentralization that we formulate is targeted toward the extent of the fiscal decentralization reforms and not to how intense these are or where they are targeted, say, basic education or health. Also, conventionally, the World Bank gives these four ratios as a measure of fiscal decentralization while IMF gives tax revenue decentralization to sub-national governments as a measure. Since the author develops a composite index of fiscal decentralization, the index is named as modified fiscal decentralization index (MFDI).
4 Under the assumption that revenue equals expenditure.

5 For India, we have considered a religious (we have taken Hindus, Sikhs, Muslims, Christians, and others as our groups) polarization index following Sengupta and Mukherjee (2018) because data availability on ethnic groups in India is a constraint and also available in a scattered manner. For China, we make use of the data on 56 ethnic groups as available in the Chinese CENSUS and accordingly interpolate/extrapolate to suit our specifications.
6 This is very close to the data that we for India and China for 2013-14 standing at 21.4% and 14.32%, respectively.
7 "Governments that are closer to the people, as a rule, should be able to provide services more efficiently than a remote, centralized authority" (Oates, 1972).

References

Ahmad, E., & Brosio, G. (Eds.). (2009). *Does Decentralization Enhance Service Delivery and Poverty Reduction?* London: Edward Elgar Publishing.

Akai, N., & Sakata, M. (2002). Fiscal decentralization contributes to economic growth: evidence from state-level cross-section data for the United States. *Journal of Urban Economics*, 52(1), 93–108.

Bardhan, P. (2006). Awakening giants, feet of clay: a comparative assessment of the rise of China and India. *Journal of South Asian Development*, 1(1), 1–17.

Barro, R. J. (1990). Government spending in a simple model of endogenous growth. *Journal of Political Economy*, 98(5, Part 2), S103–S125.

Baskaran, T., & Feld, L. P. (2013). Fiscal decentralization and economic growth in OECD countries: is there a relationship?. *Public Finance Review*, 41(4), 421–445.

Bird, R., & Rodriguez, E. R. (1999). Decentralization and poverty alleviation. International experience and the case of the Philippines. *Public Administration and Development: The International Journal of Management Research and Practice*, 19(3), 299–319.

Bonet, J. (2006). Fiscal decentralization and regional income disparities: evidence from the Colombian experience. *The Annals of Regional Science*, 40(3), 661–676.

Chen, X., & Qiu, Y. J. J. (2016). Methods for Nonparametric and Semiparametric Regressions with Endogeneity. *Annual Review of Economics*, 8, 259–290.

Davoodi, H., & Zou, H. F. (1998). Fiscal decentralization and economic growth: A cross-country study. *Journal of Urban Economics*, 43(2), 244–257.

Dreze, J., & Sen, A. (1989). *Hunger and Public Action*. Oxford: Clarendon Press.

Desai, M. (2005). India and China: an essay in comparative political economy. In *India's and China's Recent Experience with Reform and Growth* (pp. 1–22). London: Palgrave Macmillan.

Francis, P., & James, R. (2003). Balancing rural poverty reduction and citizen participation: The contradictions of Uganda's decentralization program. *World Development*, 31(2), 325–337.

Jin, Y. (2009). A comparative study of fiscal decentralization in China and India. Retrieved from https://scholarworks.gsu.edu/cgi/viewcontent.cgi?article=1061&context=econ_diss

Kakwani, N., & Son, H. H. (2016). Measuring Social Tension. In *Social Welfare Functions and Development* (pp. 45–76). London: Palgrave Macmillan.

Ladd, H. F., & Doolittle, F. C. (1982). Which level of government should assist the poor? *National Tax Journal (pre-1986)*, 35(3), 323–332.

Lee, S. (2007). Endogeneity in quantile regression models: A control function approach. *Journal of Econometrics, 141*(2), 1131–1158.

Martinez-Vazquez, J., & McNab, R. M. (2003). Fiscal decentralization and economic growth. *World Development, 31*(9), 1597–1616.

Mukherjee, S., & Karmakar, A. K. (2019). A Tri-Variate Nexus of Microfinance-Growth-Inequality: The South-Asian Experience. In *Handbook of Research on Microfinancial Impacts on Women Empowerment, Poverty, and Inequality* (pp. 247–265). IGI Global.

Mukherjee, S., & Karmakar, A. K. (2018). Military Spending, Terrorism, and Economic Growth Vinculum in India: An Empirical Morphology of the Post-Reform Period. In *Handbook of Research on Military Expenditure on Economic and Political Resources* (pp. 382–402). IGI Global.

Nathan, H. S. K., Mishra, S., & Reddy, B. S. (2008). An alternative approach to measure HDI. *Indira Gandhi Institute of Development Research (IGIDR), Working Paper, WP-2008-001.*

Oates, W. E. (1972). *Fiscal Federalism.* New York: Harcourt Brace Jovanovich.

Oates, W. E. (1993). Fiscal decentralization and economic development. *National Tax Journal, 46*(2), 237–243.

Oates, W. E. (1999). An essay on fiscal federalism. *Journal of Economic Literature, 37*(3), 1120–1149.

Panda, B., & Thakur, H. P. (2016). Decentralization and health system performance – A focused review of dimensions, difficulties, and derivatives in India. *BMC Health Services Research, 16*(6), 561.

Rao, M. G. (2016). Poverty alleviation under fiscal decentralization. Retrieved from http://www1.worldbank.org/publicsector/decentralization/cd/PovertyAlleviation.pdf

Sacchi, A., & Salotti, S. (2014). The effects of fiscal decentralization on household income inequality: some empirical evidence. *Spatial Economic Analysis, 9*(2), 202–222.

Sengupta, R., & Mukherjee, S. (2018). Crime, deprivation and social sustainability — Evidence across States in India. *Indian Journal of Human Development, 12*(3), 354–377.

Sepulveda, C. F., & Martinez-Vazquez, J. (2011). The consequences of fiscal decentralization on poverty and income equality. *Environment and Planning C: Government and Policy, 29*(2), 321–343.

Khanna, T. (2007). CHINA-INDIA the power of two. *Harvard Business Review, 85*(12).

Thornton, J. (2007). Fiscal decentralization and economic growth reconsidered. *Journal of Urban Economics, 61*(1), 64–70.

Weber, M. (1947). *The Theory of Economic and Social Organization.* Trans. A. M. Henderson and T. Parsons. New York: Oxford University Press.

Zhang, T., & Zou, H. F. (1998). Fiscal decentralization, public spending, and economic growth in China. *Journal of Public Economics, 67*(2), 221–240.

Zhang, X. (2006). Fiscal decentralization and political centralization in China: Implications for growth and inequality. *Journal of Comparative Economics, 34*(4), 713–726.

8 The Culture of Corruption in Pakistan and Afghanistan
Impacts on Socio-Economic Profiles

Debasish Nandy

Introduction

In terms of corruption, both Pakistan and Afghanistan hold a negative position. Corruption generates crimes. Corruption has penetrated both the social and political life of Pakistan and Afghanistan resulting in an increasing number of crimes. Corruption and crime cannot be eliminated at a time, but corruption can be reduced by taking strict measures. Different methods and policies are to be taken at various levels to combat corruption. It is also essential to ensure social, administrative, and institutional reforms to eliminate corruption. It is a time-consuming process. Despite taking some anti-corruption initiatives, the rate of success is very much dissatisfactory because of the fragile infrastructure of the government. Porta and Vannucci (1997) argued that corruption infiltrates the governance system with deep-rooted and it is structural problems. The relationship between corruption and good governance is antagonistic. In Pakistan, bureaucratic neutrality is absent and Afghanistan also has the same experience. The administration has been highly corrupted in both countries. Political corruption influences the policy-making process. The corruption leads to uneven development that resulted in discontent among the various ethnic groups. Both Pakistan and Afghanistan are multi-ethnic countries but decades-long ethnic conflicts have fragmented the societies.

Corruption is well connected with terrorism. Terror financing has been one of the discourses in the study of the International Political Economy today. Various terrorist groups are collecting and disbursing money through illegal means. Black money is reaching the hands of terrorists like Jaish-e-Mohammad, Lashkar-e-Tobia, Al-Qaida, Taliban, and others. A parallel black economy generates a new dimension of corruption in Pakistan and Afghanistan. The responsibility of states cannot be denied. The state authority of Pakistan has been accused of funding terrorist groups. This is called 'state-sponsored terrorism'. This foreign aid-based economy has witnessed the drainage of money go in vain. During the Taliban regime, the Afghan economy was running through illegitimate means. Corruption and violation of the code of conduct remain an integral part of Afghanistan. There are several areas in Pakistan where corruption is institutionalized. Over the years, Pakistan and Afghanistan have been vehemently criticized by the

DOI: 10.4324/9781003245797-9

global community for conducting corrupt acts. I have chosen these two states due to having some affinity with the nature of society, politics, and the economy. How corruption impacted on socio-political profiles of both countries has been critically highlighted in this study.

Review of Literature

Abbasi (2011) has argued that due to corrupt practices, a negative impact has been noticed in investment in Pakistan. Ali (2018, April 6) has critically analyzed the role of anti-corruption measures. In their working paper, Banerjee and Pande (2009) highlighted the corrupt practices of politicians. Bhavnani and Condra (2012), in their report *Why People Vote for Corrupt Politicians Evidence from Survey Experiments in Afghanistan?*, argue that the voting behavior of Afghanistan is influenced by a corrupt culture. Porta and Vannuccin (1997) have critically discussed political corruption. Galli (2019) has done research work on facts behind the corruption in Afghanistan in a project on Facts about the corruption of Afghanistan. Javaid (2010), in his article, elaborately discusses the scenario of corruption in Pakistan. Khan (2016) has mentioned the taken measures by the Pakistani government in combating terrorism. Nandy (2017) has critically discussed the impact of corruption in Pakistan. Paul (2014) has shed light on the militarization process of Pakistan in his famous book titled *The Warrior State: Pakistan in the Contemporary World*. Sattar (2011), in his working paper, has questioned the role of civil society in Pakistan. Shaikh (2009) has attempted to project a dismal picture of Pakistan. The report of Transparency International on Pakistan and Afghanistan (2017 and 2019) has been studied to justify this study.

Research Questions Sources of Data and Methodology

There are two research questions in this study—(1) How Pakistan and Afghanistan are continuing the legacy of corruption? (2) How does corruption impact socio-economic profiles?

The study has been conducted using content analysis and comparative methods to identify the commonalities and differences in the system of corruption practiced in these two countries. Both primary and secondary data are used as the foundation for the current investigation. To gather information and conduct analysis, books, journals, reports, newspapers, and websites have been examined. To comprehend the true situation, the author spoke with some Afghan and Pakistani experts and policymakers during this study. They have offered significant evidence to support my analysis.

Contextualizing Corruption

In the present global order, corruption is a virus with widespread impact on all parts of the world with variable degrees. As per the analysis of

Transparency International (2015), corruption is considered the most demanding issue in the contemporary world. The cost of corruption has four-dimensional effects—(1) Corruption is usually affected by political milieu, democracy, and rule of law; (2) the economic cost of corruption is very dangerous and it negatively affects national wealth; (3) the social cost of corruption has a long-term effect because it reduces citizens' trust in the political system and administration; (4) corruption degrades the image of the country to the global community. As a complex and multi-faceted phenomenon, the term corruption has been defined in many ways. Kaufmann and Vicente (2011) and Kaufmann, Kraay and Mastruzzi (2010) have defined corruption as 'the abuse of public office for private gain'. Nye (1967) defined corruption through the prism of behavior. Corruption has been analyzed through the Normative Approach also. As per the Normative Approach, any sort of unethical and illegal behavior of officers is treated as corruption. According to Klitgaard (1988), to understand corruption, the Cultural Constraint Theory of Corruption is very relevant. Certain cultural norms and values influence the members of the society, officials, and discussion-makers (Buttle et al., 2016). The culture of corruption inherits generation-wise in a country so to an existing value system.

The Experience of Pakistan

The roots of corruption in Pakistan are a very old systematic problem (Dogar, 2017). During the British period, the British administration used to reward the feudal lords and landowners who showed their loyalty to the colonial power. The loyal landowners were rewarded lands, and titles that resulted in nepotism, and corruption. In the post-independence period, two major things played a fundamental role in rampant corruption in Pakistan— (1) accumulation of wealth within a little elite group. Pakistani society is divided into two parts—'haves' and 'haves not' and (2) lack of governability in every sphere of the state. It was quite difficult to think that in the era of globalization, Pakistan remains a feudalist country. The distribution of wealth is unequal. Due to not having a sizable middle class, Pakistan has witnessed economic disparity between haves and haves not which creates a culture of corruption (Sayeed, 2010).

Pakistan is industrially backward and economically challenged. Due to the shortage of resources in comparison to demands, the Pakistani government is unable to fulfill the basic need of the people. To avail these facilities from the government, when citizens approached the officers, bribes were demanded. In the 1970s, the adaption of nationalization policy created new opportunities for corruption and gave birth to a new breed of corrupt government officers. Pakistan witnessed reckless corruption in the 1980s (Javaid, 2010).

In 2017, a survey was conducted by the World Economic Forum and it mentioned in its report that corruption was the most problematic factor in doing business in Pakistan (World Economic Forum Annual Meeting, 2017).

Systematic corruption has been manifested in all sectors, especially in police services, bureaucracy, and tax administration. Surprisingly, the rate of corruption is also very high in the judicial system, public land and revenue department, services sector, public procurement, customs administration, etc. According to a survey by Transparency International (2017) the practice of nepotism, lack of merit-based recruitment, embezzlement of public funds, and tax evasion collectively made a strong base of corruption. However, the culture of corruption intensified in Pakistan in many ways. First, in Pakistan, bribery has been common practice in government service. Second, corruption has been a common social practice. For saving time and costs from frequent visits, common people offered bribes to government employees. Third, without offering bribes, it is very difficult to get any government contract or tender. So, contractors use to pay bribes to the concerned authority to get desirable contracts. In Pakistan, corruption is alleged as a widespread virus and it has become a way of life in Pakistan (Islam, 2004). Corruption has been institutionalized in Pakistan, making the country extremely inefficient (Abbasi, 2011).

Responsibility of the Political Leaders

The culture of corruption has been injected into Pakistani politics for a long time. Several Pakistani leaders have been accused of financial corruption. The former Pakistani Prime Minister Nawaz Sharif has been accused of financial misconduct several times. He belonged to a very rich family in Punjab province. He was the President of the Pakistan Muslim League-N. In 1977, Sharif was appointed as the Minister of Finance in Punjab. He became the Chief Minister of Punjab in 1985. Later on, he became the Prime Minister of Pakistan in 1990. There is a strong allegation against Sharif that he convinced Inter-Services Intelligence (ISI) for manipulating elections by spending money. In 1993, Nawaz Sharif was dismissed by the then President of Pakistan, Ghulam Ishaq Khan, on charges of corruption. He became the Prime Minister of Pakistan for the second time in 1997. The second term regime of Nawaz Sharif was also marked by confrontations with Judiciary and the Military. Mr. Sharif was overthrown by Musharraf in 1999. In 2017, Sharif was accused in the Panama Papers trial. As a result, Nawaz Sharif was once again banned from public office. He and his daughters were sentenced to imprisonment for a gross financial scam. The Panama Papers was leaked in 2016. The Supreme Court of Pakistan dismissed him from his position in July 2017.

Benazir became the first female Prime Minister of Pakistan after the death of General Zia-ul-Haq in a plane crash. Before completing two years in the post of Prime Minister, she was dismissed on the allegation of corruption. Benazir Bhutto became the Prime Minister of Pakistan for the second time in 1993. She simultaneously acted as the minister of finance. The practice of nepotism was started by her through the appointment of her husband, Asif Ali Zardari as the minister of investment in 1996. The culture of family domination in the political economy was indifferently started by Mrs. Bhutto. Asif Ali Zardari was accused of so many illegal financial transactions, and misuse of government funds. Through using personal influence, he leaked defense contacts. He had privatized power plant projects and state-owned industries. He received bribes for approving broadcast licenses. He also took money granting an export monopoly among selected businessmen. Benazir Bhutto's family illegally purchased property worth US$2.5 million in London. This is very unfortunate that due to the charges of corruption; no Pakistani Prime Minister has ever completed a five-year tenure. Pervez Musharraf was forced to reign in 2008 by the domestic democratic forces and the Western powers. The issue of corruption was also raised against Musharraf. Usually, elected governments are blamed for corrupt practices. The military–civil alliance has immensely helped to establish military supremacy. Shaikh (2009) notes that over the decades, the supremacy of the military made it the prime institution of the country. In the name of security, through armaments, the Pakistan military has institutionalized its domination in big financial deals. The frequency of corruption in the arms industry has been increasing gradually (Henriksson, 2007). The big arms deals are subject to a huge amount of money. In Pakistan, the corruption in arms deals is operated jointly by top-ranked army officers and politicians (Nagin, 2013).

Responsibility of Judiciary and Other Regularity Bodies

The role of the judiciary as the safeguard of a country is inevitable. Constitutionally, Pakistan perceived a system of 'separation of powers'. But in practice, the judicial system of Pakistan is dominated and influenced by the military elites. In many cases, the judges were ousted by the military rulers. Pervez Musharraf also suspended the Chief Justice of Pakistan. Political obligations are very common in the judiciary. One of the basic logics behind the military coup in the world is corruption. To stop the rampant corruption and foster development in the country, the military used to take over the administration of the country. Pakistan has experience with long military regimes. In 1999, the military government of Pakistan led by Pervez Musharraf adopted a new anti-corruption law through the National Accountability Ordinance. To eliminate corruption a powerful anti-corruption agency was established by the Musharraf government. After the establishment of the National Accountability Bureau (NAB), anti-corruption surveillance has been cooperatively stronger (Musharraf, 2006). One of the reasons for the economic crisis in Pakistan is defaulted and fraudulent bank loans. Musharraf's government had introduced some provisions to tackle this problem. The deliberate default generates corruption.

The NAB of Pakistan has been closely investigating cases of financial corruption, especially faulty loans. As per the record of NAB, from October 1999 to December 2016, about 627 persons had been identified and charged for defaulting the loans, and about 300 influential persons were alleged for leading luxurious life beyond their valid income, 700 people were accused of misusing public offices, and 1,500 individuals were accused corrupt practices (Ali, 2018). There is a very old hostility between the judiciary and the executive in Pakistan. The judiciary of Pakistan is not free from acquisition. Nawaz Sharif was troubled with appointing authority and judiciary. In April 2001, the accountability law of Musharraf was challenged by the Supreme Court. In a verdict, the Supreme Court condemned for delegation of excessive to the chief of the anti-corruption organization. The army and the judiciary strongly argued and also pressurized to extend their control over the NAB. The basic motto of elimination of corruption was defocused due to the rivalry of exercising power by the judiciary.

Role of Civil Society in the Anti-Corruption Movement

Some South Asian Scholars are rather interested to interpret the role of civil society in some particular countries as an infant stage. Pakistan is a warrior state as described by T.V. Paul. He had observed that since its independence the basic tendency of the Pakistan state is to spend much more money on the military sector. The citizens of Pakistan have been ruled by the military for more than 30 years. Inter-religious riots, ethnic conflicts, and continuous state-sponsored terrorism have collectively jeopardized society. In absence of democracy, human rights, accommodative policy, and human security, the formation of civil society in Pakistan is a natural phenomenon. Civil society performs the role of a watchdog of democracy and transparency. Civil society organizations usually raise their voice for the development of education, health care, upliftment of the vulnerable sections of the society, and prevention of corruption, environmental issues, etc. (Nalpat, 2010). Civil society influences public opinion as a Fifth Estate of Governance (Vikram, 2010). The role of civil society in Pakistan in the anti-corruption movement is not satisfactory.

Nikhat Sattar, a Pakistani Scholar has rightly observed that in the 1980s, during Zia-ul-Haque's regime, some significant civil society movements took place in different parts of Pakistan. The NGOs had played a key role in those movements. The basic demands of those movements were to ensure human rights. The 1990s witnessed the impressive growth of NGOs. Due to the organization of massive civil movements on different issues, several civil activists, writers, and intellectuals, journalists had been sentenced to different prisons. Sanctions were imposed on free thinkers and media. The Federal administration had taken several brutal policies with the help of a corrupted police force (Sattar, 2011).

Religious-Based Terrorism and Corruption

The Islamic Republic of Pakistan emerged based on religion. For Pakistan, religion has failed to establish social harmony. Rather, religion has been wrongly used by the state in a narrow sectarian manner. Pakistan has been experiencing intra-religious conflicts within Islam. However, the process of Islamization of politics, initiated by Pakistani leadership at the cost of development and modernization has converted Pakistan into a 'warrior state'.

Pakistan's ongoing war-making efforts have deeply affected its prospects for emerging as a tolerant, prosperous, and unified nation-state. This has major implications not only for Pakistan but also for global and regional security orders (Paul, 2014). The Pakistani case is exceptionally extraordinary. The nexus between the ISI, the Army and the jihadists has made the country jeopardize security not only for the common people of Pakistan but to some extent for South Asian security also. Syed Abdul Alla Maududi (1903–1978) was responsible for spreading fundamentalism in Pakistan. His speeches and writings were able to inject communal and narrow sectarian thought into the entire socio-political structure of Pakistan (Nandy, 2017). The Islamist political parties are immensely responsible for the radicalization of society. Just after independence, the Muslim League was not only a political party in Pakistan but also a power-mobilization factor (Nandy, 2017). However, Jamaat-e-Islam as a political party was established to mobilize the society in a wrong way which resulted in the emergence of several terrorist groups like Lashkar-e-Taiba, Harkatatul Mujahidin, and Jaish-e-Mohammad.

The radical Islamic terrorist groups are not only a security threat to Pakistan it is very alarming for the Pakistani economy. Lashkar-e-Taiba is accused of transferring and generating money through several illicit channels—(1) through the hawala banking network funds are being received and transferred to and from Pakistan and the Middle East; (2) through fraud letters of credit, Pakistani militant groups are doing illegal money laundering business. With the help of corrupt bank officials and customs officials, Laskar-e-Taiba cadres are generating funds; (3) fake currency is a comparatively easier method of producing and distributing counterfeit currency. Trading network in the Terai deals in fake Rs. 500 and Rs. 1000 Indian notes and trading them at a 2:1 rate on the underground market (Miklian, 2009).

Corruptions in Different Sectors

Shaikh (2009) has argued that corruption in Pakistan is often regarded as the new evil that marked a break with the values of an older and more glorious period. Corruption has entered every sector and several punitive actions have been taken by the state organs against the corrupted institutions and personnel. The government enterprises of Pakistan are often accused of corruption. So many prime government organizations of Pakistan have been accused of corruption, such as Pakistan Steel, Punjab Bank, Rental Power Plants, National Insurance Company Limited, Pakistan International Airlines, Railway and Water and Power Development Authority, and Karachi Electric Supply Corporation (KESC). The reliability of the Pakistani police in society is highly questionable. As per the report of Transparency International (2013) police administration of Pakistan is the most corrupt institution. The genuine crimes and illegal acts are hidden by police by accepting bribes and favors. The government officers used to demand bribes for providing public services and licenses. The majority of citizens of Pakistan offer bribes for illegally reducing their utility bills which caused the drainage of government revenues that stops developmental projects.

In the Pakistani military, corruption has been a common practice. It is the most powerful institution in Pakistan. The military elites of Pakistan predominantly influence the entire system of the country. During military regimes, the military directly intervenes in economic affairs as decision-makers and during civil governments, the military indirectly determines the big deals in Pakistan. In 2016, former Army Chief, General Raheel Sharif sacked six Army officers due to connections with corruption. During the Nawaz Sharif regime, the sacked military officers are also sent to Frontier Corps in Baluchistan on deputation. The government of Pakistan has taken some initiatives to stop rampant corruption (National Anti-Corruption Strategies, 2002). Due to economic, cultural, and political causes, police corruption in Pakistan has been institutionalized (Lyon, 2004).

Afghanistan

The state-building process has not been completed in Afghanistan due to ethnic conflicts, terrorism, misgovernance, poverty, unemployment, and rampant corruption (Mullen, 2009). The decades-long war in Afghanistan led to forced migration. Being a war-torn country, it has witnessed outward illegal migration. In different phrases, the flow of migration has been accelerated to neighboring countries, especially, Pakistan and Iran. After the death of Najibullah in 1994, recorded numbers of Afghans have illegally migrated to comparatively secure and developed countries. With the advent of the Taliban regime in 1996, a tremendous security crisis started in Afghanistan. In 2002, with the fall of the Taliban, record numbers of Afghan people returned to Afghanistan. An international reconstruction and development initiative began to aid Afghans in rebuilding their country after decades of war. Afghanistan has continuously been challenged by underdevelopment, lack of infrastructure, few employment opportunities, and widespread poverty. As a vulnerable state, Afghanistan has been passing through a huge financial crisis since its very inception. Corruption has immensely affected the socio-economic development of Afghanistan. Politics and corruption are synonymous. The post-conflict society of Afghanistan has witnessed enormous corruption in voting behavior (Bhavnani and Condra 2012). This study argues that the lack of administration, absence of financial transparency, illiteracy, weak vigilance system, nexus between financial institutions and political leaders, and uneven development made this country highly corrupted. The lack of governance and unemployment corruption escaped the entire society. After establishing the Hamed Karzai regime in 2002, the culture of corruption was started as an instrument of economic gain.

Due to the lack of industrialization and economic challenge, Afghanistan is immensely dependent upon foreign aid. In the post-Taliban era, Hamid Karzai and Ashraf Ghani governments have failed to prevent corruption at the administrative and political levels. Reckless corruption caused the drainage of budgetary allocation for development. The misuse of foreign aid by politicians and administrators has been a common financial culture in Afghanistan. As per the report of Transparency International (T.I.) (2019), Afghanistan ranked 173 out of 180 countries and scored 16 out of 100. Transparency International has recommended that the Afghan government limit the level of corruption with the help of the National Unity Government (NUG) and civil society.

Corruption in Various Sectors

Corruption in Afghanistan disrupted basic services and the development process. It promotes the trafficking of narcotics and creates socio-political instability. The government has adopted an anti-corruption strategy and enacted reforms in the legal code in Afghanistan. In every sector, corruption has been injected in Afghanistan (Razaq and Shahim, 2014).

Judicial System

The judicial system of Afghanistan is highly corrupted. Bribery has been one of the common features of the Afghan judicial system. Judiciary is the protector of citizens' rights and it prevents illegal activities through verdicts. The judicial system of Afghanistan is very fragile and it cannot work independently The Afghan people have no faith in the judiciary. They do not expect to get justice from the judiciary. They consider the judiciary as the most corrupt institution. The verdicts are often directed by the government, politicians, police, and economically influential people.

Government

The public sector of Afghanistan is incapable to provide even basic services to citizens. Due to the highly centralized administrative system, the allocation of public funds and state resources is decided through a lengthy bureaucratic procedure with frequent delays. The political recommendations-based recruitment procedure generated widespread corruption. In 2012, almost 50% of Afghan citizens had paid bribes to the government staff for availing of public service. In 2012, 3.9 billion bribes were paid by Afghan citizens to public servants (Lamb and Brooke, 2012). The Afghan government is reluctant to about making the public sector apolitical and corruption-free.

Education

The impact of corruption on the educational system has highly alarming. The appointment of teachers and staff depends upon bribes. On the other hand, the trained and most eligible teachers are often unable to get jobs. At a higher level, nepotistic influence is highly existing. According to the national corruption survey, the Ministry of Education is the second-most corrupt institution in Afghanistan (Integrity Watch 2018). Usually, the Taliban are against of modern education system.

Health

The healthcare system in Afghanistan is not only fragile but also highly corrupted. The access to public healthcare facilities often depend upon bribes. Despite corruption and risks, the healthcare system has been improved. The health care system in Afghanistan is not only inferior but also highly corrupted. The access to public healthcare facilities often depend upon bribes.

Security

The fragile security system of Afghanistan is highly corrupted. The police are also perceived as highly corrupt. Afghan police administration witnessed anonymous police personnel; monthly salaries are disbursed in their name (Galli 2019).

Responsibility of Judiciary and Other Governmental Agencies

Being a vulnerable and war-torn country, Afghanistan has gone through a lot of crises over the decades. The foreign aid-based economy is highly corrupted for so many reasons. Due to the legacy of corruption, its socio-economic profile is very low. The role of the judiciary and other governmental vigilance agencies is very vital to stopping corruption. This section will try to analyze the role of the judiciary and other agencies in the growing tendency of corruption.

Corrupt Practices among the Politicians

Nepotism has been one of the common features of Afghan politics. The politicians of Afghanistan are highly attached to illegal activities and financial misconduct. A large number of Afghan PMs and ministers use to run private businesses in the name of their relatives. Afghanistan of the poorest countries in the world, but the ruling political elites of Afghanistan lead luxurious lifestyles through illegal money (Torabi and Lorenzo, 2008). The anti-corruption commission has found that around 8,000 officers have illegal money and property which is not justified by their actual income.

Taken anti-Corruption Measures

The fragile Afghan administration has taken some measures to stop corruption. First, the government of Afghanistan has formed an anti-corruption institutional framework to prevent and fight against large-scale corruption comprehensively (Azizi, 2021). Against this institutional backdrop, the government of Afghanistan has taken some key steps in recent years to strengthen its framework for preventing and countering corruption. Second, by enacting a new penal code and adopting an Afghan anti-corruption strategy, the Afghan government has initiated to minimize anti-corruption activities. Third, in March 2016, after the establishment of the High Council for Rule of Law and Anti-Corruption, the degree of corruption has been reduced. It is the highest body of anti-corruption efforts. It has three committees that are working on various issues related to corruption. But these committees are highly politically controlled, which makes obstacles to taking any steps against corrupted ruling elites. Fourth, an Anti-Corruption Commission has been formulated to judge corruption-related cases. Fifth, the Major Crimes Task Force is working to identify the top-level corrupted officers. In 2010, this task force ordered the arrest of a senior member of the National Security Council. This commission is not so active in taking action against all corrupted executives and officers and there is also a lack of clarity about its mandate. Fifth, by April 2018, the ACJC had completed 34 cases and by 2019, it had ruled in 57 cases (UNAMA, 2020). The performance of this agency is highly questionable. It lacks the capacity to provide security to the witnessed people. The personnel of these agencies has a background of corruption. Finally, in the anti-corruption strategy, the Afghan government has given priority to five sectors: (i) through anti-corruption reforms, political leaders will have to be free from corruption; (ii) elimination of corruption in the security sector; (iii) introduction of the merit system in recruitment, (iv) prosecution against corrupt persons, and (v) initiatives for tracking illegal money flows.

Research Outcome and Concluding Remarks

There is no doubt that corruption is rampant and prevalent in Pakistan and Afghanistan. As we've seen, it has a complex personality and is unregulated by the expansion of numerous laws and bureaus. The economic profile of both countries are very poor due to corruption and lack of transparency (World Bank, 2016). When the current anti-corruption strategies are largely viewed as ineffectual, discriminatory, and further complicated by problems with institutional capacity, there is little room for better planning. Thus, the problem of corruption and the current socio-political imbalances are inexorably intertwined. Both Pakistan and Afghanistan have a strong culture of corruption. In Afghanistan, Taliban 2.0's stunning takeover of power is largely reflective of the corruption inside the Afghan National Défense and Security Forces had weakened the resolve and fighting capacity of the U.S.-backed forces (Vittori, 2021). The culture of corruption has been represented in administrative, bureaucratic, and socio-political behaviors. It is extremely challenging to eradicate the culture of corruption in both nations. It has been discovered through comparison that these two countries' causes of corruption are distinct from one another. The anti-corruption movements have not surfaced properly in both countries. The international community has applied significant pressure on the governments of Afghanistan and Pakistan to combat corruption. There have been several measures and changes implemented, but the international community is skeptical of the outcomes thus far. In every sector, corruption is deep-rooted as an incurable disease. Discontent has grown naturally among ordinary people as a result of an underdeveloped economy and a lack of a fair distribution policy. The governments of Pakistan and Afghanistan have consistently been portrayed as unstable political systems. The common people in Pakistan are left defenseless and vulnerable, with no hope for peaceful development, as it seems as though both politicians and Army officers are never able to satiate their appetite for power and wealth. As a result, the country swung for decades into a cradle of political anarchy and unlawful rule. The highest levels of corruption continue to be a huge problem for the nation and obstruct real social improvements. A policy change has become necessary for the country's progress, along with the strengthening of democratic institutions, particularly the judiciary. For both countries, the government is responsible for rampant corruption. The governmental agencies have been accused for lack of transparency (Rose-Ackerman and Palifka, 2016).

Recommendations

It is a difficult task to stop corruption in Pakistan and Afghanistan. It is a time-taking process, but anti-corruption actions are to be initiated urgently. Although Imran Khan and Ashraf Ghani's governments are approaching to end the legacy of corruption, to stop corruption from the entire system of both countries, some recommendations can be made. First, it is immediately required to establish an independent judicial service commission. Second, clear and wide-ranging codes of conduct are recommended for the senior leadership of Pakistan and Afghanistan. Third, training on ethics and anti-corruption is to be provided for the government's staff. Fourth, the installation of anti-corruption assistance services is to be ensured. Fifth, the vibrant civil society movement is highly recommended for the elimination of corruption from society. And that can be helpful to uplift the socio-economic profiles of both countries.

References

Abbasi, A. (2011). Public Sector Governance in Pakistan: Board of Investment. *International Journal of Politics and Good Governance*, 2(2).

Ali, Z. (2018, April 6). Anti-corruption Institutions and Governmental Change in Pakistan. *South Asia Multidisciplinary Academic Journal*. https://doi.org/10.40C0/samaj.4499

Azizi, W. (2021). How Corruption Played a Role in the Demise of the Afghan Government. *The Diplomat*.

Banerjee, A.V., & Pande, R. (2009). Parochial Politics: Ethnic Preferences and Politician Corruption. *Working Paper*. MIT and Harvard University.

Bhavnani, R. R. & Condra, L. N. (2012). *Why People Vote for Corrupt Politicians Evidence from Survey Experiments in Afghanistan?* International Growth Centre Political Economy Grant Final Report, 1–8.

Buttle, J. W., Graham, D. S. and Meliala, A. E. (2016). A Cultural Constraints Theory of Police Corruption: Understanding the Persistence of Police Corruption in Contemporary Indonesia. *Australian and New Zealand Journal of Criminology*, 49(3), pp. 437–454.

Della Porta, D., & Vannucci, A. (1997). The Perverse Effects of Political Corruption. *Political Studies*, 45(3), 516–538.

Dogar, A. S. (2017). Corruption remains a systemic problem in Pakistan. *The Tribune*.

Galli, S. (2019, July 15). Fact about the corruption of Afghanistan, Kabul, Afghanistan. *10 Facts About Corruption in Afghanistan*. The Borgen Project.

Henriksson, E. (2007). *Corruption in the Arms Trade: Undermining African Democracy*. International Peace Bureau Disarmament for Development, Geneva, p. 13.

Integrity Watch (2018). https://iwaweb.org/ accessed on 22nd December 2020.

Islam, N (2004). Sifarish, sycophants, power, and collectivism: administrative culture in Pakistan. *International Review of Administrative Sciences*. 70(2).

Javaid, U. (2010). Corruption and Its Deep Impact on Good Governance in Pakistan. *Pakistan Economic and Social Review*. 48(1), pp. 123–134.

Kaufmann, D., Kraay, A., & Mastruzzi, M. (2010). Response to What do the worldwide governance indicators measure? *The European Journal of Development Research*. 22(1), 55–58.

Khan, F. (2016). Combating corruption in Pakistan. *Asian Education and Development Studies*, 5(2), 195–210, https://doi.org/10.1108/AEDS-01-2016-0006

Klitgaard, R. (1988). *Controlling Corruption*. Berkeley: University of California Press, p. 70.

Miklian, J. (2009, January 27). Illicit Trading in Nepal: Fuelling South Asian Terrorism South Asia. Working Paper No. 3. International Peace Research Institute, Oslo.

Mullen, R. D. (2009). Afghanistan in 2008: State Building at the Precipice. *Asian Survey*. 49(1), 28–38.

Musharraf, P. (2006). *In the Line of Fire: A Memoir*. London: Pocket Books, p. 150.

Lamb, R. D. and Brooke, Shawn. (2012). Political Governance and Strategy in Afghanistan. *Centre for Strategic & International Studies*. 28.

Lyon, S. M. (2004). *An Anthropological Analysis of Local Politics and Patronage in a Pakistani Village*. New York: Edwin Mellen Press.

Nalpat, M. D. (2010, February 16). Civil Society Awakens, *The Times of India* of India.

Nandy, D. (2017). *Understanding Pakistan*. New Delhi: Kunal Books, pp. 118–119.

National Anti-Corruption Strategy (NACS) (2002). Islamabad, Pakistan.
Nagin, D. S. (2013). Deterrence in the Twenty-First Century. *Crime and Justice.* 42(1), 199–263. Doi:10.1086/670398.
Nye, J. S. (1967). Corruption and political development: A cost-benefit analysis. *American Political Science Review*, 61(2), 417–427.
Paul, T. V. (2014). *The Warrior State: Pakistan in the Contemporary World.* Random House Publishers India Private Limited. Gurgaon, p. 184.
Razaq, I. M., & Shahim. (2014). Kabuli, National Corruption Survey 2014. *Integrity Watch Afghanistan.*
Rose-Ackerman, S., & Palifka, B. J. (2016). *Corruption and Government: Causes, Consequences, and Reform.* Cambridge University Press.
Sattar, N. (2011). *Has Civil Society Failed in Pakistan?* SPDC Working Paper No. 6. p. 7.
Sayeed, A. (2010). Contextualizing Corruption in Pakistan. *Social Science and Policy Bulletin*, 2(1), 2–10.
Shaikh, F. (2009). *Making Sense of Pakistan.* Hurst and Company, London, p. 133.
Torabi, Y. & Lorenzo, D. (2008). Afghanistan: Bringing Accountability Back In: From Subjects of Aid to Citizens of the State. Kabul: Integrity Watch Afghanistan. 13 http://reliefweb.int/sites/reliefweb.int/files/resources/4B61D4642FC36F2C4925746A000520E0-Full_Report.pdf
Transparency International: Pakistan. (2017). Strategic Plan 2017–2020. *Action Plan for Transparency and Accountability.* http://www.transparency.org.pk/pdf/TI-P_Strategy_2017-2020.pdf
Transparency International. (2015). *National Integrity System Assessment Afghanistan 2015*, 23–26.
Transparency International. (2019). CPI 2019 Global Heights. https://www.transparency.org/en/news/cpi-2019-global-highlights accessed on 26th December 2020.
United Nations Assistance Mission in Afghanistan. (UNAMA). (2020). *Afghanistan's Fight Against Corruption: Crucial for Peace and Prosperity*, https://unama.unmissions.org/sites/default/files/afghanistans_fight_against_corruption_crucial_for_peace_and_prosperity_june_2020-english.pdf, accessed on 25 October 2022.
Vikram S. V. (2010, June 10). Public Opinion- the Fifth Estate, *The Times of India of India.*
Vittori, J. (2021). *Corruption and Self-Dealing in Afghanistan and Other U.S.-Backed Security Sectors.* Carnegie Endowment for International Peace.
World Bank (2016). Ease of Doing Business Ranking, Available at http://www.doingbusiness.org/rankings
World Economic Forum Annual Meeting 2017. (17–20 January 2017). https://www.weforum.org/events/world-economic-forum-annual-meeting-2017, accessed on 25 October 2022.

9 Do Emerging Market Economies Have Sustainable Development?
A Panel Vector Autoregression Analysis

Adem Gök and Nausheen Sodhi

9.1 Introduction

Nations at either of the ends of development levels have shown a detrimental impact of economic growth on environmental quality. At low levels of development, nations' economic growth is largely dependent on natural resources, often leading to their inefficient utilization. In these nations, a subsequent improvement in their growth is linked to environmental degradation. This phenomenon has been explained in the first half of the upward slope of the inverted U-shaped Kuznets curve, which shows that at initial levels of economic growth, environmental quality keeps falling as growth picks up till a certain level (Kuznets, 1955). However, studies pertaining to understanding the relationship between growth and environmental quality in advanced nations have shown mixed results. While the latter part of the Kuznets curve states that after a certain level of growth, further improvements in economic growth lead to a fall in environmental degradation, some studies in the literature have also shown a link between higher growth levels and environmental degradation. This ambiguity raises doubts about the temporal concept of sustainable development, given first by the World Commission on Environment and Development in 1987 in the report 'Our Common Future' (Brundtland, 1987). It defines sustainable development as 'development that meets the needs of the present without compromising the ability of future generations to meet own needs'.

Although it seems somewhat unambiguous what relation holds between economic growth and environmental quality for the least and most developed nations, the same cannot be said for the emerging market economies When it comes to the impact that such economies' growth has on their environment, it is yet to be studied whether they learned from past mistakes of the advanced nations or whether they followed a similar developmental path (dependent on natural resources) of the underdeveloped nations or whether they stand separate of the two. Have they been able to strike the right balance between furthering economic growth and maintaining environmental quality? Have they been able to convert negative externalities of growth to positive externalities? In other words, are the emerging market economies' developmental practices sustainable? Sustainable development

DOI: 10.4324/9781003245797-10

practices take care of the trade-off between present economic needs and negative externalities having long-term detrimental impacts on the environment.

However, the relationship between development and sustainability is linked closely to the concept of sustainable development. The temporal concept of sustainable development relates to the positive influences of past development levels on future developmental prospects. But, with some studies showing negative externalities of growth in the advanced nations, the concept of sustainable development will have to be re-defined. Keeping in mind the applicability of past environmental theories to date, an incremental approach to re-defining sustainability is required. But given the magnitude of environmental degradation, policy changes require a transformative approach, such as linking the same to sustainable development goals (SDGs). The three pillars of sustainability as given by Edward B. Barbier (1987) include economic, social and environmental aspects. In their simplest form, these pillars seem to suffice in conceptualizing sustainability. But with institutional complexities growing as a by-product of development, the aspect of governing these complexities must not be ignored in this conceptualization. Hence, this study attempts to re-defining the pillars of sustainability and further studies the link it has with development. These pillars include governance, environment and socio-economic aspects. Numerous studies show that there exists a strong relationship between these pillars and development in nations. They are both a cause and effect of development. The present study empirically analyzes the two-way effect that exists been these three pillars of sustainability and development, so much so that conceptualizing sustainable development has been hypothesized based on this two-way relationship.

The chapter is structured into five sections. The next section presents literature pertaining to sustainable development, the three pillars of sustainability and their two-way relationship with development. The third section puts forth a theoretical perspective and the fourth section explains the empirical analysis taken up, along with results and discussion. The last section concludes the study.

9.2 Literature Review

Studies on sustainability inherently link it to a stable desirable outcome, with the definition of desirable flexible over the course of time. In this sense, sustainable development aims at attaining long-term development goals with an onset of self-sustenance, such that resource use never ratchets down for future generations. With this temporal aspect, the sustainability of development can be said to be a factor of pre-existing levels of development. It can further be said that a variable becomes dependent on itself over the course of time. Hence, if a nation is poor because it is poor (Nurkse, 1952), can a nation also be rich because it is rich? In other words, do past levels of development affect current/future levels of development? This has been hypothesized in the present study to understand the role that past development levels play in future developmental prospects of nations.

Income inequalities that exist in nations also impact their levels of development. With the gap between the rich and poor increasing to all-time highs, the subsequent impact on development shows in the differing development rates across these nations. The richest 1% in the world have more than twice as much wealth as 6.9 billion people. Along with that, the income growth rates at the bottom have slowed down, adding further to the increase in the wealth gap. Cingano (2014) explores if such trends in incomes across different segments of society would impact economic performance. Using 30 years of data for OECD nations, the analysis shows that income inequalities impact subsequent growth negatively and it is statistically significant. The paper also finds evidence to back the 'human capital accumulation theory' to show that human capital development can impact the link that income inequalities have on growth. It suggests that policies for income inequalities should harmonize social outcomes and sustain long-term growth. Redistributive taxation policies prove to be an effective tool to achieve that. The study by Bruckner & Lederman (2015) gave different results for countries with different income levels. Their study shows that for poor nations, high income inequality raises their economic growth while for middle- and high-income countries, it decreases their growth. They also add that this link between income inequality and growth is affected significantly by human capital accumulation. Their study is based on the analysis by Galor and Zeira (1993) who also examined the relationship between inequality and aggregate output; and predicted differing effects of inequality on aggregate output across countries with different income levels. Lahouij (2017) examined this relationship for selected oil-importing MENA countries using panel data for the years 1980–2007. The paper shows that income inequality decelerates the rate of change of economic development. But it suggests judicious use of policy tools as the link between income inequalities and economic development would be different if the sample changes to, for example, a combination of oil-exporting and oil-importing MENA countries. Kandek & Kajling (2017) examine data from 2010 to 2015 for 357 metropolitan cities in America to study the relationship between regional inequality and local economic growth. Their study is an important addition to the literature on regional economics, owing to their city-level approach, which is not studied widely due to the lack of availability of data. The results show that the Gini coefficient has a positive significant relationship with GDP per capita growth, but an insignificant negative relationship with GDP per capita.

On the impact that governance has on development, studies have shown both direct and indirect linkage between the two. And similar to the previous set of studies on inequality and growth, there have also been studies that show a significant role played by human development in this linkage between governance and development (UNESCAP, UNDP and ADB, 2006). Rahman (2010) studied the linkages between governance and the extent of success of the Millennium Development Goals using data for the years 2000–2008 for India. The results show that there is an indirect linkage between governance and MDGs via growth and a direct link between each MDG and certain elements of governance. Azam and Emirullah (2014) study the link between governance indicators on GDP per capita for nine nations in Asia and the Pacific in the years 1985–2012. They find that corruption and inflation rate are negatively related to GDP per capita. The importance of governance for growth has been highlighted by Kirkpatrick (2012) who reviews less developed nations' regulatory policy as impacted by donor interventions and, further, how regulation quality impacts economic outcomes. Using causal chain analysis, the study shows that poorly designed regulations can hamper economic growth, but regulation, governance and institutional framework can mitigate damages. Togolo (2006) studied the governance–growth relationship via resource course, a phenomenon of resource-abundant nations being economically weaker. An increase in resource exports leads to an appreciation of the local currency and makes agriculture exports and manufacturing sector exports less competitive internationally. Using data for the years 1980–2005 for Papua New Guinea (PNG), the study shows that in PNG, poor performance was due to a lack of efficient macroeconomic management, socio-political institutions and governance structures.

Studies on the impact of environmental quality on development also follow either a direct or an indirect approach to the relationship between the two. The role played by human development in both these approaches is significant. Mukherjee & Chakraborty (2009) study the relationship between environmental quality, economic growth and human development for 14 major Indian States during 1990–1996 and 1997–2004. Using Human Development Index (HDI) methodology, the paper constructed an Environmental Quality (EQ) index consisting of eight environment themes comprising all 63 indicators. The results show variance over time in EQ ranks of the States, which implies spatial and temporal dimensions in the environment. Using multivariate OLS regression models, the paper also tested the Environmental Kuznets Curve hypothesis, and results indicate a non-linear relationship between certain environmental themes and per capita NSDP. Between environment and HDI, there exists a slanting N-shaped relationship. The paper suggested states to follow a local approach while adopting environmental management practices and work on transforming economic growth into human well-being. Li & Xu (2021) investigate the connection between overall environmental quality and human development. To measure environmental quality and human development at the provincial level in China for the years 2004–2017, the study constructed the Environment Degradation Index (*EDI*) and HDI; and studied the relationship between them using Simultaneous Equations Model (SEM). Results showed an inverted U-shaped relationship between the two. The study also confirmed that environmental pollution delays economic growth even at the regional level. Park et al. (2009) studied the significance of environmental quality as a determinant of sustainable rural development in England. The study combines economic and environmental factors for a regional growth model. Results show that other than environmental quality, variables such as business and communications infrastructure, commuting and employment prospects play a significant role.

Theoretical background points to the co-existence of inequalities and growth. Kuznets (1955) described the inverted U-shaped Kuznets curve to show a low income inequality in the initial growth stages and higher income inequalities when growth picks up. But after a certain growth level, income inequality starts declining. This relation was later called the great U-turn by Harris et al. (1986), who confirmed the hypothesis for the case of the United States post-1970s. While in another study, Partridge et. al (1996) throw light on the applicability of the Kuznets curve, stating that it was based on the manufacturing sector as the engine of growth, whereas in the current economic growth scenario, the services sector is taking the lead. On the link between income inequalities and economic growth, studies have shown varying results for nations with different levels of development and along with that, for rural and urban areas (Fallah & Partridge, 2007). Their study shows opposite results for rural and urban areas for the impact that inequality has on economic growth. Majumdar and Partridge (2009) study the effect that economic growth has on income inequality using data for per capita income and the Gini coefficient, respectively, to show whether the results vary for rural and urban areas. Their study shows that growth may negatively impact income inequality due to the presence of higher levels of investments, employment and incomes. The differing impact in rural and urban areas is owing to differences in population density and hence, different levels of job competition, thereby reducing the access to jobs in rural areas and, hence, lower incomes. In urban areas, growth may negatively impact income inequality due to higher population density causing better networking and hence, access to better jobs. However, in urban areas, it is because of positive spillovers of higher population density in the form of more personal contacts, better networking and access to information that growth reduces income inequalities. The policy suggestion of the paper is to invest more in the provision of skilled laborers to further the economic growth, thereby reducing inequality.

Studies on the impact that development has on governance show a positive one, even at different levels of development of nations. Al-Marhubi (2004) analyzed this relationship for 86 countries using cross-section OLS estimation and found a positive significant impact of GDP per capita on the overall governance of these countries. He concluded that even though income per capita has a significant role to play in governance outcomes, it does not imply that politics and culture do not matter for governance. In fact, economic factors are the result of other factors, many of them being cultural and political in origin. In another study by Rontos et al. (2015), the impact of economic growth and human development on governance has been analyzed using cross-section OLS estimation for 173 countries for the year 2012. It found that GNI per capita has a positive significant effect on all six governance dimensions, while HDI has a positive significant impact on two governance dimensions. The link between human development and social structures is brought about by the quality of public services and the commitment on the part of the government to such policies. They concluded that human capital building is closely linked to improved governance outcomes. Hence, investing in human capital building, including health and education is essential for sustainable human development. Barro (1999) studied the relationship between certain economic and social variables and governance using panel data analysis of over 100 countries for the years 1960–1995. The study found that a rise in GDP per capita, primary schooling and life expectancy and a decrease in infant mortality significantly cause the propensity for democracy to increase, which is an important dimension of governance. He confirmed the Lipset/Aristotle hypothesis stating that a higher standard of living promotes democracy. The study by Garcia-Sanchez et al. (2013), on the determinants of governance, finds a positive significant effect of GDP per capita and literacy rates on government effectiveness. Using GMM analysis of 202 countries for the years 2002–2008, the study concluded that for countries with lower economic development, it is necessary to focus policies on the removal of political constraints; while for economies that are in transition, the educational status is the most important determinant, especially in densely populated areas.

Studies on the relationship between growth and the environment show that in the initial stages of development, an increase in GDP deteriorates environmental quality, but as income levels increase further, the detrimental impact on the environment starts to reduce. Verbeke & De Clercq (2002) estimate the impact that economic growth has on the quality of the environment using five-year 'non-overlapping emissions growth equations for sulphur and carbon dioxide'. Their study shows that it is the level of income on which the relationship between economic growth and the quality of the environment depends. Supporting the Kuznets Curve Hypothesis, it shows that after a certain level of income, economic growth leads to better environmental quality. The significance of certain other variables like black market premiums or import tariffs suggests that reducing these variables improves economic growth and environmental quality. Grossman and Krueger (1995) show that in the initial stages of economic growth, there is deterioration, followed by improvements later. Selden & Song (1994) and Holtz and Selden (1995) show an inverted U-shaped relationship between per capita emissions and per capita GDP, suggesting that emissions reduce in the long run. On various aspects of environment, Tan (2006) finds that the impact that GDP has on improving air quality is higher than it does on water quality. But GDP impacts wilderness negatively and does not impact biodiversity. But the negative impact of growth on the environment is more evident in less developed nations, owing to their high dependence on natural factors and the respective pressure of population on the same. It is also prevalent in advanced nations with a past history of over-utilization of resources on their path to development where the exploitation rate of growth exceeds replacement rates of natural resources. However, with respect to the emerging market economies, the dependence on natural resources is lower compared to less developed nations, as they are more skill driven. And they have access to information from the advanced nations, which can help them overcome unnecessary environmental hazards in their path to development. This aspect has been considered in the present study to analyze the link that exists between growth and environmental outcomes in the emerging market economies.

9.3 Theoretical Perspective

The path to conceptualizing progress from economic activity has undergone a shift from economic growth to economic development and, more recently, to sustainable development. Economic development that safeguards future livelihoods can be termed sustainable. In other words, the path to self-reinforcing development which creates institutions ensuring longevity of that path over time is sustainable development. This links economic activities closely to environmental outcomes. Initial traces of this linkage can be dated back to the 1980's World Conservation Strategy for Conservation of Nature and Natural Resources (UNEP/WWF/IUCNNR,1980) presented by the UN Environment Programme, the World Wildlife Fund and the International Union. This led to the emergence of what is now known as the three pillars of sustainability – social, economic and ecological. Sustainable development is 'development that meets the needs of the present without compromising the ability of future generations to meet own needs' (Brundtland, 1987). This definition brings out the significance of temporal aspects of development. This will be emphasized later in the chapter in the first hypothesis.

Sustainability as a concept is vast and subjective and varies depending on the source of usage. At the micro level of an individual or a household, sustainability could mean efficient utilization of financial resources, consistent with the permanent income hypothesis of Friedman (1957). At an institutional level, sustainability could be linked to assured long-term succession of the institute, be it for profit or non-profit objectives. At the national and international level, sustainability could imply and require conscious collective efforts toward achieving a self-re-enforcing developmental path which houses self-sufficiency. For environmentalists, sustainability could be linked to ecological balance, green technologies and prevalence of rule of law that safeguards the environment. Whereas, for policy-makers, sustainability could be re-defined if populist agendas so require. The subjectivity of the concept makes it essential to clearly bring about the usage of sustainability in this chapter and link the same to the literature available.

Sustainability has been used to denote outcomes without negative externalities in the long run (Brundtland, 1987). It can be linked to how a society's affairs are managed and governed to ensure sustenance. Governing for fulfilling the economic and social needs of the present without compromising on the environmental concerns in the future can make development sustainable. But no policymakers or governments can ensure sustainability without an equal share of participation from citizens at an individual level. Garrett (1968) highlighted the significant impact that an individual's self-centric approach could have on the exhaustion of the planet's natural resources. Given the level of development of a nation along with its policies to govern socio-economic growth and environmental quality, sustainable development can be determined by past levels of development and by the relationship between such development and the pillars of sustainability. That is, a country or a country group has sustainable development if it meets three criteria simultaneously.

First, development should be self-reinforcing, that is, past levels of development should be a positive significant determinant of the current level of development due to the strategic complementarity between the two. In other words, the improvement in development should be maintained due to its own structure even if there is no improvement in other variables that are contributing to development.

Hypothesis 1:

The lag of development should have a positive significant effect on the current level of development.

Second, lower income inequality, better governance quality and higher environmental quality should increase the level of development. Studies show that there is a negative impact of income inequalities on subsequent growth (Cingano, 2014; Lahouij, 2017). Although, the relationship also depends on the pre-existing level of development of the nations being studied (Galor & Zeira, 1993; Bruckner & Lederman, 2015). With respect to the impact of governance on development, studies in the literature show a positive significant effect (Togolo, 2006; UNESCAP, UNDP & ADB, 2006; Kirkpatrick, 2012; Azam & Emirullah, 2014). On the impact that environmental quality has on development, literature suggests that environmental quality impacts economic growth (Li & Xu, 2021; Mukherjee & Chakraborty, 2009). Hence, it has been summed up in the second hypothesis as follows:

Hypothesis 2:

Income inequality should have a negative significant effect, governance quality should have a positive significant effect and environmental quality should have a positive significant effect on the level of development.

Third, an increase in the level of development should reduce income inequality and improve governance and environmental quality. The first part of this statement has been empirically verified by studies which show that at a higher level of development, income inequalities witness a downfall

(Kuznets, 1955; Harrison et al., 1986). However, this relationship differs for rural areas than urban areas (Fallah & Partridge, 2007; Majumdar & Partridge, 2009). Next, on the relationship between development and governance, studies show that there is a positive significant impact of development on governance (Barro, 1999; Al-Marhubi, 2004; Garcia-Sanchez et al. 2013; Rontos et al. 2015). Lastly, on the impact of development on the environment, most studies show that it depends on the level of development existing in the nation. At the initial stages of development, economic growth causes environmental degradation, while at later stages of development, environment quality begins to improve. Hence, an inverted U-shaped relationship exists between the two (Kuznets, 1955; Selden & Song, 1994; Grossman & Krueger, 1995; Douglas & Selden, 1995; Verbeke & De Clercq, 2002). These results have been put together in the final hypothesis as follows.

Hypothesis 3:

Development level should have a negative significant effect on income inequality and it should have a positive significant effect on governance quality and environmental quality.

From the figure, the three pillars of sustainability as defined in this study have been presented with area 'S' at the center representing sustainable development. The governance aspect highlights the role of policies for better environmental and socio-economic outcomes. Area 'a' represents environmental policies, while area 'b' represents socio-economic policies. That is, sustainable development comprises aspects of governance practices for fulfilling current socio-economic needs without negatively impacting future environmental quality. In other words, sustainable development requires striking the right balance in policies for social and economic growth and the environment. The following section explains the data and variables selected along with the methodology adopted in the present study to analyze the concept of sustainable development as mentioned in the hypothesis.

9.4 Empirical Analysis

9.4.1 Data and Variables

The study analyzed whether emerging market economies have sustainable development over the period of 1996–2017 with Panel Vector Autoregression (Panel VAR) analysis. Due to the data availability, 23 emerging market economies are analyzed.

HDI is taken from HDI (2020), which is used as a proxy for development. A higher value of HDI indicates a higher development level. This study uses HDI instead of growth rate since the HDI (hdi) was created to emphasize that people and their capabilities should be the ultimate criteria for assessing the development of a country, not economic growth alone (HDR, 2020).

Gini index is taken from Solt (2020) to proxy income inequality (gini). A higher value of gini indicates higher income inequality.

Average of control of corruption, government effectiveness, political stability and absence of violence/terrorism, regulatory quality, rule of law and voice and accountability from WGI (2021) is used as a proxy for governance (gov). A higher value of gov indicates better governance quality.

CO_2 emissions (metric tons per capita) from WDI (2021) are used as a proxy for environmental quality (co2). A higher value of co2 indicates lower environmental quality.

See Part A of Appendix 9A for the summary statistics.

The results of cross-section dependency test in Part B of Appendix 9A indicate that all of the variables have cross-section dependency. Hence, Pesara's (2007) second-generation unit root test has been applied. According to the results of Pesaran (2007) unit root test in Part C of Appendix 9A, all of the variables are stationary at first difference, hence they are I(1).

9.4.2 Methodology

Panel VAR Analysis treats all variables as endogenous in order to allow unobserved individual heterogeneity (Love & Zicchino, 2006). Since our variables are endogenous, there exist bivariate causal relationships between them according to the Granger causality tests, hence panel VAR was employed to build a system of four simultaneous equations.

Since the optimal lag-length for the model has been found to be one, the following first-order panel VAR model has been used:

$$y_{it} = \Gamma_0 + \Gamma_1 y_{it-1} + f_i + d_{c,t} + e_t \qquad (9.1)$$

where y_{it} is a vector of four variables comprising hdi, gini, gov and co2 emissions (Love & Zicchino, 2006).

Fixed effects, f_i, and country-specific time dummies, $d_{c,t}$ have been introduced to allow for individual heterogeneity and country-specific aggregate macro shocks, respectively (Love & Zicchino, 2006). To eliminate fixed effects, first-differencing has been used based on two reasons. First, panel data is balanced; hence there is no need to use forward orthogonal deviation (Helmert procedure). Second, the variables are I(1), hence using first-differencing turns our data into stationary.

The model in first differences may be consistently estimated equation by equation by instrumenting lagged differences with differences and levels of the dependent variable vector from earlier periods by Generalized Method of Moments (GMM), which requires small T and large N (Abrigo and Love, 2016).

Panel VAR utilizes five different tools; stability test, Granger causality test, panel VAR, impulse response functions and forecast-error variance decomposition. Panel VAR satisfies the stability condition if all the eigenvalues lie inside the unit circle according to the result of the stability test. The Granger causality test indicates whether the variables are endogenous or not. It can also be used to order variables from more exogenous to more endogenous due to the unilateral or bilateral causal relationship between variables. Since first-order panel VAR is used, panel VAR presents the direct effects of the first lag of each independent variable on each of the four-variable dependent vector. The impulse-response functions show how one variable reacts to shocks given to another variable, while keeping shocks to the other variables nil. Impulse response functions present the overall effects of each variable. Confidence intervals have been generated with Monte Carlo simulations to calculate the standard errors of the impulse-response functions. Finally, variance decompositions have been presented to show the total effect. It shows how much of the variation in one variable is explained by the shock given to another, which is accumulated over time. The total effect accumulated over ten years has been reported (Love & Zicchino, 2006).

For panel VAR analysis, the STATA package developed by Abrigo and Love (2016) has been used in this study.

9.4.3 Estimation Results

Panel VAR satisfies the stability condition since all the eigenvalues lie inside the unit circle according to the results of panel VAR stability test in Part D of Appendix 9A.

There are at least two bi-directional causal relationships between variables according to the results of the Granger causality test in Part E of Appendix 9A, which indicate that the variables are endogenous justifying to use panel VAR technique. Since there is a bi-directional causality between hdi and the rest of the three variables, it can be concluded that a necessary but not sufficient condition is met for our second and third hypotheses.

Since the first-order panel VAR model has been defined in this study, the results of Part A of Table 9.1 and Figure 9.1 are interpreted together. While Table 9.1 presents the direct effects of the lag of each variable on the current value of the other, impulse response functions show the overall effect of each variable on the other.

The lag of HDI (hdi_{it-1}) has a positive significant effect on its current value (hdi_{it}) according to Table 9.1 or the response of HDI (hdi_{it}) to the one standard deviation shock given to its value in the previous period (hdi_{it-1}) is positive significant according to Figure 9.1. Both results support Hypothesis 1 for emerging market economies. Hence, Hypothesis 1 is valid for emerging market economies.

The lag of gini coefficient ($gini_{it-1}$) has a negative significant effect on HDI (hdi_{it}) according to Part A of Table 9.1 or the response of HDI (hdi_{it}) to the one standard deviation shock given to the gini coefficient ($gini_{it}$) is negative significant according to Figure 9.1. Both results support Hypothesis 2 for emerging market economies. The lag of governance quality (gov_{it-1}) has a

Table 9.1 Statistical Results

Part A. *Panel Vector Autoregression Results*

	hdi	gini	gov	co2
hdi (t-1)	0.846***	-8.511***	-0.812***	-9.483***
	(0.015)	(1.139)	(0.308)	(1.147)
gini (t-1)	-0.003***	0.575***	0.005	-0.405***
	(0.0008)	(0.041)	(0.011)	(0.041)
gov (t-1)	-0.011***	-0.874***	0.864***	0.814***
	(0.001)	(0.076)	(0.033)	(0.069)
co2 (t-1)	0.001***	0.147***	0.011***	0.246***
	(0.0002)	(0.010)	(0.003)	(0.023)
No. of countries/obs				23/138
Part B. Variance Decomposition				
hdi	0.696	0.066	0.047	0.029
gini	0.217	0.666	0.010	0.118
gov	0.066	0.105	0.940	0.260
co2	0.021	0.163	0.003	0.593

Notes: Four variable VAR model is estimated by GMM; country-time and fixed effects are removed prior to estimation. Column variables indicate dependent variables while row variables indicate independent variables. Reported numbers show the coefficients of regressing the column variables on lags of the row variables. Heteroskedasticity-adjusted z-statistics are in parentheses. ***, ** and * denote significance levels at 1%, 5% and 10%, respectively.

Percent of variation in the column variable (10 periods ahead) is explained by row variable.

Source: Authors' calculations.

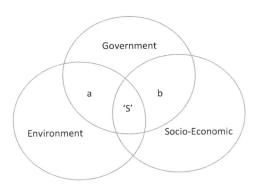

Figure 9.1 Pillars of Sustainable Development.
Source: Author's elaborations.

negative significant effect on HDI (hdi$_{it}$) according to Part A of Table 9.1 or the response of HDI (hdi$_{it}$) to the one standard deviation shock given to the governance quality (gov$_{it}$) is negative significant according to Figure 9.2. Both results do not support Hypothesis 2 for emerging market economies.

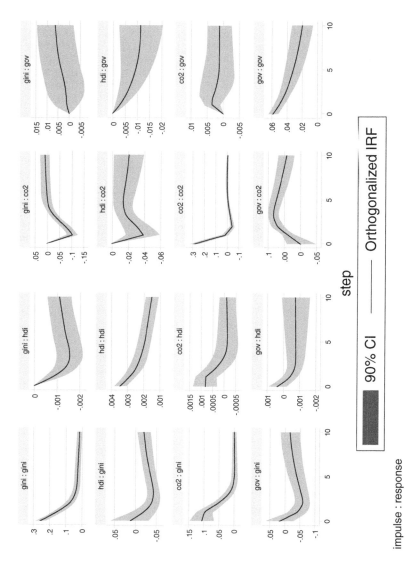

Figure 9.2 Impulse Response Functions.
Source: Author's derivations

The lag of per capita CO_2 emissions ($co2_{it-1}$) has a positive significant effect on HDI (hdi_{it}) according to Part A of Table 9.1 or the response of HDI (hdi_{it}) to the one standard deviation shock given to the per capita CO_2 emissions ($co2_{it}$) is positive significant according to Figure 9.1. Both results do not support Hypothesis 2 for emerging market economies. Since the results for the governance quality (gov_{it}) and per capita CO_2 emissions ($co2_{it}$) do not support Hypothesis 2, we conclude that Hypothesis 2 is not valid for emerging market economies.

The lag of HDI (hdi_{it-1}) has a negative significant effect on the gini coefficient ($gini_{it}$) according to Part A of Table 9.1 or the response of the gini coefficient ($gini_{it}$) to the one standard deviation shock given to HDI (hdi_{it}) is negative significant according to Figure 9.1. Both results support Hypothesis 3 for emerging market economies. The lag of HDI (hdi_{it-1}) has a negative significant effect on the governance quality (gov_{it}) according to Part A of Table 9.1 or the response of the governance quality (gov_{it}) to the one standard deviation shock given to HDI (hdi_{it}) is negative significant according to Figure 9.1. Both results do not support Hypothesis 2 for emerging market economies. The lag of HDI (hdi_{it-1}) has a negative significant effect on the per capita CO_2 emissions ($co2_{it}$) according to Part A of Table 9.1 or the response of the per capita CO_2 emissions ($co2_{it}$) to the one standard deviation shock given to HDI (hdi_{it}) is negative significant according to Figure 9.1. Both results support Hypothesis 3 for emerging market economies. Although the results for the gini coefficient ($gini_{it}$) and per capita CO_2 emissions ($co2_{it}$) support Hypothesis 3, the results for the governance quality (gov_{it}) do not support Hypothesis 3. Hence, we conclude that Hypothesis 3 is not valid for emerging market economies.

Although Hypothesis 1 is valid for emerging market economies; the lag of HDI has a positive significant effect on its current level supporting the theory of self-reinforcing human development in the sense that past levels of HDI become a significant determinant of the current HDI due to the strategic complementarity. Although decreasing income inequality leads to a higher HDI, improvement in governance and a decrease in CO_2 emissions lead to a lower HDI. Hence, Hypothesis 2 is not valid. Although improvement in HDI decreases income inequality and CO_2 emissions, improvement in HDI deteriorates governance quality. Hence, Hypothesis 3 is not valid. Hence, we conclude that development is not sustainable or there is no sustainable development that exists for emerging market economies.

9.5 Conclusion

This study analyzed whether emerging market economies have sustainable development over the period of 1996–2017 with panel VAR analysis. Although the term 'emerging' might be linked to 'sustainability' in the sense that emergence stems from sustainability, the same has been empirically tested in this chapter. Hence, the chapter is an attempt to understand the developmental choices in this particular country group.

The study brings forth a theoretical perspective that a country or a country group has sustainable development only if it meets three hypotheses simultaneously. First, development should be self-reinforcing, that is, past levels of development should be a positive significant determinant of the current level of development due to the strategic complementarity. Second, lower income inequality, better governance quality and higher environmental quality should increase the level of development. Third, an increase in the level of development should reduce income inequality and improve governance and environmental quality.

The lag of HDI has a positive significant effect on its current value supporting Hypothesis 1 for emerging market economies.

The lag of gini coefficient has a negative significant effect on HDI supporting Hypothesis 2 for emerging market economies. The lag of governance quality has a negative significant effect on HDI that does not support Hypothesis 2 for emerging market economies. The lag of per capita CO_2 emissions has a positive significant effect on HDI that does not support Hypothesis 2 for emerging market economies. Since the results for the governance quality and per capita CO_2 emissions do not support Hypothesis 2, we conclude that Hypothesis 2 is not valid for emerging market economies.

The lag of HDI has a negative significant effect on the gini coefficient, supporting Hypothesis 3 for emerging market economies. The lag of HDI has a negative significant effect on the governance quality that does not support Hypothesis 2 for emerging market economies. The lag of HDI has a negative significant effect on the per capita CO_2 emissions, supporting Hypothesis 3 for emerging market economies. Although the results for the gini coefficient and per capita CO_2 emissions support Hypothesis 3, the results for the governance quality do not support Hypothesis 3. Hence, we conclude that Hypothesis 3 is not valid for emerging market economies.

Although Hypothesis 1 is valid for emerging market economies, Hypotheses 2 and 3 are not valid. Hence, it is concluded that development is not sustainable for emerging market economies.

As policy implications, we recommend that emerging market economies should re-establish their governance structures since their inefficiencies lead to unsustainable development. Along with that, they should build renewable energy sources as improvement in CO_2 emissions from fossil fuels does not contribute to development.

Appendix 9A

Part A. Summary Statistics

Variable	Obs	Mean	Std. Dev.	Min	Max
hdi	506	0.725	0.101	0.431	0.912
gini	506	41.192	8.614	24.6	63.6
gov	506	0.029	0.587	−1.178	1.287
co2	506	6.069	7.47	0.668	47.699

Part B. Cross-Section Dependency Test

Variables	CD-Test	p-value
hdi	70.903	0.000
gini	2.574	0.010
gov	−1.814	0.070
co2	17.339	0.000

Notes: Null hypothesis is the cross-section independence. p-values close to zero indicate data are correlated across panel groups.

Part C. Unit Root Test

	Level		First-Difference	
Variable	Constant	Constant & Trend	Constant	Constant & Trend
hdi	−1.926	−2.038	−4.134***	−4.320***
gini	−0.450	−1.674	−2.824***	−2.889***
gov	−1.415	−1.633	−3.355***	−3.589***
co2	−1.143	−1.977	−3.931***	−4.093***

Notes: Null hypothesis is the presence of unit root. CIPS values are reported for Pesaran (2007). ***, ** and * denote significance levels at 1%, 5% and 10%, respectively.

Part D. Stability Test

Eigenvalue		
Real	Imaginary	Modulus
0.958	0	0.958
0.865	0	0.865
0.354	0.252	0.434
0.354	−0.252	0.434

Part E. Granger Causality Test

	hdi	gini	gov	co2
hdi		0.000	0.008	0.000
gini	0.000		0.640	0.000
gov	0.000	0.000		0.000
co2	0.000	0.000	0.000	

Notes: The numbers are the Prob > chi2 values. The null hypothesis is that the row variable does not Granger-cause column variable.

References

Abrigo, M. R., & Love, I. (2016). Estimation of panel vector autoregression in Stata. *The Stata Journal, 16*(3), 778–804.

Al-Marhubi, F. (2004). The determinants of governance: A cross-country analysis. *Contemporary Economic Policy*, 22(3), 394–406.

Azam, M., & Emirullah, C. (2014). The role of governance in economic development: evidence from some selected countries in Asia and the Pacific. *International Journal of Social Economics*.

Barbier, E. B. (1987). The concept of sustainable economic development, *Environmental Conservation*, 14(2), 101–110.

Barro, R. J. (1999). Determinants of democracy. *Journal of Political Economy*, 107(S6), S158–S183.

Bruckner, M., & Lederman, D. (2015). Effects of income inequality on economic growth, *VOX CEPR's Policy Portal*, 7.

Brundtland, G. H. (1987). Our common future—Call for action. *Environmental Conservation*, 14(4), 291–294.

Cingano, F. (2014). Trends in income inequality and its impact on economic growth, OECD Social, Employment and Migration Working Papers, No. 163, OECD Publishing.

Fallah, B. N., & Partridge, M. (2007). The elusive inequality-economic growth relationship: are there differences between cities and the countryside? *The Annals of Regional Science*, 41(2), 375–400.

Friedman, M. (1957). The permanent income hypothesis, *NBER Chapters*, 20–37.

Galor, O., & Zeira, J. (1993). Income distribution and macroeconomics. *The Review of Economic Studies*, 60(1), 35–52.

Garcia-Sanchez, I. M., Cuadrado-Ballesteros, B., & Frias-Aceituno, J. (2013). Determinants of government effectiveness. *International Journal of Public Administration*, 36(8), 567–577.

Garrett, H. (1968). The tragedy of the commons. *Science*, 162(3859), 1243–1248.

Grossman, G. M., & Krueger, A. B. (1995). Economic growth and the environment *The Quarterly Journal of Economics*, 110(2), 353–377.

Harrison, B., Tilly, C., & Bluestone, B. (1986). Wage inequality takes a great U-turn. *Challenge*, 29(1), 26–32.

HDI (2020). Human Development Index. United Nations Development Programme. http://hdr.undp.org/en/data (accessed 19 July 2021).

HDR (2020). Human Development Report. United Nations Development Programme. http://hdr.undp.org/en/content/human-development-index-hdi (accessed 20 July 2021).

Holtz-Eakin, D., & Selden, T. M. (1995). Stoking the fires? CO2 emissions and economic growth. *Journal of Public Economics*, 57(1), 85–101.

Kandek, B., & Kajling, V. (2017). Income Inequality and Economic Growth: What relation does regional income inequality have with local economic growth in US Metropolitan Areas?

Kirkpatrick, C. (2012). Economic governance: Improving the economic and regulatory environment for supporting private sector activity, *WIDER Working Paper*, No. 2012/108.

Kuznets, S. (1955). Economic growth and income inequality, *The American Economic Review*, 45(1), 1–28.

Lahouij, H. (2017). The effects of income inequality on economic growth evidence from MENA countries, 2017 Awards for Excellence in Student Research and Creative Activity – Documents. 4. http://thekeep.eiu.edu/lib_awards_2017_docs/4

Li, X., & Xu, L. (2021). Human development associated with environmental quality in China. *Plos One*, 16(2), e0246677.

Love, I., & Zicchino, L. (2006). Financial development and dynamic investment behavior: Evidence from panel VAR. *The Quarterly Review of Economics and Finance*, 46(2), 190–210.

Majumdar, S., & Partridge, M. D. (2009). *Impact of economic growth on income inequality: A regional perspective* (No. 319-2016-9872), http://dx.doi.org/10.22004/ag.econ.49270

Mukherjee, S., & Chakraborty, D. (2009). Is there any relationship between Environmental Quality Index, Human Development Index and Economic Growth? Evidences from Indian States.

Nurkse, R. (1952). Some international aspects of the problem of economic development, *The American Economic Review*, 42(2), 571–583.

Park, J. R., Stabler, M. J., Jones, P. J., Mortimer, S. R., Tiffin, J. R., & Tranter, R. B. (2009). Evaluating the role of environmental quality in the sustainable rural economic development of England, *Environment, Development and Sustainability*, 11(4), 735–750.

Pesaran, M. H. (2007). A simple panel unit root test in the presence of cross-section dependence. *Journal of Applied Econometrics*, 22(2), 265–312. https://doi.org/10.1002/jae.951

Rahman, N. (2010). Governance Process Innovation for Improved Public Service Delivery. *One World Foundation India, New Delhi*. [Online] Available: http://indiagovernance.gov.in/files/GovernanceInnovation4PublicService. pdf. (March 4th, 2013).

Rontos, K., Syrmali, M. E., & Vavouras, I. (2015). Economic, political and social determinants of governance worldwide. *Journal of Social and Economic Development*, 17(2), 105–119.

Selden, T. M., & Song, D. (1994). Environmental quality and development: is there a Kuznets curve for air pollution emissions?. *Journal of Environmental Economics and Management*, 27(2), 147–162.

Solt, F. (2020). Measuring Income Inequality Across Countries and Over Time: The Standardized World Income Inequality Database. *Social Science Quarterly*, 101(3), 1183–1199.

Tan, X. (2006). Environment, governance and GDP: discovering their connections. *International Journal of Sustainable Development*, 9(4), 311–335.

Togolo, M. (2006). 14. The 'Resource Curse'and Governance: A Papua New Guinean perspective. *IN THE PACIFIC ISLANDS*, 275.

UNESCAP, UNDP, ADB (2006). *Good governance and the MDGs*. Supporting the Achievement of the Millennium Development Goals in Asia and the Pacific (Phase II). March 2004-December 2006.

Verbeke, T., & De Clercq, M. (2002). Environmental quality and economic growth, *UG Economics & Business Administration Working Paper*, (2002/128).

WDI (2021). World Development Indicators, The World Bank, Washington D.C. https://databank.worldbank.org/source/world-development-indicators. (accessed 19 July 2021).

WGI (2021). Worldwide Governance Indicators, The World Bank, Washington D.C. https://databank.worldbank.org/source/worldwide-governance-indicators. (accessed 19 July 2021).

10 Governance Reforms from a Global Perspective
Some Dimensions

Asim Kumar Karmakar and Sebak Kumar Jana

Introduction

As recently as 35 years ago, the word 'governance' had rested almost unused. For a long time, the term 'Governance' was neglected by economists, perhaps because they expected the government to provide it efficiently. However, experience of the less developed countries and reforming economies, and observations from economic history have led economists to study non-governmental institutions of governance. It was the former British Prime Minister Harold Wilson who brought it back into general circulation, by entitling his 1976 memoirs *The Governance of Britain*, for which he was praised by reviewers for reviving an archaic word. Since then it has moved rapidly from obscurity to ubiquity. Governance is now used in various fields. Governance was introduced on the agenda by the World Bank (1989) because it needed to explain why a number of countries failed to develop despite the fact that they have adopted the neo-liberal adjustment policies imposed on them by the International Monetary Fund (IMF) and the World Bank. The answer was 'bad' governance. If we now question: What can explain the differences in the level of development between Argentina and France while both were at the same level of development and among the richest countries in the world at one time? The answer is bad governance for Argentina and good governance for France.

The New Palgrave Dictionary of Economics (Durlauf & Blume 2008) defines many senses of the word 'governance' including:

(a) the action or manner of governing; controlling, directing or regulating influence, control, sway, mastery;
(b) the state of being governed; good order;
(c) the office, function or power of governing; authority or permission to govern; the command of a body of men or ship; that which governs;
(d) the manner in which something is governed or regulated; method of management, system of regulations: a rule of practice, a discipline; and
(e) the conduct of life or business; mode of living, behavior; discrete or virtual behavior; wise self command.

DOI: 10.4324/9781003245797-11

With so many diverse meanings, it is hardly surprising that the word is used, and misused, so much for almost any context of economic decision-making or policy. But all these senses have common features: they are processes, institutions, or organizations of governing, not specific actions. Or in other words, it is not a field per se; it is an organizing or encompassing concept that bears on issues in many fields, including institutions and organizational behavior, economic development and growth, industrial organization, law and economics, political economy, comparative economic systems, or various sub-fields of these. There is a broad agreement that the quality of institutions of governance significantly affects economic outcomes (De Soto, 2000). Therefore, governance pertains to a more basic, deeper level of policymaking than any one policy choice or outcome. If outcomes are undesirable, reforms should operate on the mechanisms that produced them. Of course, it can be argued that ultimately only the actual policies matter and institutions that appear bad according to some general criteria can produce good policies, but it would be unwise to rely on such fortuitous results.

This still leaves a very large scope for the concept of governance: the political, legislative, executive, and administrative processes, institutions, and organizations that make and implement the rules and policies in a society, country, or groups of countries. We here consider only governance in its economic aspects. The importance of good governance for good economic performance is intuitively obvious and has been demonstrated in theoretical models, historical case studies, and empirical statistical analyses.

Against the above backdrop, the present chapter focuses on the efficacy and nexus between governance reforms and economic growth, along with governance reforms from global perspectives with special emphasis on what ought to be the characteristic of good economic governance.

Two Themes of Governance

Usually, there are two themes/aspects of good governance so far as historical practices in this field are concerned. First, although many countries must undertake major institutional and organizational reforms to improve the quality of governance, no country has perfect institutions and no country ever will. Property rights and contracts are never and nowhere 100% secure. Legislative and administrative institutions are everywhere plagued by multidimensional problems of asymmetric information and agency. A sensible strategy for reform will look for opportunities to improve the institutions and processes but pay due attention to these unavoidable limits. A strategically aware reformer will also watch for arguments that a proposed reform should be rejected because it is not perfect; this is sometimes offered as an excuse that hides self-interest in preserving the status quo.

Second, although all good institutions have to perform similar functions, they can take many different forms and use many different mechanisms: the formal legal system, formal state regulatory agencies, social networks with their norms of behavior and sanctions for misbehavior, business groups with their internal arbitration procedures for resolving contractual disputes and for self-regulation, and so on. Different historical, social, political, and economic circumstances call for different modes of governance. Judgment about the efficacy of a set of institutions, and efforts for reform, should be guided by this consideration of appropriateness in the context, and also by recognition of the first point that nothing's perfect and nobody's perfect.

Areas of Applications of Governance

Two areas of applications merit attention in this connection. One is corporate governance. This analyses the internal management of corporation, for example, the rules and procedures by which the corporation deals with its shareholders and other stakeholders. The second is economic governance. Its themes have been expressed by Williamson (2005) as the 'study of good order and workable arrangements.' These include the institutions and organizations that underpin economic transactions by protecting property rights, enforcing contracts, and organizing collective action to provide the infrastructure of rules, regulations, and information that are needed to lend feasibility or workability to the interactions among different economic actors, individuals, or corporate. Different economies at different times have used different institutions to perform these functions, with different degrees of success. The field of economic governance studies and compares these different institutions. It includes theoretical models and empirical and case studies of the performance of different institutions under different circumstances, of how they relate to each other, of how they evolve over time, and of whether and how transitions from one to another occur, as the nature and scope of economic activity and its institutional requirements frequently change (Ugur & Sunderland, 2011). North (1990, 1994), Williamson (2005), and Ostrom (1990) have emphasized the importance of formal and informal institutions for achieving good economic performance and growth.

Democracy is endowed with so many normative virtues, but its worth in governance is less. For example, in India, democracy itself is being marketized under the banner of neo-liberal philosophy. From the local to the central level, election campaigns are being fought on the strength of money. Contributors to election funds are increasingly viewing their contribution as an investment, expecting to maximize their rate of return with illicit favors to be obtained from the victors in election. The unholy nexus between politicians, corporate houses, and journalists fostered by lobbyists is assuming alarming proportions. If democracy is to serve the public purpose, this marketization of democracy must be stopped. The first step is the reform of what has been called 'political finance' covering the financing of elections and of party organization. Barro (1999:61) finds an inverse U-shaped relationship between economic growth and a continuance measure of democracy—'more democracy raises growth when political freedoms are weak, but depresses growth when a moderate amount of freedom is already established.'—but the fit is relatively poor. Persson (2005) argues that the precise form of democracy matters for policy design and economic outcomes: parliamentary, proportional, and permanent democracies seem to foster the adoption of more growth-promoting structural policies, whereas presidential majoritarian, and temporary democracies do not. However, Keefer (2004a:10) concludes that they affect policies but are not a crucial determinant of success: electoral rules almost surely do not explain why some countries grow and others do not, and 'the mere fact that developing countries are more likely to have presidential forms of government is unlikely to be a key factor to explain slow development.'

Democracy can be important for governance because its reliance on rules and procedures provides citizens with protection. In fact, an emerging literature argues that economic growth is better performed under suitably authoritarian regimes. Glaeser, La Porta, Lopez-de-Silanes, and Shleifer (2004) view that growth in poor countries starts because of good policies, often initiated by dictators, and that improvement of their institutions comes later. Giavazzi and Tabellini (2005) find positive feedback between economic and political reforms, but they also find that the sequence of reforms also matters, and the countries that implement economic liberalization first and then democratize do much better in most dimensions than those who follow the opposite route. In practice, of course, it is difficult to ensure exactly that an authoritarian ruler will implement good governance.

The 2009 Nobel Laureate, Ostrom (1990) on the issue of common-pool resource management, emphasizes the importance of local knowledge and communications, of appropriately designed punishments, and of incentives for individuals to perform their assigned roles and actions in the system.

Governance and Economic Growth

That good economic governance, which is efficient, effective, clean, corruption-free, freely accessible to the people, and based on simple and transparent procedures, is at the very heart of economic growth and poverty reduction, and even political legitimacy, is now part of conventional wisdom. The realization that good governance is critical came as a result of some profound changes in development thinking over the past 50 years. In the 1950s and 1960s, when many of the countries of Asia and Africa were emerging out of colonialism, the path to development, it was widely believed, lay in capital formation. In the 1970s, awareness grew that physical capital was not enough. When this too did not yield fruitful results, the missing link, it was thought, was improving social capital through education and health. Yet again, there was no breakthrough indeed. The disappointing and disquieting experience with the debt crisis in Latin America and chronic poverty and inequality among the individuals in Sub-Saharan Africa and South Asia during the 'lost decade' of the 1980s threw up the idea that the path to development lay in improving economic management and giving greater play to market forces. Again the results were mixed.

Some countries such as those in Latin America posted disappointing results despite making the transition to the market fully; on the other hand, countries in East Asia performed well despite sharply deviating in important ways from the market model. What made the difference were institutions of governance. The received wisdom is that, for growth and poverty reduction, we need physical and social capital, we need to focus on basic needs, and we need to yield to the market forces in a calibrated manner. These are all necessary, but not sufficient. They will not yield results unless they are accompanied by good governance.

There is broad agreement among social scientists that the quality of institutions of governance significantly affects economic outcomes. The importance of property rights, both from other individuals and from predation by the state itself, is generally recognized and documented (De Soto, 2000, Dixit, 2009). Democracy has many normative virtues, but its worth in governance is less. Barro (1999:61) finds an inverse U-shaped relationship between economic growth and a continuous measure of democracy—'more democracy raises growth when political freedom is weak, but depresses growth when a modern amount of freedom is already established'—but the fit is relatively poor. Persson (2005) argues that the precise form of democracy matters for policy design and economic outcomes: parliamentary, proportional, and permanent democracies seem to foster the adoption of more growth-promoting structural policies, whereas presidential, majoritarian, and temporary democracies do not (Persson, 2005:22). However, Keefer (2004b:10) concludes that they affect policies but are not a crucial determinant of success: electoral rules almost surely do not explain why some countries grow and others do not,' and 'the mere fact that developing countries are more likely to have presidential forms of government is unlikely to have key factor to explain slow development.'

What Is Good Governance?

A common question arises: What is good governance? Good Governance refers to the setting, application, and enforcement of rules but the focus is on the setting of rules that guide rule-making. From governance, governments learn that they can no longer steer directly, but learn how to manage networks in an indirect way to enable an efficient service delivery since Government is only one of many actors in the delivery of services and thus it needs to strengthen its coordinating role. In other words, economic governance is about setting rules that induce economic actors to cooperate more effectively with each other, and that support the implementation of economic policy. The World Bank articulates that

> Good governance is epitomized by predictable, open and enlightened policy-making, a bureaucracy imbued with professional ethos acting in furtherance of the public good, the rule of law, transparent processes, and a strong civil society participating in public affairs.

Poor governance (on the other hand) is characterized by arbitrary policy making, unaccountable bureaucracies, unenforced or unjust legal systems, the abuse of executive power, a civil society unengaged in public life, and widespread corruption.

In Andrew Gamble's (2000) words, it is about setting an economic constitution, i.e., the rules, constraints, and norms which economic agents accept as binding upon them. It denotes altogether the management of complex policy-making structures. In the ultimate analysis, it is the quality of governance that separates success and failure in economic development. Across countries, application of the same policies in roughly similar contexts has produced dramatically different results. In India, one can see vast differences across states in development outcomes from out of the same mix of development policies. These differences across countries as well as across regions within countries, even as they adopt similar policy packages, arise because of differences in governance (Karmakar et al., 2021:18). Indeed research shows that per capita incomes and the quality of governance are strongly correlated indicating a virtuous circle in which good governance results in economic growth and development.

Nexus between Good Governance and Economic Development

How does good governance impinge on economic development? Antipoverty programs may be totally undermined by weak accountability, corruption, and 'capture' of the programs by vested interests. An unsympathetic and oftentimes hostile government–citizen interface may alienate people from the ruling class and erode the government's credibility. Legislation promoting social development (e.g., abolition of bonded labor, minimum wages) may come to naught if the laws are not implemented without fear or favor. Efforts to promote private investment may not succeed unless the rules of the game are clear and potential investors see governmental action to be credible, rational, transparent, and predictable. Public investment priorities may be distorted by narrow parochial concerns or corrupt motives. Expenditure management systems may flounder because of weak accounting or monitoring systems. Failure to involve people in the development process may erode its benefits and compromise its sustainability.

State and Market

While talking of good governance, it is contextual to refer to the debate thrown up by economic reforms on the role of the government. Liberalization implies the state yielding economic space to the market. This has given rise to the stereotypical view that in the post-reform scenario, the government has a smaller role because the market now takes over part of what the government has been doing. This is a misperception. In the reform context, the government has, not a smaller role, but a different role, and arguably a more critical one. The state still remains today as a helpful support to the community (Rajan, 2019: 139). As has been remarked somewhat paradoxically, more market does not mean less government but different government.

It is worth mentioning in this connection that the market strategies are unable to solve all the problems of economic governance. Neither state nor the market solutions has been proven to be optimal. For economic liberals, the solution for state failure is more markets, while proponents for state intervention look at the solution for market failure to be more state. As a result of which we witness the prevalence of a zero-sum game. The move to a post-industrial society, however, involved the operation of other types of governance rejecting the sharp dichotomies in the market or state approaches. This type of governance is called heterarchical governance. This became widespread in the post-industrial society. But a hierarchical system has its own sources of failure when goals are not successfully redefined. The hierarchical system may not, in all cases, provide the best optimum mechanism through which to resolve conflicts. There are thus grounds to argue that an important role for the state still remains in coordinating a plurality of institutional arrangements in economic policy-making. This is what governance is about. Heterarchical governance refers to self-regulating networks, but in general, governance is about overall coordination (Khan, 2006: 200–221).

Role of the Government

Conceptually, the role of the government in the reform context can be divided into two broad strands. The first strand of the role of the government arises from performing those functions that the government alone can perform. In the transition to a market system, the government needs to move out of areas where markets can perform; conversely, the government needs to concentrate its efforts and resources on areas where markets do not exist or cannot perform. For example, tasks such as maintaining macroeconomic stability, promoting equity, and securing the right to property are all quintessentially government functions which, to use today's terminology, cannot be outsourced to the market. Then there are government functions which arise as a result of market failure. Market failure represents a set of conditions under which markets fail to allocate resources efficiently because of the myopic nature of the market participants. This happens typically in the provision of public goods, in the case of natural monopolies, or in situations where there are externalities or information asymmetries. For example, markets cannot be relied upon to provide external defense or internal security which is public goods. Markets cannot also be relied upon to provide a positive bias in favor of girls' education which has a positive externality, or to prevent pollution which has a negative externality.

The second strand of the role of the government in the reform context is to 'govern' the market to maximize collective welfare. Market economies are not self-regulating. They cannot simply be left on an autopilot with a government watching from the sidelines. The government has a central role in regulating the market. For example, the government has to set in place and enforce a competition law, regulate those utilities which are natural monopolies, has to set standards for quality and safety, and has to take initiatives toward consumer awareness and consumer protection. As David Osborne (2007) once articulated in his landmark book, *Reinventing Government*, the role of the government is to 'steer, but not row.'

Good Governance—Characteristics

We attemp there to reflect on some essential characteristics of good governance, and for the sake of clarity, we can group them under three heads: (i) rule of law; (ii) accountability for actions and results; and (iii) combating corruption.

Rule of Law

Rule of law has five distinct characteristics, *viz*.: first, there is a set of laws/rules known in advance; second, the laws/rules are effectively enforced or, in other words, nobody should be able to get away by breaking the laws/rules. Nonetheless, there must be widespread respect for the rule of law (Jalan, 2021:141); third, the laws/rules are enforced in a transparent and non-discriminatory manner; fourth, there are established institutional mechanisms for making new laws and for amending modifying existing laws to reflect the changing situation; and finally, the processes for making laws are participatory and consultative.

But serious shortcomings emerge in the enforcement of laws. First, the rich and the powerful can get away by breaking the law because they can 'manipulate' the system. Second, the poor and vulnerable get caught in the spokes of law enforcement even when they are innocent.

Accountability for Results and Actions

The government is the trustee of public resources and is responsible for using them for maximizing collective welfare. This requires that there are institutional mechanisms not only for determining how the resources are allocated but also for demanding accountability for results. Modern democracies are beginning to embrace a wider and more direct concept of accountability. Increasingly, the trend is toward accountability in terms of standards of performance and service delivery of public agencies to citizen groups that the agencies are required to serve.

We have seen, in the Indian case, several positive movements in the direction of increasing the accountability of the government. First, there has been the deepening of decentralization through the 73rd and 74th Amendments to the Constitution. The rising demand for decentralization around the world has come as part of the broader process of liberalization of the economic system. The underlying rationale for liberalization is similar to that for decentralization: that power over the production and delivery of goods and services should be rendered to the lowest unit capable of capturing the associated costs and benefits. Decentralizations, if effectively enforced can aid good governance by giving 'voice' to people not only to determine how their common pool resources should be spent but also to demand accountability for those expenditures. It is equally important that delegation must go hand in hand with capacity building.

The second recent initiative toward enforcing accountability for results is the output/outcome budgeting. This is an important reform as it links outlays of expenditure to actual results on the ground. For example, in India, enormous amounts of money are spent on primary schools and teachers, but what use is all this expenditure if there is no improvement in enrolment (which is an output) and in literacy levels (which is an outcome)? By explicitly indicating results to be achieved through public outlays, the government is not only imposing a discipline on itself but is also providing a reference frame for rendering accountability.

The third initiative in India toward enhancing accountability is the right to information. The right to information fills the important gap between 'demand' for accountability and 'supply' of accountability by providing public access to information relating to the functioning of public agencies. Evidence around the country shows that the right to information has checked malpractices, prevented waste and leakage of resources, and enforced accountability for results. But the problem may come from another side. For example, the administrative cobweb, with multiple agencies and no clear-cut demarcation of functions, creates insurmountable problems and delays for all those who have to deal with a government agency for any purpose, large or small (Jalan, 2021:148).

Combating Corruption

Concern about corruption is very old. In 350 BC, Aristotle articulated in *The Politics* that 'to protect the treasury from being defrauded, let all money be issued openly in front of the whole city, and let copies of the accounts be deposited in various wards.' There are similar references in Kautilya's *Arthashastra*. Corruption, broadly defined, is the abuse of public office for private gain. Accordingly, this definition covers all the pernicious maladies—bribery, nepotism, extortion, and blackmarket. The negative consequences of corruption are well known: corruption is anti-national, anti-development, and anti-poor. Corruption, a common problem faced by many governments, impedes growth, inhibits potential investment, increases inefficiency, and breeds vested interests. The international community feels that corruption, particularly systemic corruption, impinges on the rights of people; in fact, it is regarded as a violation of human rights (Atal and Choudhary, 2014:3). Most importantly, corruption, like inflation is a regressive tax and hurts the poor the most. Admittedly, corruption is pervasive across all countries, all cultures, and all settings. But it varies in degree, in kind, and, most importantly, in its damaging impact. The costs of corruption are decidedly heavy and also tragic. It is also an important fact that in poorer countries with all-round scarcities, corruption is more pervasive.

Although economists are increasingly engaged in the task of estimating the impact of corruption on growth and development, there are no definitive answers. Several studies do show a negative correlation between the corruption index and the investment rate or the rate of growth. However, there are three problems associated with such studies: first, there is no standard definition of corruption; second, there are as yet no standard ways of quantifying the extent of corruption; most studies base their measure of corruption on surveys of corruption perception; and third, it is difficult to estimate the counterfactual—what would growth have been in the absence of corruption?

Notwithstanding these conceptual and empirical problems, there is wide acknowledgment that corruption imposes heavy costs on society. In particular, there are five types of costs: (i) loss of public resources through leakages in taxes, duties, fees, and other levies; (ii) misallocation of public resources as investment choices are often driven by opportunities for corruption; (iii) low investment because of lower trust and confidence in public institutions; (iv) high costs and low quality of public services; and (v) increased insecurity and vulnerability of the poor, erosion of confidence in public institutions, breakdown of the rule of law, and ultimately threat to the legitimacy of the state itself.

Demand for corruption, i.e., the opportunity for corruption, as is well known, is higher in regulated and controlled environments which allow politicians and bureaucrats to dispense patronage. For example, India's pre-reform License-Permit-Quota Raj of the socialist era had fostered corruption because of the rents available in dispensing licenses, permits, and quotas. Similarly, citizen–government interface provides opportunities for corruption. In tax administration, for example, corruption depends on five factors: the complexity of tax laws, the monopoly power of revenue officials, the degree of discretion available to tax officials, the degree of transparency in the system, and finally the role of the political leadership. Quite evidently, the demand for corruption goes down if the opportunities for rent-seeking and dispensing patronage are minimized. It is indeed true that with liberalization and increased prosperity, scarcities have diminished in many areas. In many matters such as the allocation of telephone connections and the purchase of railway tickets, one does not face corruption to the extent one did 25 years ago (Agarwala, 2014:294).

The implementation of economic reforms in India, for example, since 1991 has reduced opportunities for rent-seeking. The introduction of e-governance systems has increased transparency, no doubt. Even as these have been positive developments, the incidence of corruption, especially at the cutting-edge level continues to be high. In 2020, Transparency

International, an international watchdog body ranks India in the 86th position with a score of 40 among 180 countries in the Corruption Perception Index at par with African and Caribbean countries like Burkina Faso, Morocco, and Trinidad and Tobago. Delia Ferreira Rubio, Chair, Transparency International says that COVID-19 is not just a health and economic crisis. It's a corruption crisis. And they're currently failing to manage and not to speak on attaining the UN's Sustainable Development Goals (SDGs). Critics often ask how India is growing so fast in spite of so much corruption. That is a wrong question. The right question will be to turn this one and ask, how much faster India would be growing if corruption were controlled.

Corruption operates at three levels: one is business–government level corruption, second is corruption in public services, and the third type is the one that involves a large number of voters in this case (Rao, 2013:5–6). Corruption emerges from the lack of transparency in the system, lack of good quality of governance, etc. One has to accept it as an unavoidable part of democracy and governance structures. Combating corruption is critical to improving the quality of life of the people. So far as the Indian case is concerned, though in India, from time to time, several Committees and Commissions set up by the government since independence, like Gorwala Committee, 1951, Bakshi Committee, 1952, and other Commissions and Committees, and Santhanam Committee on Corruption, were appointed to investigate corruption, no great progress was visible so far. For example, administrative reforms—reducing delays in decision-making, improving the behavior of the officials vis-à-vis the public, and ensuring commitments to India's development goals—have not focused on re-examining and/or altering the rules or structures as the essence of tackling corruption. In our opinion, a two-fold strategy is needed to arrest corruption. First, opportunities for corruption must be reduced. This can happen as we carry forward our economic reforms and reduce all forms of controls which result in rent-seeking opportunities. As scarcity of supply of goods and services is replaced by greater abundance, the pervasive nature of corruption that India witnesses can be restricted. Reforms and growth can go hand-in-hand in reducing opportunities for corruption. Second, the government agencies charged with combating corruption must show an increased determination in identifying corrupt officials and politicians and getting them convicted. Unless the conviction rate goes up, indulging in corruption will be treated as a low-risk violation. Above all, the public has a major responsibility. They must show in a decisive way their disapproval of people who are corrupt. This is particularly relevant at the time of casting the vote. The estimates of governance indicators for India during the period 1996–2020 are presented in Table 10.1.

Table 10.1 and Figure 10.1 show that all the indicators have fluctuating trends except voice and accountability, rule of law, and government effectiveness. Voice and accountability and rule of law follow a downward trend in the entire period whereas government effectiveness has a rising trend.

Table 10.1 Estimates of governance indicators for India (ranges from −2.5 (weak) to 2.5 (strong) governance performances)

Year	Voice and Accountability	Political Stability and Absence of Violence/Terrorism	Government Effectiveness	Regulatory Quality	Rule of Law	Control of Corruption
1996	0.48	−0.97	−0.11	−0.55	0.31	−0.38
1998	0.39	−1.20	−0.06	−0.46	0.35	−0.25
2000	0.35	−1.00	−0.13	−0.16	0.33	−0.35
2002	0.43	−1.21	−0.12	−0.35	0.00	−0.52
2003	0.45	−1.51	−0.09	−0.35	0.13	−0.42
2004	0.40	−1.28	−0.16	−0.43	0.04	−0.41
2005	0.41	−1.01	−0.11	−0.29	0.13	−0.36
2006	0.44	−1.06	−0.10	−0.28	0.18	−0.28
2007	0.45	−1.15	0.12	−0.30	0.09	−0.40
2008	0.46	−1.11	−0.02	−0.39	0.09	−0.34
2009	0.46	−1.35	−0.01	−0.33	0.01	−0.45
2010	0.44	−1.28	0.03	−0.38	−0.04	−0.47
2011	0.44	−1.33	0.01	−0.34	−0.09	−0.54
2012	0.40	−1.29	−0.17	−0.47	−0.07	−0.51
2013	0.43	−1.23	−0.17	−0.47	−0.06	−0.52
2014	0.41	−1.00	−0.21	−0.45	−0.06	−0.43
2015	0.43	−0.95	0.09	−0.39	−0.05	−0.35
2016	0.44	−0.95	0.07	−0.31	−0.03	−0.28
2017	0.39	−0.76	0.09	−0.25	0.00	−0.24
2018	0.35	−0.99	0.28	−0.23	0.03	−0.18
2019	0.27	−0.77	0.17	−0.16	−0.03	−0.25
2020	0.15	−0.86	0.39	−0.14	−0.02	−0.24
Average	0.403182	−1.10273	−0.00955	−0.34	0.0563	−0.37136

Source: Presented by the authors using the data of World Bank, www.worldbank.org.

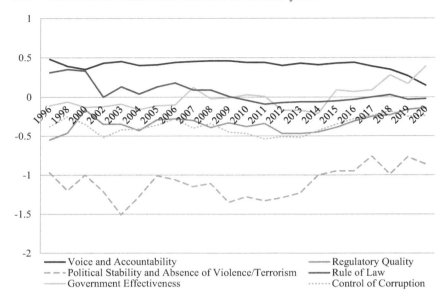

Figure 10.1 Trends of different governance indicators.
Source: Sketched by the authors using the data of the World Bank.

Computing the average values of all the six governance indicators for India for the entire period (as given in the last row of Table 10.1), it is observed that only voice and accountability and rule of law have positive values, which means they are, on average, high. But all others' average values are negative with a high magnitude of political instability followed by high corruption and poor regulatory quality. The impacts of these poor governances may be costly to the overall development of the country.

Conclusion

Theories and models about the state in development focus on setting an institutional framework for economic policy-making. They thereby study the conditions of governance and debate how some economies are less governed than others. Because governability varies, one unique model of governance cannot be applied universally, and this is true for economic constitutions.

Good governance is a combination of transparent and accountable institutions, strong skills and competence, pecuniary and professional integrity, and a fundamental willingness to do the right thing. The test of good governance is ultimately the quality of service at the cutting-edge level. Good policies are necessary, but not sufficient. They need to be accompanied by good governance. Each and every public functionary, be they part of the executive, judiciary, or legislature has the responsibility of making his or her contribution to good governance. Only then will the country be able to achieve the goals of growth and poverty reduction.

References

Agarwala, R. (2014). *India 2050: A Roadmap to Sustainable Prosperity*. New Delhi: SAGE Publications India Pvt. Ltd.

Atal, Y., & Choudhary, S. K. (2014). *Combating corruption: The Indian case*. New Delhi: Orient Black Swan.

Barro, R. (1999). *Determinants of Economic Growth: A Cross Country Empirical Study*. Cambridge, MA: MIT Press.

De Soto, H. (2000). *Mystery of capital: Why Capitalism Triumphs in the West and Fails Everywhere Else*. New York: Basic Books.

Durlauf, S., & Blume, L. E. (2008). *The New Palgrave Dictionary of Economics*. London: Palgrave Macmillan.

Gamble, A. (2000). "Economic Governance," in Pierre, John (Ed.), *Debating Governance: Authority, Steering and Democracy*, Oxford University Press: Oxford.

Giavazzi, F., & Tabellini, G. (2005). Economic and political liberalizations. *Journal of Monetary Economics*, 52(7), 1297–1330.

Glaeser, E. L., La Porta, R., Lopez-de-Silanes, F., & Shleifer, A. (2004). Do institutions cause growth? *Journal of Economic Growth*, 9, 271–303.

Jalan, B. (2021). *The India Story: An Epic Journey of Democracy and Development*. New Delhi: Rupa.

Karmakar, A. K., Ghosh, A., & Jana, S. K. (2021). Understanding the workings and dynamics of governing the global political economy. In Ghosh, A. (ed.), *Resilient Strategies for Good Governance in the COVID Era*, Chapter 2, 17–44. Registrar: Netaji Subhas Open University, Kolkata.

Keefer, P. (2004a). A review of the political economy of governance: From property rights to voice. World Bank Policy Research Working Paper No. 3315.

Keefer, P. (2004b). What does political economy tell us about economic development—and vice versa? *Annual Review of Political Science*, 7, 247–274.

Khan, M. H. (2006). Corruption and Governance, in Jomo, K. S. and Fine, Ben (eds.), *The New Development Economics*, Tulika Books, New Delhi, pp. 200–221.

North, D. C. (1990). *Institutions, Institutional Change, and Economic Performance*. Cambridge, UK: Cambridge University Press.

North, D. C. (1994). Economic performance through time. *The American Economic Review*, 84(3), 359–368.

Osborne, D. (2007, June). Reinventing government: What a difference a strategy makes. In 7th Global Forum on Reinventing Government: Building Trust in Government (pp. 26–27).

Ostrom, Elinor. (1990). *Governing the Commons: The Evolution of Institutions for Collective Action*. Cambridge, UK: Cambridge.

Persson, T. (2005). *Forms of Democracy, Policy, and Economic Development*. Working paper No. 11171. Cambridge, MA: NBER.

Rajan, R. G. (2019). *The Third Pillar: How Markets and the State Leave the Community Behind*. Uttar Pradesh, India: HarperCollins Publishers India.

Rao, N. B. (2013). *Good Governance: Delivering Corruption-Free Public Services*. New Delhi: Sage Publications India Pvt. Ltd.

Ugur, M., & Sunderland, D. (Eds.). (2011). *Does Economic Governance Matter? Governance Institutions and Outcomes*. Edward Elgar Publishing.

Williamson, O. (2005). The Economics of Governance. *American Economic Review*, 95, 1–18.

World Bank. (1989). *World Development Report 1989: Financial Systems and Development*. New York: Oxford University Press.

11 Effectiveness of Social-Sector Expenditure and Governance on Economic Development

A Comparative Study between Developing and Developed Economies

Madhabendra Sinha, Durlav Sarkar, Anjan Ray Chaudhury and Arindam Metia

Introduction

It is a notable fact that the governance and the public expenditures in specific sectors of the economy may swiftly alter human development in terms of quality of life, degree of well-being, and access to essential social services (Anand and Ravallion, 1993). Therefore, social-sector expenditure and governance on economic development fulfil the ultimate objective of human development. However, economic growth is considered the only objective of economic policy (Vasylieva et al., 2020). As many countries' fiscal and monetary liberalization measures to address the global economic slowdown are limited, effective policymaking is of utmost importance. This demands a shift from short-term goals and toward a long-term economic growth strategy (World Bank, 2020b). The primary purpose of social expenditure and governance in economic growth is to create a model for long-term development. People and prosperity are the most important of the five pillars of the sustainable development objective: people, wealth, the planet, peace, and partnership.

As country-wise health-related issues and humanity's activities impact the future, significant insight is more important than ever. Another significant concern in terms of social expenditure is the digital issues for emerging countries, including educational expenses. Since sustainable finance is a prerequisite for sustainable development, flow factors (such as the debt service cost-to-export income ratio) take precedence over stock variables when assessing a country's debt situation (such as the debt-to-GDP ratio). Moreover, volatility is an inherent nature of finance (Andersen et al., 1999). As a result, policymakers should invest significantly in development institutions intended to assist their countries in integrating more equitably and effectively into regional and global value chains, which may boost domestic value-added and access to technology and resources, as well as diversify economic activity, allowing social-sector expenditure and governance in economic development to have the most impact while posing the

DOI: 10.4324/9781003245797-12

minimum risks. Several econometric studies have demonstrated a significant relationship between long-term economic development and good governance.

It can be observed that the government's rhetoric of the developing nations in poverty reduction and social development does not necessarily lead to a growth trajectory. The experience of the African and Asian courtiers (Guisan and Exposito, 2010; Craigwell et al., 2012) shows that the amount of funds allocated for social development does not necessarily translate into economic development, social development, and irradiation poverty at large. The existence of corruption also acts as a catalyst towards the non-channelling of the development finances to the target group. In this context, developmental expenditure needs to be decomposed in order to find the long-run and short-run effects of this expenditure on the social development of the economies. The impact of social-sector spending on legislative bargaining is quite apparent. Studies indicate that higher social spending has a pro-incumbency effect on democratic processes (Persson et al., 2000; Sáez and Sinha, 2010). To support this argument, one must assume that the poorer agents benefit more from social-sector spending than the rich. This is a plausible assumption and can be justified on the ground that credit constraints and coordination problems can reduce the ability of the poor to invest in human capital.

There are several channels through which health determines aggregate productivity (Bloom and Canning, 2000). The productivity of a healthy workforce is expected to be high since workers in good health have more incredible physical and mental energy. Health-related downtime is likely to be minimal if the workforce is healthy. Good health leads to longer life expectancy which may encourage investment in education. Consequently, labour force participation and per capita income may increase. And longer life expectancy due to good health may promote saving for retirement, facilitating increased physical capital accumulation. The rhetoric of the successive governments of India in social-sector development and poverty elevation has been not sufficiently financed and has merely kept the social sector afloat (Kaur and Misra, 2003). On the one hand, the new pattern of the tax system has resulted in an increased untied fund to the states and the states have not shown enough ability to use this new economic independence. The expenditure on human development has not been monitored, resulting in expenses without reaching its goal. At the centre of the debate on social development, it is not necessary the fund allocation but a mechanism that will ensure the fund reaches its end destination through a proper monitoring mechanism.

Convergence in public expenditures for a panel of 17 European Union (EU) member countries during 1990–2012 was also explored. Applying the transition modelling and econometric convergence tests to various public expenditures, the results did not support the hypothesis that all countries converge to a single state of equilibrium (Apergis et al., 2013). Multiple food assistance programs alleviate catastrophic household exposure, encouraging savings (Lentz and Barrett, 2013). This promotes investment and the adoption of better technologies that contribute to economic growth and improved incomes. Further, school-feeding programs may encourage school attendance. The resulting improvement in educational attainment enhances income-earning opportunities in adulthood and boosts labour productivity. It has been shown that every dollar spent on social security generates nearly two dollars of economic output in the United States. This substantial positive effect was attributed to the positive impact of expenditure on social security programs such as unemployment benefits on aggregate demand (Koenig and Myles, 2013).

The discussion, as mentioned above, concludes that the concerns such as social-sector expenditure and governance in economic development, education, and healthcare are among the top priorities of any dominant economic strategy. As the globalization processes entail the connectivity of social and economic development parameters in different countries, we argue that development should proceed under a sustainable governance structure, which would positively impact the economy across numerous channels. Moreover, good governance fosters growth, which in turn enhances governance. Understanding the current disparities in social-sector expenditure and governance on economic growth is critical for successfully controlling the social development process. In this context, the present study aims to capture the differences in scenarios of developing and developed countries empirically from macroeconomic points of view over the period of 2001–2019 by utilizing some advanced panel data econometric methods.

The remaining part of the study is structured as follows. The next section presents brief surveys of some previously conducted associated studies followed by a concrete presentation of empirical illustrations. The last section presents the conclusion of the study.

Related Literature

The economic theories count a few studies analyzing the issues related to the impacts of social-sector spending and governance. Solow (1956) predicted that there would be cross-country convergence in the long run to a standard steady-state value of per capita income since a country starting with a relatively high value of per capita income at the initial time point will grow at a relatively low pace compared to a country which begins with a relatively low level of per capita income. Barro and Sala-i-Martin (1992) and other endogenous growth theoreticians developed that countries with different levels of other indicators except for per capita incomes at the initial time point will not converge to a common steady-state point. Individual countries will connect to their steady-state values of incomes.

Some empirical studies also enabled the link of particular government expenditure components to social-sector productivity and economic growth. Still, most of these efforts were not successful due to a lack of a meticulous theoretical framework (Diamond, 1989). Landau (1983, 1986), Barro (1989, 1991), and Grier and Tullock (1989) found a negative relationship between social expenditures and economic growth. Ram (1986) and Aschauer (1989) have found a positive relationship, while Kormendi and Meguire (1985) observed no significant association. The studies conducted in the nineties show significant positive relationships between the two.

Baum and Lin (1993) examined the impact of three different government expenditures on the growth rate of per capita GDP using cross-section data from both developed and developing countries between 1975 and 1985. This study determined that expenditures on defence, welfare, and education have different impacts on economic growth. The growth rate of educational expenditures has a significant positive impact on economic growth in all cases. The growth rate of welfare expenditures has a negative and insignificant impact on economic growth in all cases. The growth rate of defence expenditures positively impacts economic growth significantly for one subset of countries but is negligible for another subgroup.

Lindert (1994, 1996), Husted and Kenny (1997), and Snyder and Yackovlev (2000) showed that the democratic process, voting pattern, and social spending are statistically related. Most of these studies documented that the higher the turnaround of women and young voters to exercise their rights, the greater the statistical significance between social spending and government formation by the political entity in power. Mauro (1998) showed a negative relationship between corruption indices and expenditure on education in a study of cross-sectional economies. The study was started with the assumption that the more spending on the infrastructure of education, the greater the share of money tilted towards corruption. This was, however, negated. In an allied study, Grossman (2017) considered health an essential aspect of human capital that facilitates participation in the market and non-market production at the individual level.

A study by Ravallion (2000) on Ghana tried to find out if the economic conditions affect social spending shows that an increase in total expenditure is not statistically significant with the social expenditure; however, a cut in total expenditure produces a considerable difference in the social spending statistically and the elasticity is greater than unity. In yet another study, Tavares and Wacziarg (2001) revealed both positive and negative effects of democracy on human development. Specifically, the results show that democracy promotes growth by improving the accumulation of human capital and, less robustly, by lowering income inequality. On the other hand, it hinders growth by reducing the rate of physical capital accumulation and, less robustly, by raising the ratio of government consumption and the gross domestic product (GDP).

Gupta et al. (2002) pointed out that recent studies show that corruption is associated with higher military spending and lower government spending on education and healthcare. This suggests that policies aimed at reducing corruption may lead to changes in the composition of government outlays toward more productive spending. However, little empirical evidence has been presented to support the claim that public spending improves education and health indicators in developing and transition countries. The paper uses cross-sectional data from 50 such countries to show that increased public expenditure on education and healthcare is associated with improvements in both access to and attainment in schools, and reduces mortality rates for infants and children. The education regressions are robust to different specifications, but the relationship between healthcare spending and mortality rates is weaker.

In their study, Kaur and Misra (2003) examined the amount and efficacy of social-sector investment in the fields of education and health from 1985–1986 to 2000–2001 for a sample of 15 non-special category states in order to better understand the importance of human capital and the necessity for public spending on social sectors. Empirical data indicate that public investment in education has been beneficial but concentrated on elementary schools rather than senior schools. The linkage is more prominent for poorer regions than for non-poor states. The relationship between government spending and health outcomes is weaker, implying that health spending is insufficient. The lack of an adequate infrastructure system appears to have a major impact on infant mortality. In the case of health, state investment has had a minor role compared to education in eliminating gender and rural–urban inequalities.

Kaufmann and Kraay (2008) investigated the relationship between governance and development and analyzed national performance in terms of governance quality using an extensive World Bank data set spanning over 200 countries from 1996 to 2003. The study concludes that governance indicators can help synthesize and summarize a vast number of different governance metrics. Kwon and Yi (2009) looked into Korea's economic development and change, focusing on multifunctional governance. From 1965 to 1990, the study looked at public assistance programs, employees by sector from 1966 to 1990, and school enrollment from 1959 to 2003. According to the study, the government can set priorities for almost any institution, with economic growth at the top of the value hierarchy for institutions in each field. In Greece, Sakellaridis (2009) further provided evidence of the negative relationship between government expenditure on social security and economic growth.

Guisan and Exposito (2010) examined the correlation between public spending on healthcare, education, and a variety of variables in African and Asian nations using data from 132 countries and found that low levels of socio-economic development result in deficient healthcare expenditure. Health awareness is improved through education. A higher level of education equates to a higher level of socio-economic growth. International collaboration to promote investment and industrial development is another aspect of socio-economic progress. The state of one's health is a significant element in determining one's level of contentment with life's indicators. So, the study showed that in the backdrop of MDG, the primary way to improve health expenditure is to increase expenditure on education. The beneficial effects of education on health include preventive measures addressed to avoid malnutrition, water contamination, and other adverse circumstances, and curative measures through more quantity and quality of health services.

Craigwell et al. (2012) showed that investment in human development is considered a means of improving the quality of life and sustaining economic growth in the Caribbean. The purpose of this chapter is to assess the efficacy of public spending on healthcare and education by evaluating the life expectancy and school enrolment rates of these countries. Using a data set containing 19 Caribbean countries from 1995 to 2007 for healthcare and from 1980 to 2009 for education, a Panel Ordinary Least Squares model was employed. The results revealed that health expenditure has a significant positive effect on health status, while spending on education has no appreciable influence on primary or secondary school enrolment. Carter et al. (2013) found that public expenditure on social security had no statistically significant effect on GDP per capita in Barbados. Pereira and Andraz (2015) evidenced that an increase in public expenditure on social security has adverse macroeconomic effects. Their analysis based on data from 12 European Union countries and VECM indicated that public expenditure on social security had a significant and negative impact on output.

Sinha et al. (2018) found that with the bi-directional relationship, developed nations witness the positive impact of defense expenditure on economic growth. Still, in the case of developing countries, the exact result is negative. Also, in the case of SAARC countries, Mahapatra et al. (2018) documented that defense spending positively influences economic growth. In a time series analysis, Mukhopadhyay et al. (2018) observed a significant interlinkage between public expenses in the defence sector and the growth of the Indian economy, but the exact relationship is found to be insignificant in China. According to Soni (2019), the eventual aim of all developmental efforts is human development, which encompasses quality of life, well-being, and access to adequate social services. People can contribute to economic development if they have good health, education, skills, and governance. Das et al. (2019) have shown that social-sector expenditure and HDI have long-run associations as well as bilateral causal interplays in the states of India.

Amusa and Oyinlola (2019) studied the relationship between government expenditure and economic growth in Botswana. From 1985 to 2016, this paper, using a multivariate approach, identifies that the total public expenditure negatively impacts the growth of the economy. On disaggregating the expenditure, it shows that both recurrent and non-recurrent expenditure positively impacts the short-run development of the state. Their study showed the diverse effect of public expenditure on the economy, i.e., how small open finances for non-resources reliant on small SSA economies depend on the composition of the social-sector expenditure of the country. Using data on selected developing nations in Asia, Sinha et al. (2021) evidenced that different types of government policies significantly influence FDI inflows and other open economy macroeconomic variables, which are closely linked with economic output and growth.

In light of the above-mentioned discussion, the present study aims to carry out a comparative analysis between developing and developed economies where the effectiveness of governance and social-sector expenditure on economic development are examined over the last two decades, and that type of study is sporadic in the available literature.

Empirical Illustrations

To conduct empirical analyses, two separate panels have been made over the period of 2000–2019 for 52[1] developing and 49[2] developed nations selected on the basis of the World Bank classifications of countries as per the levels of income, where the developing countries are selected from the lower-middle and upper-middle-income groups and the developed countries are chosen from the higher-income group. The Worldwide Governance Indicators (WGI) (2020) database of the World Bank (2020a) provides country-wise data on governance (GOV). We collect the data on the suitable measure of the government expenditure on the social sectors (GEX), the domestic capital formation (DCF), the human capital formation (HCF), the volume of international trade (TRD) (exports + imports) and the per capita GDP (PCI) (as the suitable measure of the economic development) from the World Development Indicators (WDI) (2020) database of the World Bank (2020b). All considered variables in the study are measured in the constant prices and adjusted with the purchasing power parity.

Now in order to fulfil the fundamental objective, the study carries out the testing of a general null hypothesis as stated below:

- *GEX and GOV have no impact on the PCI; and no difference in scenarios between developing and developed countries is observed.*

We utilize the estimation technique of the generalized method of moments (GMM) in a dynamic panel structure for conducting the empirical analyses which was referred to by Arellano and Bond (1991). In this connection, the panel unit root tests as proposed by Levin et al. (Levin-Lin-Chu) (LLC) (2002) and Im et al. (Im-Pesaran-Shin) (IPS) (2003) have to be applied first in order to verify the stochastic properties of variables. Now, to inspect the effectiveness of GEX and GOV on PCI disjointedly in developing and developed groups of countries on a comparative basis, the fundamental model to be estimated is hereby proposed as the Equation (11.1).

$$\Delta PCI_{it} = \beta_1 \Delta PCI_{it-1} + \beta_2 \Delta GEX_{it} + \beta_3 \Delta GOV_{it} + \beta_4 \Delta x'_{1it} + \Delta \varepsilon_{it} \quad (11.1)$$

In Equation (11.1), x'_{1it} denotes the components matrix of a group of control variables including DCF, HCF, and TRD. All other notations used in Equation (11.1) follow their standard meanings. As the study mainly focuses on GEX and GOV in order to explore their dynamic impacts on PCI, the initial estimation process of Equation (11.1) has to be performed without considering x'_{1it} and consequently all independent control regressors are to be incorporated sequentially to check the robustness of the main outcomes. As per Arellano and Bond (1991) framework of the dynamic panel model, the cross-section units (N) should be greater than the time series units (T) to attain consistent outcomes. From this fact, the current empirical analysis is expected to be trustworthy as it is dealing with the data on 52 developing and 49 developed economies over the period of 20 years (i.e., N = 52/49 and T = 20).

To estimate the effect of GEX and GOV on PCI, first, we employ Levin et al. (LLC) (2002) and Im et al. (IPS) (2003) panel unit root tests. Those test statistics are calculated for all underlying panels of the selected developing and developed countries. The lag lengths of variables are selected by the minimum Akaike (1969) information criterion (AIC). Both the individual-level effects and also linear trends as the exogenous variables are incorporated in the estimated GMM equations. It is found that all considered variables in the case of both developing and developed groups of nations are non-stationary at the level in terms of both LLC (2002) and IPS (2003) tests, as Table 11.1 indicates. But, their first-differenced forms of those variables are found to be stationary as referred by both types of tests statistics.

We use the first-differenced equations of Arellano and Bond (1991) specified GMM estimations to administer the unobserved heterogeneities involved in the estimated models, where PCI is treated as the dependent variable, GEX and GOV are considered as the focused independent regressors, and DCF, HCF, and TRD are used as control instruments. The lag value of the dependent variable captures the dynamism of economic development measured by the per capita GDP. Table 11.2 presents the outcomes of the estimated models regressing GEX and GOV on PCI by incorporating DCF, HCF, and TRD as control variables in the dynamic panel framework for the panel of selected developing countries.

In Table 11.2, Model 1 shows the initial regression model only estimating impacts of GEX and GOV on PCI followed by sequential inclusions of earlier mentioned control variables as captured by Models 2 and 3,

Table 11.1 Results of LLC (2002) and IPS (2003) Panel Unit Root Tests

Series	LLC (2002) Level	LLC (2002) First Difference	IPS (2003) Level	IPS (2003) First Difference
Developing Countries				
PCI	2.58	−5.32*	−2.64	−5.49*
GEX	−2.27	−5.91*	−1.99	−5.73*
GOV	−2.11	−5.45*	−1.46	−5.68*
DCF	−1.55	−6.14*	−1.63	−6.06*
HCF	−2.01	−5.67*	−0.97	−5.80*
TRD	−0.76	−5.83*	−1.92	−5.79*
Developed Countries				
PCI	0.99	−5.12*	−1.44	−6.01*
GEX	−1.33	−5.77*	−1.57	−5.82*
GOV	−2.31	−5.82*	−1.79	−5.72*
DCF	−1.58	−6.22*	−1.63	−5.95*
HCF	−3.01	−6.86*	−2.86	−6.73*
TRD	1.44	−5.78*	−1.72	−6.02*

* represents the stationary at 5% level of significance.
Source: Authors' estimation using WGI (2020) and WDI (2020) databases.

respectively. Finally, Model 4 ends the estimation process by checking the robustness by incorporating all focused as well as control variables simultaneously in a single regression equation. The Arellano–Bond specified second-order auto-correlation (AR(2)) text authenticates the correct specification of the model. The p-values of Sargan (1958), Hansen (1982), and Wald (1947) tests make sure that instruments are exogenous. The outcomes also favour the estimation process that the number of observed instruments is lower than the number of cross-section units in specified models. Findings of the core empirical exercises as presented in Table 11.2 make known that GEX and GOV have positive and significant impacts on PCI at their first-differenced forms. Moreover, PCI is also directly influenced by DCF, HCF, and TRD in the selected developing countries. It is also observed that GOV is more effective than PCI compared to GEX. All results are found to be consistent and robust over the specified models as estimated and as different diagnostic tests report.

Table 11.3 presents similar type of outcomes in the case of developed countries. The results of the dynamic panel GMM estimations on selected 49 developed nations also imply that PCI is positively influenced by GOV, GEX, DCF, HCF, and TRD, as we have observed in developing economies. However, it is noteworthy that, like developing countries, GOV is not found to be more effective than PCI as compared to GEX in the case of developed countries.

Table 11.2 Results of Dynamic Panel GMM Estimations for Developing Countries

Dependent Variable: ΔPCI_{it}

Method: Dynamic Panel GMM

Variables	Model 1	Model 2	Model 3	Model 4
ΔPCI_{it-1}	0.1644*** (0.00)	0.1702*** (0.00)	0.1531*** (0.00)	0.1493*** (0.00)
ΔGEX_{it}	0.0217*** (0.00)	0.0209*** (0.00)	0.0192** (0.01)	0.0185*** (0.00)
ΔGOV_{it}	0.0401*** (0.00)	0.0334** (0.01)	0.0382** (0.02)	0.0378** (0.01)
ΔDCF_{it}		0.0512*** (0.00)	0.0494** (0.02)	0.0407** (0.01)
ΔHCF_{it}		0.0388** (0.02)		0.0279** (0.03)
ΔTRD_{it}			0.0289** (0.01)	0.0197** (0.02)
Observations	988	988	988	988
No. of Instruments	8	7	9	8
Arellano–Bond Test for AR(2)	0.26	0.21	0.28	0.22
Sargan Test p-value	0.19	0.25	0.31	0.33
Hansen Test p-value	0.23	0.40	0.18	0.27
Wald Test p-value	0.00	0.00	0.00	0.00

Source: Authors' estimation using WGI (2020) and WDI (2020) databases.

Note: ** and *** indicate the statistical significance at 5% and 1% level, respectively. p-values are in parentheses.

Table 11.3 Results of Dynamic Panel GMM Estimations for Developed Countries

Dependent Variable: ΔPCI_{it}

Method: Dynamic Panel GMM

Variables	Model 1	Model 2	Model 3	Model 4
ΔPCI_{it-1}	0.1927*** (0.00)	0.1801*** (0.00)	0.1843*** (0.00)	0.1788*** (0.00)
ΔGEX_{it}	0.0331*** (0.00)	0.0318*** (0.00)	0.0292** (0.01)	0.0306** (0.01)
ΔGOV_{it}	0.0287*** (0.00)	0.0299** (0.02)	0.0225** (0.01)	0.0297*** (0.00)
ΔDCF_{it}		0.0411** (0.01)	0.0362*** (0.00)	0.0384** (0.01)
ΔHCF_{it}		0.0371*** (0.00)		0.0212*** (0.00)
ΔTRD_{it}			0.0155*** (0.00)	0.0128** (0.03)
Observations	931	931	931	931
No. of Instruments	9	8	7	9
Arellano–Bond Test for AR(2)	0.23	0.16	0.19	0.28
Sargan Test p-value	0.21	0.24	0.21	0.23
Hansen Test p-value	0.20	0.36	0.27	0.18
Wald Test p-value	0.00	0.00	0.00	0.00

Source: Authors' estimation using WGI (2020) and WDI (2020) databases.

Note: ** and *** indicate the statistical significance at 5% and 1% level, respectively. p-values are in parentheses.

Conclusions

The study conducts a comparative analysis between developed and developing nations to catch up on the scenarios by employing dynamic panel system GMM methods using the WGI (2020) and the WDI (2020) databases of the World Bank (2020a, b) on the selected developing and developed countries over the emerging period of economic reform from 2000 to 2019. Empirical outcomes imply that different measures of governance are more effective than the social-sector expenditures to promote economic growth in developing nations as compared to developed economies.

Based on the empirical investigations, analyzing the effects of the social-sector expenditure of government as well as governance on economic development comparatively between developed and developing countries across the world during the era of globalization has been found to be a prominent issue of research. From the macro aspects of development, the social-sector spending under a good governance system could have positive multiplier impacts on the economy through various channels including the contribution to an enhancement of investments in education, healthcare, etc. Such investments augment productivities and get a higher level of returns by contributing to higher economic growth. The consistency of the current research is comparable with different previous studies including Kaufmann and Kraay (2008) and Amusa and Oyinlola (2019).

Notes

1 Argentina, Armenia, Bangladesh, Bhutan, Bolivia, Botswana, Brazil, Cambodia, China, Colombia, Costa Rica, Cuba, Ecuador, Egypt, Ethiopia, Fiji, Georgia, Ghana, Guatemala, Honduras, India, Indonesia, Iran, Jamaica, Jordan, Kazakhstan, Kenya, Kyrgyzstan, Malaysia, Maldives, Mexico, Micronesia, Mongolia, Morocco, Myanmar, Nepal, Nigeria, Oman, Pakistan, Peru, Philippines, South Africa, Sri Lanka, Tajikistan, Thailand, Turkmenistan, Uganda, Ukraine, Uzbekistan, Venezuela, Vietnam, and Zimbabwe.
2 Australia, Austria, Bahrain, Barbados, Belgium, Bermuda, Brunei Darussalam, Canada, Chile, Croatia, Cyprus, Denmark, Estonia, France, Germany, Greece, Greenland, Guam, Hong Kong, Hungary, Iceland, Ireland, Israel, Italy, Japan, Kuwait, Latvia, Luxembourg, Macao SAR, Malta, Mauritius, Monaco, Netherlands, New Caledonia, New Zealand, Norway, Palau, Poland, Portugal, Romania, Singapore, South Korea, Spain, Sweden, Switzerland, United Arab Emirates, United Kingdom, United States of America, and Uruguay.

References

Akaike, H. (1969). Fitting autoregressive models for prediction. *Annals of the Institute of Statistical Mathematics*, 21(1), 243–247.

Amusa, K., & Oyinlola, M. A. (2019). The effectiveness of government expenditure on economic growth in Botswana. *African Journal of Economic and Management Studies*, 10(3), 368–384.

Anand, S., & Ravallion, M. (1993). Human development in poor countries: on the role of private incomes and public services. *Journal of Economic Perspectives*, 7(1), 133–150.

Andersen, T. G., Bollerslev, T., & Lange, S. (1999). Forecasting financial market volatility: Sample frequency vis-a-vis forecast horizon. *Journal of Empirical Finance*, 6(5), 457–477.

Apergis, N., Christou, C., & Hassapis, C. (2013). Convergence in public expenditures across EU countries: evidence from club convergence. *Economics & Finance Research*, 1(1), 45–59.

Arellano, M., & Bond, S. (1991). Some tests of specification for panel data: Monte Carlo evidence and an application to employment equations. *The Review of Economic Studies*, 58(2), 277–297.

Aschauer, D. A. (1989). Is public expenditure productive?. *Journal of Monetary Economics*, 23(2), 177–200.

Barro, R. J. (1989). A Cross-Country Study of Growth. *Saving and Government*. NBER Working Paper No. 2855.

Barro, R. J. (1991). Economic growth in a cross section of countries. *The Quarterly Journal of Economics*, 106(2), 407–443.

Barro, R. J., & Sala-i-Martin, X. (1992). Convergence. *Journal of Political Economy*, 100(2), 223–251.

Baum, N. D., & Lin, S. (1993). The differential effects on economic growth of government expenditure on education, welfare and defense. *Journal of Economic Development*, 18(1), 175–185.

Bloom, D. E., & Canning, D. (2000). The health and wealth of nations. *Science*, 287(5456), 1207–1209.

Carter, J., Craigwell, R., & Lowe, S. (2013). Government expenditure and economic growth in a small open economy: A disaggregated approach. *Central Bank of Barbados*, 1–28.

Craigwell, R., Bynoe, D., & Lowe, S. (2012). The effectiveness of government expenditure on education and health care in the Caribbean. *International Journal of Development Issues*, 11(1), 4–18.

Das, R. C., Mandal, C. & Patra, A. K. (2019). Linkage between Social Sector's Spending and HDI: Study on individual as well as panel data of Indian states, *Review of Social Economy*, 357–379, https://doi.org/10.1080/00346764.2019.1671605

Diamond, J., & Heller, P. S. (1989). Government expenditure and economic growth: An empirical investigation. IMF Working Paper No. 1989(045).

Grier, K. B., & Tullock, G. (1989). An empirical analysis of cross-national economic growth, 1951–1980. *Journal of Monetary Economics*, 24(2), 259–276.

Grossman, M. (2017). 2. The Human Capital Model. In *Determinants of Health* (pp. 42–110). Columbia University Press.

Guisan, M., & Exposito, P. (2010). Health expenditure, education, government effectiveness and quality of life in Africa and Asia. *Regional and Sectoral Economic Studies*, 10(1), 115–126.

Gupta, S., Verhoeven, M., & Tiongson, E. R. (2002). The effectiveness of government spending on education and health care in developing and transition economies. *European Journal of Political Economy*, 18(4), 717–737.

Hansen, L. P. (1982). Large sample properties of generalized method of moments estimators. *Econometrica*, 50(4), 1029–1054.

Husted, T. A., & Kenny, L. W. (1997). The Effect of the Expansion of the Voting Franchise on the Size of Government. *Journal of Political Economy*, 105(1), 54–82.

Im, K. S., Pesaran, M. H., & Shin, Y. (2003). Testing for unit roots in heterogeneous panels. *Journal of Econometrics*, 115(1), 53–74.

Kaufmann, D., & Kraay, A. (2008). Governance indicators: Where are we, where should we be going?. *The World Bank Research Observer*, 23(1), 1–30.

Kaur, B., & Misra, S. (2003). Social sector expenditure and attainments: An analysis of Indian states. *Reserve Bank of India Occasional Papers*, 24(1), 105–143.

Koenig, G., & Myles, A. (2013). *Social Security's Impact on the National Economy*. Washington DC: AARP Public Policy Institute.

Kormendi, R. C., & Meguire, P. G. (1985). Macroeconomic determinants of growth: cross-country evidence. *Journal of Monetary economics*, 16(2), 141–163.

Kwon, H. J., & Yi, I. (2009). Economic development and poverty reduction in Korea: Governing multifunctional institutions. *Development and Change*, 40(4), 769–792.

Landau, D. (1983). Government expenditure and economic growth: a cross-country study. *Southern Economic Journal*, 783–792.

Landau, D. (1986). Government and economic growth in the less developed countries: an empirical study for 1960–1980. *Economic Development and Cultural Change*, 35(1), 35–75.

Lentz, E. C., & Barrett, C. B. (2013). The economics and nutritional impacts of food assistance policies and programs. *Food Policy*, 42, 151–163.

Levin, A., Lin, C. F., & Chu, C. S. J. (2002). Unit root tests in panel data: asymptotic and finite-sample properties. *Journal of econometrics*, 108(1), 1–24.

Lindert, P. H. (1994). The rise of social spending, 1880–1930. *Explorations in Economic History*, 31(1), 1–37.

Lindert, P. H. (1996). What limits social spending? *Explorations in Economic History*, 33(1), 1–34.

Mahapatra, S. S., Sinha, M., Chaudhury, A. R., Dutta, A., & Sengupta, P. P. (2018). Defense expenditure and economic performance in SAARC countries. In *Handbook of Research on Military Expenditure on Economic and Political Resources* (pp. 46–58). IGI Global.

Mauro, P. (1998). Corruption and the composition of government expenditure. *Journal of Public economics*, 69(2), 263–279.

Mukhopadhyay, P., Sinha, M., & Sengupta, P. P. (2018). Public Expenditure on Defense and Economic Development: A Comparative Study on India and China In *Handbook of Research on Military Expenditure on Economic and Political Resources* (pp. 170–181). IGI Global.

Pereira, A. M., & Andraz, J. M. (2015). On the Long-Term Macroeconomic Effects of Social Security Spending: Evidence for 12 EU Countries. *Journal of International Business and Economics*, 3(2), 63–78.

Persson, T., Roland, G., & Tabellini, G. (2000). Comparative politics and public finance. *Journal of Political Economy*, 108(6), 1121–1161.

Ram, R. (1986). Government size and economic growth: A new framework and some evidence from cross-section and time-series data. *The American Economic Review*, 76(1), 191–203.

Ravallion, M. (2000). Are the poor protected from budget cuts? Theory and evidence for Argentina. *Theory and Evidence for Argentina (July 31, 2000)*. World Bank Policy Research Working Paper, (2391).

Sáez, L., & Sinha, A. (2010). Political cycles, political institutions and public expenditure in India, 1980–2000. *British Journal of Political Science*, 40(1), 91–113.

Sakellaridis, G. (2009, June). An empirical investigation of social protection expenditures on economic growth in Greece. In *Paper for the 4th Hellenic Observatory PhD Symposium on Contemporary Greece, Hellenic Observatory. European Institute, LSE Hellenic Observatory, European Institute* (Vol. 2526).

Sargan, J. D. (1958). The estimation of economic relationships using instrumental variables. *Econometrica, 26*(3), 393–415.

Sinha, M., Chakraborty, P., Laha, S. S., & Bhuimali, A. (2021). Government Policies and Inflows of Foreign Direct Investment in Developing Asia: A Dynamic Panel Study. In *Optimum Size of Government Intervention* (pp. 120–132). Routledge India.

Sinha, M., Chaudhury, A. R., & Sengupta, P. P. (2018). Dynamics of public expenditure on defense and economic growth pattern in developed and developing countries. In *Handbook of Research on Military Expenditure on Economic and Political Resources* (pp. 131–143). IGI Global.

Snyder, J., & Yackovlev, I. (2000). *Political and economic determinants of changes in government spending on social protection programs.* Cambridge, United States: Massachusetts Institute of Technology. Mimeographed document.

Solow, R. M. (1956). A contribution to the theory of economic growth. *The Quarterly Journal of Economics, 70*(1), 65–94.

Soni, M. (2019). Social Sector Expenditure in India: A regional Analysis, *Research Review International Journal of Mutidisciplinary, 4*(6), 1.

Tavares, J., & Wacziarg, R. (2001). How democracy affects growth. *European Economic Review, 45*(8), 1341–1378.

Vasylieva, T. A., Bilan, S., Bahmet, K. V., & Seliga, R. (2020). *Institutional development gap in the social sector: Cross-country analysis,* 69–80.

Wald, A. (1947). An essentially complete class of admissible decision functions. *The Annals of Mathematical Statistics,* 549–555.

World Bank. (2020a). *Worldwide Governance Indicators (WGI) 2020.* World Bank, Washington, DC.

World Bank. (2020b). *World Development Indicators (WDI) 2020.* World Bank, Washington, DC.

12 Some Issues on Health, Urbanization and Wage Inequality in the Aftermath of the Pandemic

An Introspection

Debashis Mazumdar and Mainak Bhattacharjee

12.1 Introduction

The COVID-19 pandemic and the associated socio-economic crises are posing huge challenges before the governments and the common people in the affected regions of the world, raising many novel issues and imposing wrenching trade-offs. Though this crisis is global, its impacts are deeply local. The policy response to both crises, viz. the health shock as well as the socio-economic shock, needs to be rapid, even if it is rough around the edges. But countries cannot expect to pull this off on their own. Instead, the global crisis requires global solidarity and coordination. There is no denying the fact that every government needs to respond to this health emergency with decisions based on evidence, provide people with the best accurate information and provide free or affordable COVID-19 testing and treatment through vaccines and other medicines evolved in recent times. These health services should be backed by adequate health infrastructure, particularly in the public sector since higher costs of availing health services from private healthcare service providers may not fulfil the affordability principle in this regard, particularly in developing nations. It is normally assumed that a country with higher health expenditure per capita and a higher share of public expenditure on health can fight out the casualty of this pandemic in a better way. Table 12.1 reflects this scenario across nations.

12.2 Review of Literature

Islam and Maitra (2012) estimate, using a large panel data set from rural Bangladesh, the effects of health shocks on household consumption and how access to microcredit affects households' response to such shocks. The prime finding remains that even though general consumption remains stable in many cases when households are exposed to health shocks, households that have access to microcredit appear to be more resilient. The most important instrument used by households appears to be the sale

DOI: 10.4324/9781003245797-13

Table 12.1 Global scenario of health spending and COVID-19 pandemic

Country	Health expenditure per capita (2016) (US$)	Health Exp. as percentage of GDP (%) (2017)	COVID death as percentage of total cases (%) (as on May 5, 2020)
USA	9869.74	17.06	5.76
Germany	4714.26	11.24	4.21
Canada	4458.21	10.57	6.34
France	4263.36	11.31	14.87
UK	3958.01	9.63	15.08
Spain	3259.8	8.87	11.14
Israel	2837.14	7.41	1.46
Italy	2738.71	8.84	13.72
S. Korea	2043.86	7.6	2.35
Saudi Arabia	1147.33	5.23	0.67
Russia	469.13	5.34	0.93
China	398.33	5.15	5.59
India	62.71	3.53	3.38

Source: Compiled by the authors on the basis of WHO and World Bank database.

of productive assets (livestock) and there is a significant mitigating effect of microcredit: households that have access to microcredit do not need to sell livestock to the extent households that do not have access to microcredit need to, in order to insure consumption against health shocks. Thus, the study posits the case for those microcredit organizations and microcredit per se having to play the role of insurance.

In another study, Haren and Simchi-Levi (2020) project that the brunt of COVID-19 on global supply chains will occur in mid-March 2020, forcing thousands of companies to throttle down or temporarily shut assembly and manufacturing plants in the USA and Europe. The study indicates that the most vulnerable companies are those which rely heavily or solely on factories in China for parts and materials. Besides, the activity of Chinese manufacturing plants has been found to be plummeting past month and is expected to remain depressed for months. The study highlights how mounting pressure to reduce supply chain costs induces companies to pursue strategies such as lean manufacturing, offshoring and outsourcing. Such austerity measures smacks of severe dampening of manufacturing in light of flagrant supply-chain disruption.

Hartley and Rebucci (2020) present an event-study analysis of 24 COVID-19 QE announcements made by 21 global central banks on their local ten-year government bond yields. The findings indicate that the average developed market QE announcement had a statistically significant −0.14% 1-day impact, which is slightly smaller than past interventions during the Great Recession era. In contrast, the average impact of emerging market QE announcements was significantly larger, averaging −0.28% and −0.43% over 1-day and 3-day windows, respectively. Moreover, the study comes with an estimate where an overall average 1-day impact of −0.23%

averaged over developed and emerging bond markets. Besides, the study posits that all ten-year government bond yields in our sample rose sharply in mid-March 2020, but fell substantially after the period of QE announcements.

Hevia and Neumeyer (2020) envisage how emerging economies must navigate the COVID-19 pandemic amid collapsing exports, dwindling remittances and tightening international credit conditions. The study asserts that developing countries will be harder hit by the pandemic as many policy measures to fight it will be less effective. This is because their governments will have difficulties issuing debt to smooth the COVID-19 shock as they struggle to credibly commit future tax revenues to pay for a fiscal expansion today.

Hofmann et al. (2020) indicate that borrowing through domestic currency bonds has not insulated emerging market economies (EMEs) from the financial shock unleashed by COVID-19 in what is revealed by an uptick in EME local currency bond spreads coupled with sharp currency depreciations and capital outflows. However, EMEs with monetary policy frameworks that are equipped to address the feedback loop between exchange rate depreciation and capital outflows stand a better chance of weathering the financial fallout from the COVID-19 pandemic.

Tanberg et al. (2020) discuss the role public investment spending can play in the fiscal response to the COVID-19 pandemic in two aspects: cuts or postponements in public investment spending to make room for emergency spending in the immediate response to the pandemic; and the scaling up of public investment spending to support economic recovery and growth. The fundamental highlights are regarding the key challenges facing countries at different levels of economic development and capacity, and it proposes concrete measures to address the two aspects. Besides, it proposes that both during the immediate crisis and the recovery phase, there is a need for strong prioritization and project selection processes, accompanied by clear policy objectives, dedicated coordination mechanisms and high transparency.

12.3 A Theoretical Model

The model developed herein is based on Jones (1965, 1971) and Beladi and Marjit (1996) and consists of five sectors – (a) an overall health sector (X), (b) a manufacturing sector (Z), (c) a defence sector (Y), (d) construction sector and (e) a rural sector producing primary goods (R). Of these, X, Y and R are open to trade, with X and R on the export side and Y on the import side. Moreover, the health sector uses import inputs, such as active pharmaceutical ingredients and medical instruments (M_X). In this model, two skilled types of labour have been considered – S_1, used specifically in X and S, used in Z, C and Y. Moreover, there are two types of capital as well – K_1, used in X and K, used in Z, C, Y and R. Besides, there is unskilled labour being (L_u) used in C and R, while its price in the former sector is

Some Issues on Health, Urbanization and Wage Inequality 191

fixed and in latter it is competitively determined. Hhere, we assume that defence goods production is carried out in state-owned enterprise with no private sector, but it imports raw materials and finished goods as well along with its price being administered and negotiated, i.e., $P_Y = \overline{P_Y}$. To this, let us suppose that S_Y and K_Y are, respectively, the amount of skilled labour and capital being used in Y which are exogenously given as per the government's production plan and needs. Hence, the residual amount of S and K are allocated competitively among Z, C and R which have perfectly industrial structures. However, the health sector is oligopolistic in nature with the price of health services being determined by a markup rule. Now, it is assumed that this markup is diminishing in government pricing policy on health and medical research along with administered import procurement, taken together as G_X. Moreover, the sectors are assumed to have fixed-coefficient production technology. Moreover, the model encompasses the phenomenon of rural–urban migration from R to C and the rural sector derives raw materials from Z. All of the primary factors are fixed in supply and fully employed. The price of Z is exogenously given in line with the international price and so is the price of imported inputs to the health sector and the price of the primary goods, i.e., P_M and P_R. These apart, unskilled wage in construction sector is fixed as per the minimum wage legislation ($\overline{W_U}$). Thus, the overall model discussed hitherto can be summarized in terms of the following equations:

$$P_X = \left(a_{SX}^1 W_S^1 + a_{KX}r + a_{MX}P_M\right)\left(1 + m(G_X)\right) \tag{12.1}$$

$$P_Y = \overline{P_Y} \tag{12.2}$$

$$P_Z = a_{SZ}W_S + a_{KZ}r \tag{12.3}$$

$$P_C = a_{SC}W_S + a_{UC}\overline{W_U} + a_{KC}r \tag{12.4}$$

$$P_R = a_{UR}W_U + a_{KR}r + a_{ZR}P_Z \tag{12.5}$$

$$\overline{W_U}\left(\frac{a_{UC}C}{L_{UC}}\right) = W_U \tag{12.6}$$

$$a_{SX}^1 X = S_1 \tag{12.7}$$

$$a_{SZ}Z + a_{SC}C = (1 - \beta_{SY})\overline{S} \tag{12.8}$$

$$a_{KX}X + a_{KZ}Z + a_{KC}C + a_{KR}R = (1 - \beta_{KY})\overline{K} \tag{12.9}$$

$$C_d = \alpha_c\left(\frac{P_X X + P_Z Z + P_C C + P_R R + \overline{P_Y}Y}{P_C}, \varepsilon\right), 0 < \alpha_c < 1 \tag{12.10}$$

$$P_X = P_X\left[\alpha_X\left(\frac{P_XX + P_ZZ + P_CC + P_RR + \overline{P_Y}\overline{Y}}{P_X}, \gamma\right)\right], P_X' < 0, 0 < \alpha_X < 1 \quad (12.11)$$

[Note: Equations (12.10) and (12.11), respectively, denote the demand and inverse demand functions of C and X and, β_{KY} and β_{SY} are, respectively, the fixed share of total K available and total S available in the economy devoted to defence production. Further, α_c and α_X are, respectively, the expenditure shares of C and X]

Let us now explain the model. The Equations (12.7)–(12.10) solve X, Z, C and R. Given, C, (12.6) determines W_U and given that, (12.5) determines r. Now, given the value of r, Equations (12.3) and (12.4) determine P_C and W_S. Again, for given r and given P_X Equation (12.1) determines W_S^1. Finally, Equation (12.11) determines P_X. This is how the whole system is solved.

12.4 Impact of Health Crisis or Pandemic on the Economy

The advent of the pandemic has led to an upsurge in morbidity and mortality among people. This eventually has led to a contraction of the labour force. Now, as it happened to be in the case of India, the prevalence of the pandemic was more in urban areas than in rural areas, particularly in the first wave of it. Moreover, as the lockdown was declared by the government, the mobility of the labour force went into troubled water hampering production in almost all sectors. Moreover, disruption in the supply chain was emergent within the border and across the border and this leads to a supply crisis of critical input into production like active pharmaceutical ingredients (API) and other items, pushing the whole production into doldrums wide across and throughout the world as well. Against this backdrop, we present the comparative results as the following.

(a) *Increase in morbidity/mortality rate (denoted by φ) and fall in the supply of S_1 and S*

To trace the impact aforementioned, we have performed total differentiation and 'hat' algebra in line with Jones (1965) on the output subsystem including the demand equation for C (i.e., from (12.7) to (12.10)) and got the following results.

$$\beta_{SX}\hat{X} = \varepsilon_{s1}^\varphi\hat{\varphi}, \varepsilon_{s1}^\varphi < 0 \quad (12.12)$$

$$\beta_{SZ}\hat{Z} + \beta_{SC}\hat{C} = (1 - \beta_{SY})\varepsilon_s^\varphi\hat{\varphi}, \varepsilon_s^\varphi < 0 \quad (12.13)$$

$$\beta_{KX}\hat{X} + \beta_{KZ}\hat{Z} + \beta_{KC}\hat{C} + \beta_{RX}\hat{R} = 0 \quad (12.14)$$

Some Issues on Health, Urbanization and Wage Inequality 193

$$\hat{C} = \frac{\alpha_C \left(\emptyset_X \hat{X} + \emptyset_Z \hat{X} + \emptyset_R \hat{X} \right)}{(1-\alpha_C)\emptyset_C} + \frac{\alpha_C \left[\emptyset_X \widehat{P_X} - (1-\emptyset_C)\widehat{P_C} \right]}{(1-\alpha_C)\emptyset_C} \quad (12.15)$$

[Note: β_{ij} is employment share of factor 'i' in sector 'j', $\emptyset_j$ denotes the share of sector 'j' in GDP, α_C is the aggregate propensity to spend on C]

Solving these equations, we get

$$\hat{X} = \left(\frac{\varepsilon_{s1}^\varphi}{\beta_{SX}} \right) \hat{\varphi} < 0 \quad (12.16)$$

$$\hat{Z} = \left(\frac{\pi_2 \pi_5 + \pi_1 \pi_6}{\pi_0 \pi_5 - \pi_1 \pi_4} \right) \hat{\varphi} + \left(\frac{\pi_3 \pi_5 - \pi_1 \pi_7}{\pi_0 \pi_5 - \pi_1 \pi_4} \right) \left[\emptyset_X \widehat{P_X} - (1-\emptyset_C)\widehat{P_C} \right] \quad (12.17)$$

$$\hat{R} = -\left(\frac{\pi_0 \pi_6 + \pi_4 \pi_2}{\pi_0 \pi_5 - \pi_1 \pi_4} \right) \hat{\varphi} + \left(\frac{\pi_0 \pi_7 - \pi_4 \pi_3}{\pi_0 \pi_5 - \pi_1 \pi_4} \right) \left[\emptyset_X \widehat{P_X} - (1-\emptyset_C)\widehat{P_C} \right] \quad (12.18)$$

where,

$$\pi_0 = \left[\beta_{SZ} + \beta_{SC} \left\{ \frac{\alpha_C}{(1-\alpha_C)} \right\} \frac{\emptyset_Z}{\emptyset_C} \right] > 0$$

$$\pi_1 = \left[\beta_{SC} \left\{ \frac{\alpha_C}{(1-\alpha_C)} \right\} \frac{\emptyset_R}{\emptyset_C} \right] > 0$$

$$\pi_2 = \left[(1-\beta_{SY})\varepsilon_s^\varphi - \left(\frac{\beta_{SC}}{\beta_{SX}} \right) \left\{ \frac{\alpha_C}{(1-\alpha_C)} \right\} \left(\frac{\emptyset_X}{\emptyset_C} \right) \varepsilon_{s1}^\varphi \right]$$

$$\pi_3 = \left[\left(\frac{\beta_{SC}}{\emptyset_C} \right) \left\{ \frac{\alpha_C}{(1-\alpha_C)} \right\} \right] > 0$$

$$\pi_4 = \left[\beta_{KZ} + \beta_{KC} \left\{ \frac{\alpha_C}{(1-\alpha_C)} \right\} \frac{\emptyset_Z}{\emptyset_C} \right] > 0$$

$$\pi_5 = \left[\beta_{KR} + \beta_{KC} \left\{ \frac{\alpha_C}{(1-\alpha_C)} \right\} \frac{\emptyset_R}{\emptyset_C} \right] > 0$$

$$\pi_6 = \left[\left(\frac{\beta_{KX}}{\beta_{SX}} \right) + \left(\frac{\beta_{KC}}{\beta_{SX}} \right) \left\{ \frac{\alpha_C}{(1-\alpha_C)} \right\} \left(\frac{\emptyset_X}{\emptyset_C} \right) \right] \varepsilon_{s1}^\varphi \hat{\varphi} < 0$$

$$\pi_7 = \left[\left(\frac{\beta_{KC}}{\varnothing_C}\right)\left\{\frac{\alpha_C}{(1-\alpha_C)}\right\}\right] > 0$$

Now, let us examine the aforementioned. To begin with, given $\beta_{SZ} > 0$, it is obvious that $\pi_0 > \pi_1$. Now, assuming the construction sector to be more K-intensive than R, it is arguable that $\pi_4 > \pi_5$. This very case coupled with the requirement for the stability of the solution of $\hat{Z}$ and $\hat{R}$, it stands emphatic quite sufficiently that $(\pi_0\pi_5 - \pi_1\pi_4) < 0$. Now, assuming that the sectoral share of Z is greater than R in GDP, $\pi_2 > |\pi_6|$ while lingering on the same argument it stands sufficiently clear that $\pi_5 > \pi_1$, depending on the degree of K-intensive nature of agriculture and allied activities which can be taken as a contemporary development, at least so in the case of India. Hence, we have, $(\pi_2\pi_5 + \pi_1\pi_6) > 0$. This makes the immediate outcome of the advent of the pandemic and consequential stasis in social and economic mobility to wreck a negative repercussion on manufacturing (as indicated by the first term of (17)). Again if the manufacturing sector is relatively skill-intensive as compared with K to an extent more than that of the construction sector being relatively capital-intensive compared to skill, then it is opportune to argue that $\pi_4 < \pi_0$. However, if, the construction sector posits a more or less balanced factor intensity between S and K, then the above argument becomes more cogent. Thus, ceteris paribus, we get $\hat{X}, \hat{Z}$ and $\hat{R} < 0$. Hence, in light of (15), we get to conjecture, ceteris paribus, about the contraction in the construction sector too as an immediate fallout of the pandemic. These arguments now can be collated to extend a conjecture on the contraction of the construction sector as well; henceforth an economy-wide supply-induced recession can be indicted as the foregone backlash of the pandemic in the immediate time. This contraction will squeeze up the real GDP, given the prices, and hence lead to a decline in real aggregate income. This will now spawn an effective demand paucity in the economy and will compound the problem already in space. In particular, as what can be said in light of Equations (12.10) and (12.11), there would be a reduction of spending on construction as well as on health, manufacturing goods and primary goods. But in context elasticity, spending contraction will be most pronounced in construction and other non-essential items. This explains that $\widehat{P_C} < 0$. However, due to the consumption of hygiene goods and medicines (life-saving and general) out of preventive concern among people, expenditure on heath goods can be supposed to increase on the net and thus, we may have $\widehat{P_X} < 0$. These will have secondary implications on the output contractions in the sectors concerned. This is what is essentially indicated by the second term in (15), (17) and (18). Now, if the $|\widehat{P_X}| < |\widehat{P_C}|$, as quite likely development, then given that $\varnothing_X < (1-\varnothing_C)$, we have

$\left[\varnothing_X \widehat{P_X} - (1-\varnothing_C)\widehat{P_C}\right] > 0$. Given, as obvious from above, $\pi_1 < \pi_3$ and $\pi_5 > \pi_7$; we have the second term of (17) being negative; henceforth, the manufacturing will contract furthermore. Again, as already explained, $\pi_7 > \pi_3$; henceforth, the second term in (18) is also negative. However, the situation may be a bit ambiguous for the construction sector as is evident from the Equation (12.15). However, if the effective demand problem is dominant and so are the adverse spill-over effects (operating through the demand channel) of the contraction in X, Z and R, the contraction in the construction sector would get amplified over and above the negative immediate effect. Now, the bout of contraction in all the sectors will have implications for factor returns. The skilled and unskilled labour and capital released due to the contraction cannot be redeployed through factor substitution in each of the sectors, for they operate on fixed coefficient production technology.

Thus, we have $\widehat{W_S^1}, \widehat{W_S}, \hat{r}$ and $\widehat{W_U} < 0$. This would accentuate the effective demand problem which will set in a negative multiplier effect on the overall real economic activities. Moreover, the essential commodities that have price inelastic demand may witness a price rise and that, in turn, would pave the way to economy-wide stagflation consequent on output contraction.

(b) *Pandemic and reverse migration of unskilled workers (i.e., $\widehat{L_{UC}} < 0$)*

Here, we shall consider an exposition of how reverse migration of unskilled workforce whets up the income inequality between skilled and unskilled workers. To this end, we perform total differentiation and 'hat' algebra on Equations (12.3)–(12.6), the result of which is as follows.

$$\theta_{SZ}\widehat{W_S} + \theta_{KZ}\hat{r} = 0 \qquad (12.19)$$

$$\theta_{SC}\widehat{W_S} + +\theta_{KC}\hat{r} = \widehat{P_C} \qquad (12.20)$$

$$\theta_{UR}\widehat{W_U} + +\theta_{KR}\hat{r} = 0 \qquad (12.21)$$

$$a_{UC}\hat{C} = \widehat{W_U} + \widehat{L_{UC}} \qquad (12.22)$$

Solving these equations, we get the following results:

$$\hat{r} = \frac{\widehat{P_C}}{\left(\dfrac{\theta_{KC}}{\theta_{SC}} - \dfrac{\theta_{KZ}}{\theta_{SZ}}\right)\theta_{SC}} < 0, \text{ since } \widehat{P_C} < 0 \qquad (12.21.1)$$

$$\widehat{W_S} = -\left(\frac{\theta_{KZ}}{\theta_{SZ}}\right)\left[\frac{\widehat{P_C}}{\left(\frac{\theta_{KC}}{\theta_{SC}} - \frac{\theta_{KZ}}{\theta_{SZ}}\right)\theta_{SC}}\right] > 0 \qquad (12.22.2)$$

$$\widehat{W_U} = a_{UC}\hat{C} - \widehat{L_{UC}} + \left(\frac{\theta_{UR}}{\theta_{KR}}\right)\left[\frac{\widehat{P_C}}{\left(\frac{\theta_{KC}}{\theta_{SC}} - \frac{\theta_{KZ}}{\theta_{SZ}}\right)\theta_{SC}}\right] \qquad (12.23)$$

Let us now explain the above results. Begin with (21), due to the contraction in the construction sector for the want of unskilled workers moving homeward, demand for K will fall in as much as C is K-intensive. Moreover, due to the shift in demand away from real estate, the price will fall, i.e., $\widehat{P_C} < 0$. These together, result in excess of K driving r down and that explains $\hat{r} < 0$. Capital released by C may be absorbed partly in Z which in turn is skill-intensive and that would drive up skilled wages and thus, we get $\widehat{W_S} > 0$. On the other hand, the situation with unskilled wages is even worse as the migrated worker would remain job-less or work for a meagre pittance and all these things add up to cause $\widehat{W_U} < 0$. This particular case is a bit ambiguous and moreover, the unskilled wage may remain unchanged with $\widehat{L_{UC}} < 0$ depending on the enforcement of wage regulation in rural areas and the absorptive capacity of agriculture. More precisely, if the K-employment in agriculture is below its capacity, then absorption of migrated unskilled labour may come with $\widehat{W_U} > 0$ towards the $\overline{W_U}$. This therefore will counter the negative forces and may mitigate the fall in unskilled wages. However, the wage inequality between skilled and unskilled wages in the urban sectors or non-agricultural sectors can potentially get widened.

12.5 Contraction of the Construction Sector Led by Fall in Demand

Here in this section, we shall contemplate the consequence of the pandemic on construction. With the worsening of income conditions of people across all economic tiers due to appalling job separation and lofty pay cuts, demand for real estate has got dented with real estate developers pilling up unsold houses. Thus, we have the following results:

$$a_{SX}dX = 0 \qquad (12.24)$$

$$dC = \alpha_{c\varepsilon}d\varepsilon \qquad (12.25)$$

$$a_{SZ}dZ + a_{SC}dC = \alpha_{c\varepsilon}d\varepsilon \qquad (12.26)$$

$$a_{KX}dX + a_{KZ}dZ + a_{KC}dC + a_{KR}dR = 0 \qquad (12.27)$$

Now, given $d\varepsilon < 0$, as what denotes the negative demand shock to the construction sector, we get $dC < 0$ from (25). On the other hand, from (24), we get $dX = 0$. However, from (26), we get $dZ = -\left(\dfrac{a_{SC}}{a_{SZ}}\right)dC > 0$. While from (27), we get an uncertain picture of the sign of dR, which essentially hinges on the magnitude contraction of C relative to Z and the capital intensity of production in C compared with Z. Let us now expound on the above dispensation at length. Following the contraction of the construction, the skilled and unskilled labour along with the capital will find redeployment in manufacturing enabling it to expand. This explanation however stands contingently on the factor intensity of C and Z for each of the factors common between them, given that factor coefficients are fixed. In that case, a disproportionality problem will arise in the sense that the factor which will be relatively scarce will have its price being rising, while the relatively abundant factor will see a falling price. Thus, as it stands, the contraction of the construction sector will pave to factor price adjustments and given the fixed coefficient nature production function of Z and C, such adjustments will have substantial implications for the income distribution. At this juncture, the analysis of this section coincides with that of the previous one, so far, the context of the reverse migration of unskilled labour is concerned. The retrenched unskilled would revert back homeward to the rural sector and that will the rural wage further down. Now, this fall in rural wage will be furthered if the rural sector contracts. Thus, it is obvious here that the contraction of the constructor will trigger an intersectoral wage inequality.

12.6 Data Analysis

Herein, we review the correlation coefficient of health expenditure as a percentage of GDP in 2017 (HLTHGDP) and COVID death as a percentage of total confirmed cases (as on May 5, 2020) (COVID) across some selected nations including India; we find a positive correlation where Spearman's correlation coefficient is also statistically significant. A similar result is also obtained in the case of per capita health expenditure (2016) (HELTPC) and COVID death as a percentage of total confirmed cases (as on May 5, 2020) (COVIDD) (Table 12.2). This seems to be counter-intuitive in the sense that a country that has a credibility of spending relatively higher (both public and private) share on health is expected to fight against any pandemic more efficiently with lesser casualties. But the situation is completely different. An explanation for this puzzling result might be the ineffectiveness of the existing treatment to cure the COVID-affected patients, the mindset of the people to compromise their freedom of movement and adhere to the government lockdown and social-distancing rules, the share of migrant labourers and the intensity of cross-border movement of workers, the possible distribution of the health expenditure among primary, secondary and tertiary healthcare

Table 12.2 Associations between COVID mortality and health spending

A: Association between COVID mortality and health spending (as percentage of GDP)

Measure of association	Variable	COVIDD	HLTHGDP
Spearman's rho	COVIDD	1.000	0.604[1] (0.029)
Karl Pearson's product moment correlation coefficient	HLTHGDP COVIDD HLTHGDP	. 1 .	. 0.389[2] (0.189) .

B: Association between COVID mortality and health spending (per capita)

Measure of association	Variable	COVIDD	HLTHPC
Spearman's rho	COVIDD	1.000	0.500[3] (0.082)
Karl Pearson's product moment correlation coefficient	HLTHPC COVIDD HLTHPC	. 1 .	. 0.301[3] (0.318) .

Notes
1 Significant at 10% (two-tail)
2 statistically insignificant
3 statistically insignificant at 10%

Source: Computed by authors.

services, the quality of support services provided by the government to the common people and health activists, the climatic condition in the country (it is apprehended that this virus becomes less fatal in hot and humid atmosphere), the type of this virus after mutation (medical researchers are of the opinion that the type of this virus found in Europe seems to be more virulent compared that found in Asian countries), the pattern of vaccination across nations, etc.

Given the novelty of this virus, the medical world was in complete darkness about its possible treatment and most countries have been operating still now on a trial-and-error basis in applying necessary treatment. Even the effectiveness of the recently developed vaccines differs because of the quick mutations in this virus. Hence, the health infrastructure, though needed to give better support to the affected people, failed to check the morbidity. Further, in most nations, this virus has affected urban people more in comparison with their rural counterparts. Thus, if the distribution of health expenditure has been more in favour of primary health in rural areas (though this is not the case in developed countries), then also the urban centres would be incapable of tackling this problem. The mindset of the people and the level of democracy in a nation can also be a possible factor behind the initial spread of this virus since the people at large would not want to sacrifice their freedom of movement across regions and a democratic government may not take drastic steps to restrict such movements and business activities at the initial stage of this crisis (as happened in the USA). Greater incidence of cross-border movements of people in any region, if not restricted in time, can also raise the intensity of this crisis.

Further, as against such inter-country comparisons, we can have an intra-country comparison of the impact of this virus. Let us consider 15 major states of India and look into the existing status of health infrastructure in those states along with the incidence of death due to COVID-19. The urbanization (share of urban population to the total population as per the 2011 census) pattern in each state has also been taken into account.

Here, we observe a clear-cut negative correlation between the per capita public health expenditure across states (in 2014–15) (WBHLEPC) and the incidence of COVID death (WBCOVID). On the other hand, we get a positive correlation between the level of urbanization across states (WBURB) and the number of COVID cases (as on May 5, 2020) (WBCOV) (Table 12.3). However, the negative correlation of mortality due to COVID with per capita health spending has been found to be insignificant which is perhaps because of the presence of idiosyncratic variation in epidemiological factors among the states.

Table 12.3 Associations between COVID mortality and health spending & urbanization

A: Association of COVID mortality with urbanization across the states in India

Measure of association	Variable	WBCOVID	WBURB
Spearman's rho	WBCOVID	1.000	0.532[1] (0.041)
	WBURB	.	.
Karl Pearson's product moment correlation coefficient	WBCOVID	1.000	0.499[2] (0.058)
	WBURB	.	.

B: Association of COVID mortality with per capita health expenditure across the states in India

Measure of association	Variable	WBCOVID	WBHLEPC
Spearman's rho	WBCOVID	1.000	−0.163[3] (0.562)
	WBHLEPC	.	.
Karl Pearson's product moment correlation coefficient	WBCOVID	1	−0.237[3] (0.394)
	WBHLEPC	.	.

Notes
1 Significant at 10% (two-tail)
2 statistically insignificant
3 statistically insignificant at 10%

Source: Computed by authors.

The linear regression analysis of morbidity and mortality from COVID-19 (as in Table 12.4) reveals a significant causal effect of urbanization on the degree of incidence of COVID-19 epidemic across the states in India, in particular, every 1% rise in urbanization rate translates into over 9% in morbidity from COVID-19 and over 10% increase in mortality rate, on an average across the states. Moreover, it is hereby evident from the partial regression coefficient of per capita health spending being statistically significant that the role of health spending as a preemptive factor against the pervasion of COVID-19 is a justified case only after having controlled the impact of urbanization.

In this regard, the regression analysis envisages a lower incidence of COVID-19 in terms of morbidity to the tune of more than 0.4% and that in terms of mortality to the tune of more than 0.3%, on average across the states. This in turn implies that the effectiveness of health spending in staving off the backlash of COVID-19 in a given region depends crucially on the extent of urbanization of persistent in that region. Moreover, this finding hints at the virulence or predominance of COVID-19 being significantly spatial in nature and thereof holds a strong bearing on urban planning.

The COVID scenario has given us a new wake-up call. We must prepare ourselves accordingly keeping in mind the real sustainable development goals with added importance to natural balance. Both short-term and long-term policy initiatives would be needed particularly in developing nations. At first, a fiscal space has to be created through an increase in revenues of the government and through avoiding wasteful expenditure.

Table 12.4 Linear regression analysis of the causality of COVID-19 Pandemic across the Indian states

Independent variable	Dependent variable	
	Incidence of COVID-19 (in log) as of May 5, 2020	Mortality from COVID-19 (in log) as of May 5, 2020
Intercept	6.5324*	3.1679#
	(0.0003)	(0.0981)
Per capita health expenditure (in Rs.) as of 2014–2015	−0.0043*	−0.0032*
	(0.0456)	(0.0392)
Urbanization	0.09921*	0.1141*
	(0.0105)	(0.0218)
R^2	0.4327	0.3683
Adjusted R^2	0.3382	0.2631
F-statistic (overall significance)	4.5772*	3.4992*
	(0.0333)	(0.0634)

* significant at 10%
# insignificant at 10%

Source: Computed by authors.

The government has to allocate more resources to public health, economic stimulus and the social safety net. This, in turn, would mean that the government has to revise its priorities reflected in budget revenue, spending and financing. By doing so, they can contain increases in fiscal deficits and surges in public debt. It is true that defence expenditure is one of the important segments of the government budget and it is also true that India's military budget figure, either as a percentage of GDP or in terms of per capita military expenditure, falls far short of the developed countries of the world. Still, we can think in terms of a health infrastructure equivalence of military expenditure (Table 12A.1).

Governments should use stimulus funds and incentives for a significant section of the population that need them the most. This would mean channelling sizeable parts of such stimulus packages to small and informal businesses, the vulnerable and poor, and avoiding the use of stimulus funds and incentives that enrich the well-off. Small and Medium Enterprises (SMEs) and informal enterprises are the most affected businesses, with informal workers who consist of about 90% of the workforce of India. They are expected to be the hardest hit by the economic shock. The International Labour Organization (ILO) estimated a devastating 6.7% loss in working hours globally in the second quarter of 2020, equivalent to 195 million full-time workers, 125 million of which are in Asia and the Pacific. Migrants, displaced people and informal workers are facing a stark trade-off between safeguarding their lives and livelihoods. About 100 million migrant workers in India were on the move in search of safety and basic sustenance, defying a nationwide lockdown. During the lockdown period in India, the unemployment rate surged up to 23.52% during April 2020 in comparison with the pre-COVID unemployment rate of 7.6% during December 2019 (CMIE, 2019, 2020). The urban unemployment rate was found to be more pronounced in comparison with the rural unemployment rate.

In view of such an unprecedented situation, governments should make it easier to conduct business by improving public services and making them accessible through digital technology. They should support small- and medium-sized and informal enterprises. If we make an international comparison between the fiscal stimulus declared by some COVID-affected countries, we find that India's present position is 5th in that ranking (Statista, 2020) (Table 12A.2).

12.7 Conclusion

We now have an opportunity to build a new, just and fair social contract between governments and people. This includes universal social safety nets and health insurance. The fiscal stimulus package must also address this issue. A sustainable solution to the present crisis needs global coordination among countries and optimization of the COVID-19 response. This endeavour would make development more sustainable. The global spread of the virus in our interconnected world offers little chance of success if each country takes a piecemeal approach towards health and economic response on its own. To make the response more effective and reduce the cost of the crises, strong coordination and cooperation among governments are needed, coupled with clear and transparent communication between the stakeholders. These will help enhance governance and build public trust inside and across borders.

Appendix 12 A

Table 12A.1 Health infrastructure equivalence of military expenditure

Sl. No.	Military expenditure on	Cost (US$ million)	Health infrastructure equivalence	Numbers
1	Virginia class submarine	2800	Fully equipped ambulance	9180
2	FREMM Class Frigate	936	Doctors' appointment	10662* (in a year)
3	F-35 Fighter Jet	89	ICU Bed Maintenance	3244* (in a year)
4	Trident-II Missile	31	Masks	17 million
5	Leopard -2 Tank	11	Ventilators	440

Source: Greenpeace International (* Based on OECD's yearly estimate for a doctor's salary & maintenance cost of ICU p.a.).

Table 12A.2 Post-COVID fiscal stimulus package across countries

Sl. No.	Country	Fiscal stimulus as percentage of GDP (%)
1	Japan	21.1
2	USA	13.0
3	Sweden	12.0
4	Germany	10.7
5	India	10.0
6	France	9.3
7	Spain	7.3
8	Italy	5.7
9	UK	5.0
10	China	3.8
11	South Korea	2.2

Source: STISTA Infographics Bulletin (2020), USA (website).

Table 12A.3 Incidence of COVID across the Indian states vis-à-vis health spending and urbanization

States	Per capita public exp. on health in 2014–2015 (Rs.)	Health exp. as percentage of GSDP in 2014–2015 (%)	Urbanization (2011)	COVID Cases (May 5, 2020)	COVID death	Death as percentage of confirmed cases (%)
Andhra Pradesh	1030 (7)	1.92	33.36	2018	45	2.23 (7)
Assam	1137 (5)	1.83	14.09	65	2	3.08 (10)
Bihar	530 (15)	1.45	11.29	747	6	0.80 (4)
Gujarat	1156 (4)	0.8	42.6	8541	513	6.01 (16)
Jharkhand	750 (11)	1.14	24.05	160	3	1.88 (6)
Karnataka	1043 (6)	0.7	38.67	862	31	3.60 (13)
Kerala	1437 (1)	0.97	47.7	519	4	0.77 (3)
MP	722 (12)	1.14	27.63	3785	221	5.84 (15)
Maharashtra	931 (9)	0.61	45.22	23401	868	3.71 (14)
Odisha	913 (10)	1.19	16.69	414	3	0.72 (2)
Punjab	1001 (8)	0.78	37.48	1877	31	1.65 (5)
Rajasthan	1303 (2)	1.52	24.87	3988	113	2.83 (9)
Tamil Nadu	1162 (3)	0.73	48.8	8002	53	0.66 (1)
UP	665 (13)	1.36	22.26	3573	80	2.24 (8)
West Bengal	665 (14)	0.82	31.87	2063	190	9.21 (16)
India Average	973	0.98	31.1	70756	2293	3.24 (12)

Source: National Health Profile 2017, GoI; Mahalaya Chatterjee (2017): Regional Variation in Urbanization in India & the Emergence of New Towns, Center for Urban Economic Studies, CU; Covid Tracker: GoI Portal (figures in round brackets show ranking).

References

Beladi, H. and Marjit, S. (1996). An Analysis of Rural-Urban Migration and Protection, *Canadian Journal of Economics*, 29(4), 930–40.

Chatterjee, M. (2017). *Regional Variation in Urbanization in India & the Emergence of New Towns, Center for Urban Economic Studies, Calcutta University, Kolkata.* http://www-sre.wu.ac.at/ersa/ersaconfs/ersa14/e140826aFinal01459.pdf

CMIE (2019). "Unemployment in India: A Statistical profile", Centre for Monitoring Indian Economy, Mumbai, September-December, 2019.

CMIE (2020). "Unemployment in India: A Statistical profile", Centre for Monitoring Indian Economy, Mumbai, January-April, 2020.

Haren, P., and D. Simchi-Levi. (2020). "How Coronavirus Could Impact the Global Supply Chain by Mid-March." Harvard Business Review, February 28. https://hbr.org/2020/02/how-coronavirus-couldimpact-the-global-supply-chain-by-mid-march

Hartley, J., and A. Rebucci. (2020). "An Event Study of COVID-19 Central Bank Quantitative Easing in Advanced and Emerging Economies." Available at: https://papers.ssrn.com/sol3/papers.cfm

Hevia, C., and Neumeyer. P. A. (2020). "A Perfect Storm: COVID-19 in Emerging Economies." Vox CEPR Policy Portal, April 21. Available at https://voxeu.org/article/perfect-storm-covid-19-emergingeconomies

Hofmann, B., I. Shim, and H. S. Shin. (2020). "Emerging Market Economy Exchange Rates and Local Currency Bond Markets Amid the Covid-19 Pandemic." BIS Bulletin No. 5, Bank for International Settlements, Basel.

Islam, A., and P. Maitra. (2012). Health Shocks and Consumption Smoothing in Rural Households: Does Microcredit Have a Role to Play? Journal of Development Economics 97(2): 232–242.

Jones, R. W. (1965). The Structure of Simple General Equilibrium Models. *Journal of Political Economy*, (73).

Jones, R. W. (1971). A Three-Factor Model in Theory, Trade and History," In J. Bhagwati, et al., Eds, Trade, Balance of Payments and Growth, North-Holland

Statista (2020). "The Statista Infographics Bulletin", USA, website: https://www.statista.com

Tanberg, E., and R. Allen. (2020). "Managing Public Investment Spending During the Crisis." Special Series on COVID-19. May. International Monetary Fund, Washington, DC.

13 Healthcare in India with Respect to Sustainable Development Goals

A Comparative Study within South Asian Countries

Bappaditya Biswas and Rohan Prasad Gupta

Introduction

The phenomenon of any disease not only impacts the overall well-being of an individual but also burdens the family members. Besides, it has a negative impact on public resources which in turn weakens the entire society. Achievement of health for all is a constitutional obligation in India. The Directive Principles of State Policy under the Indian Constitution outline improvement of public health as one of the primary duties of the State. Despite the constitutional provisions, India's progress towards universal healthcare has been rather dilatory. Most developing countries experience the challenge of providing proper healthcare services within its healthcare development plans. In spite of constitutional obligations and developmental demands, India's response towards international efforts on improving healthcare services and progress towards universal health standards has been rather slow.

The Sustainable Development Goals (SDGs) are a global strategy to eradicate poverty, safeguard the environment and secure everyone's prosperity. They constitute 17 objectives with 169 targets. They are the yardstick by which overall progress is assessed and offers a focus for the international community's development activities. The 17 goals are interconnected and are inclined to achieve the sustainable development of the masses (United Nations 2017). The goal of sustainable development is to strike a balance between economic, environmental and social demands, aiming to flourish in the present and the future and to ensure economic development, social equity and justice, and environmental protection. SDGs are inclined towards is long-term, integrated strategy to creating and attaining a healthy community by tackling economic, environmental and social concerns together while avoiding excessive use of natural resources.

Goal 3 under the SDGs focuses on the issue of good health and well-being, that is, to ensure healthy lives and promote well-being for all at all ages. Agenda of 2030's Goal 3 includes all major health priorities such as services related to reproductive, maternal and child health; communicable, non-communicable and environmental diseases; universal health coverage;

DOI: 10.4324/9781003245797-14

and access to safe, effective, quality and affordable medicines and vaccines (Amin-Salem et al. 2018). Various emerging health issues of the dynamic world are addressed under Goal 3 of the SDG.

In this article, an attempt has been made by the authors to empirically analyze India's position in fulfilling Goal 3 of the SDG and to make a comparative cross-country analysis which aims to highlight the current position, future prospects as well as the existing gap in policy measures regarding good health and well-being of the masses. In this context, the latest announcements and policy measures regarding the significant progress in providing universal access to affordable healthcare solutions have also been analyzed.

Various national health parameters, such as premature mortality, infant mortality rate, under-five mortality rate, communicable diseases, basic health facilities and affordable healthcare services have been used to understand India's progress towards universal health standards (Abel et al. 2016). This chapter also intends to perform a cross-country analysis of South Asian countries on progress in healthcare services with respect to the SDGs by evaluating the achievements, policies and challenges.

Moreover, the chapter also aims to understand the role of *Gram Panchayats* and Accredited Social Health Activist (ASHA) workers in providing healthcare services to rural India. Analysis of the parameters is expected to reveal that the position of India with respect to health indicators is continuously improving and there is a lot to progress in this respect.

In this present scenario, the entire world is struggling with the outbreak of the COVID-19 pandemic. India along with the other South Asian nations is experiencing a major hit due to this pandemic. All South Asian nations, including India, witnessed loopholes in their healthcare infrastructure as well as poor pandemic management system (Aayog 2017). Irrespective of the efforts to effectively achieve the goals of SDG 3, that is, to promote good health and well-being, South Asian countries need to develop more effective methods for implementing, monitoring and measuring the progress of SDGs.

Review of Literature

The authors have reviewed several literatures available in the related fields which are given below.

Gupta and Biswas (2021) studied the relationship between the social sector financing and the economic growth and well-being in India. The authors used multiple regression models to analyze the impact of social infrastructure financing on various socio-economic indicators in India. They also analyzed the past trends of the social sector expenditure and the policy measures taken in the new normal. The study concludes that there exists a positive and significant relationship between the social infrastructure expenditure and economic growth and well-being in India.

Azis et al. (2021) analyze the relationship between healthcare expenditure and maternal mortality in South Asian Countries. Their findings reveal that the prevailing healthcare system implemented naming South Asian nations is not adequate for reducing maternal mortality. Moreover, the study indicates that the growth rate of population has a significant long-term effect on maternal mortality which infers that an increase in population growth has dampened efforts towards reducing maternal mortality among South Asian countries. Further, the study concludes that economic growth, sanitation and clean fuel technologies have significant impacts on lowering maternal mortality rates.

Shahbaz et al. (2021) analyze the non-linear impact of economic growth drivers on CO_2 emissions with respect to the SDG framework for India. Their findings reveal that the prevailing economic growth pattern in India is unsustainable in terms of environmental aspects and parameters and the reason underlying such outcomes is its dependence on fossil fuel-based energy consumption and imported crude oil. On the basis of their results, they recommend certain policy measures to improve the present scenario.

Razzaq et al. (2020) analyze the roles of different stakeholders in SDG implementation and identify where gaps may lie at national and regional levels among South Asian countries. The study reveals that implementation of SDGs varies across South Asian countries and concludes that some of the nations have initiated the adoption of SDGs with development plans and programs while others have established national-level institutional structures and coordination channels for achieving the goals.

Khetrapal and Bhatia (2020) aim to analyze the impact of the COVID-19 pandemic on the health system and SDG 3. They observed that the impact of this pandemic will be long-lasting and all spheres of human lives will be negatively impacted and the achievement of all developmental activities including ambitious and aspirational SDGs will be slowed down. They further conclude that all SDGs are being impacted and health-related SDG 3 is also severely hit because all the SDGs are interlinked and complementarity to each other.

Asadullah et al. (2020) contribute to the debate on the SDGs progress by evaluating the Millennium Development Goal (MDG) achievements in South Asia and the policy and institutional challenges deriving from such experience. They used cross-country regressions and aggregate indicators pertaining to the achievements of SDGs. Their study revealed that the achievement of MDGs saw steady improvement in social indicators in South Asia with fruitful outcomes. They further revealed that government expenditure by South Asian nations significantly increased and would make considerable progress in achieving the SDGs.

Haldar and Hembram (2020) evaluate the feasibility of attaining the SDGs with respect to health and well-being in India at the sub-national level based on health indicators of MDGs. The study analyzes a wide range of state variations of health indicators set for MDG in India as well as the national level performance of MDG target for health indicators and suggested that all the states have been experiencing a decline of health deprivation, but the pace of decline is not uniform; consequently, some major states are not performing well compared to the national average.

Filho et al. (2020) discuss how the coronavirus pandemic may influence the SDGs and could affect their implementation. They employed a critical contextual approach associated with systems theory to examine the macro impacts (economic, social and environmental) in this context. Their findings depict those strong concerns in dealing with COVID-19 are disrupting other disease prevention programs and as a consequence, problems such as mental health are also likely to be overlooked. They also conclude that due to the wide areas of influence of the COVID-19 pandemic, it will hamper the process of the implementation of the SDGs and there is a need to put an emphasis on the implementation of the SDGs so that the progress achieved to date is not jeopardized.

Pandey (2019) intends to establish a relationship between health and sustainable development. Various parameters such as investments in health, country's economic output through their effects on educational achievement and skills acquisition, labour productivity and decent employment, increased savings and investment, the demographic transition and impacts on the earth's ecosystem have been analyzed. On the basis of the analysis of different parameters, the findings indicate that the contribution of health to sustainable development, and the critical importance of the multi-sector determinants of health, a "health-in-all-policies" approach could be adopted and the researcher concludes that good health is thus an end in itself and it plays an integral role in human capabilities and well-being.

Panda and Mohanty (2019) measured the progress in selected health-related indicators of SDGs in the states of India by social and economic groups and predicted their likely progress by 2030. They analyze various health indicators which include health outcomes, nutrition, healthcare utilization and determinants of health to fulfil their research objectives.

Dhaliwal (2019) critically analyzed the issues related to the sustainable healthcare services provided in India. The researcher identified various serious concerns regarding the mortality rates, prevention and treatment of dangerous diseases such as AIDS, TB and malaria where India needs to re-frame its healthcare policies. The study thus recommends that along with the public sector, that is, government financing, support of the private sector and other foundations along with International institutions is equally necessary to facilitate sustainable healthcare in India.

Paul and Sana (2018) examine the effect of infrastructure investment on the economic growth of India. The study identifies that infrastructure investment and economic growth of India are integrated in the long run, which implies that there is a long-run relationship between them. The study concludes that there exists a significant degree of influence of infrastructural development on the economic growth of India. Their findings indicate that the variables are having co-integration but there is no long-term and short-term causality between GDP and GCF, which represent that there exists a long-term association between the GDP and GCF but no causal relationship has been found.

Agarchand and Laishram (2017) identify the shortcomings in the Indian PPP procurement process using the key principles of sustainability. They review the challenges and the perspectives of key sustainability principles and then discuss them with the key stakeholders through focused interviews. They identify that the hurdles in the way of achieving the SDG targets lack of stakeholder and local participation; high bidding and transaction cost; high user charges; improper risk allocation; lack of transparency and accountability; goal conflicts between public and private sectors; and lack of skill and knowledge about sustainability.

Research Gap

On extensive review of available literatures, it is witnessed that there are numerous research works have been conducted related to the performance and target achievements of SDGs by various countries across the globe. But, with respect to India, limited research works have been carried out to analyze India's progress towards achievement of SDG 3 targets and ensuring universal health standards. Further very limited studies have been conducted to make a cross-country analysis among South Asian countries with respect to the achievements in healthcare services. Hence, the present study intends to bridge this gap which is believed to be having significant socio-economic implications.

Research Objectives

The present study is based on the following research objectives:

1 To understand the relationship between the social infrastructure financing and SDG 3 target achievements in India.
2 To evaluate various government schemes related to good health and well-being in India.
3 To make a cross-country analysis among South Asian countries with respect to their performance in achieving SDG 3 goals.

Research Questions

Based on the research objectives, the following research questions have been framed:

1 Whether there is any relationship between the social infrastructures financing with the achievement of SDG 3 targets in India?
2 What are the various government schemes promoted by the Indian Government to support the good health and well-being among the masses in India?
3 Whether there is any variation among South Asian Countries with respect to their performance in achieving SDG 3 goals?

Research Hypotheses

To test the research objectives statistically, the following Research Hypotheses have been formulated:

1 H_{N1}: There is no significant correlation between government expenditure on the healthcare sector and SDG 3 indicators.
2 H_{N2}: There is no significant variation in performance indicators related to various SDG 3 parameters among South Asian countries.
3 H_{N3}: There is no significant variation in mean ranks of indicators related to various SDG 3 parameters among South Asian countries over the study period.

Database and Methodology

The present study is based on empirical analysis of secondary data for a period of 20 years from 2000–2001 to 2020–2021. The data have been collected from the websites of Sustainable Development Goals Index maintained by United Nations, NITI Aayog, India and from the Economic Survey of India reports. Other supporting data has been collected from various UN reports on SDGs, India Voluntary National Review (VNR) reports and Budget documents of India.

For the purpose of analysis, government expenditure in the healthcare sector has been selected as an independent variable, which is considered as the dummy or representative variable representing the social infrastructure financing in India under the study. The dependent variable in this study includes twelve indicators out of fourteen indicators which are used to calculate the SDG 3 rank by the United Nations. Two of the indicators are not included in the present study due to the unavailability of data with respect to the present study period.

The dependent variables are age-standardized mortality rate attributed to non-communicable diseases – female (per 1,000 live births), age-standardized mortality rate attributed to non-communicable diseases – male (per 1,000 live births), neonatal death (per 1,000 live births), infants lacking immunization – DTP (percentage of one-year-olds), infants lacking immunization – measles (percentage of one-year-olds), mortality rate – female adult (per 1,000 people), mortality rate – male adult (per 1,000 people), mortality rate, under-five (per 1,000 live births), mortality rate – infant (per 1,000 live births), malaria incidence (per 1,000 people at risk), tuberculosis incidence (per 100,000 people) and lifetime risk of maternal death (%).

According to WHO, age-standardized mortality rate represents the weighted average of the age-specific mortality rates per 100,000 persons, where the weights are the proportions of persons in the corresponding age groups of the WHO standard population. Neonatal death means the number of deaths during the first 28 completed days of life per 1,000 live births in a given year or another period.

To understand the relationship of healthcare financing in India with SDG 3 target achievements correlation and simple linear regression has been used to analyze whether there is any relationship between the selected dependent variables and the independent variable healthcare expenditure. The comparative study is based on South Asian countries which include Bhutan, Maldives, Sri Lanka, Nepal, Bangladesh, India, Pakistan and Afghanistan.

For cross-country analysis, single-factor ANOVA has been used to analyze whether there is any variation among South Asian countries with respect to the selected indicators in achieving SDG 3 goals. Further, the mean ranks of the indicators related to South Asian countries have been calculated to analyze their performance variation in achieving SDG 3 targets with respect to the country-wise achievement and the selected study period. For this Friedman test, a non-parametric version of two-way ANOVA has been used to test the ranked (ordinal) data.

Data Presentation and Analysis

Social Infrastructure Financing in India and SDG 3

In India, the majority of the basic social infrastructure relating the education, healthcare, housing, urban development, welfare of SCs, STs and OBCs, labour welfare, social security, nutrition, etc., are financed by the government, both central and state, followed by the non-profit organizations, private sector and public–private partnerships (Armeanu et al. 2018). The expenditure on social infrastructure by the Centre and States combined as a percentage of GDP increased from 6.2% to 8.8% during the period 2014–2015 to 2020–2021.

This increase is witnessed across all social sectors. In the case of education, it increased from 2.8% in 2014–2015 to 3.5% in 2020–2021 and in the case of health, it increased from 1.2% to 1.5% during the same period. It is also witnessed that the relative importance of social sector financing in government budget which is measured in terms of the percentage of expenditure on social infrastructure out of the total budgetary expenditure has also increased to 26.5% in 2020–2021 from 23.4% in 2014–2015 (Budget Documents of Union and State Governments, Reserve Bank of India).

The increase in social sector infrastructure, with respect to the healthcare sector, has a positive impact on the selected indicators of Goal 3 of the SDGs which includes the good health and well-being of the masses (Aziz et al. 2021, David 2018, Gautham et al. 2020 and Khalid et al. 2021). The regression results support the notion which is given in Table 13.1.

The information in the table clearly depicts that all the adjusted R-squared values are more than 0.50, that is, the independent variable explains more than 50% change in the dependent variables, statistically significant at 5% level. This indicates that there may be a significant and positive impact of the government healthcare infrastructure expenditure on India's progress

Table 13.1 Correlation and Regression Analysis

Dependent / Independent	Correlation Value	Sig. Value (5% Level)	Healthcare Expenditure (Adjusted R-Square)	F Sig. (5% Level)
Age-standardized mortality rate attributed to non-communicable diseases – female (per 1,000 live births)	−.732	.002	.533	.001
Age-standardized mortality rate attributed to non-communicable diseases – male (per 1,000 live births)	−.863	.001	.619	.000
Neonatal death (per 1,000 live births)	−.832	.003	.632	.006
Infants lacking immunization – DTP (percentage of one-year-olds)	−.622	.001	.587	.000
Infants lacking immunization – measles (percentage of one-year-olds)	−.732	.000	.544	.019
Mortality rate – female adult (per 1,000 people)	−.832	.013	.627	.011
Mortality rate – male adult (per 1,000 people)	−.532	.000	.522	.003
Mortality rate, under-five (per 1,000 live births)	−.732	.000	.611	.000
Mortality rate – infant (per 1,000 live births)	−.732	.009	.523	.003
Malaria incidence (per 1,000 people at risk)	−.632	.001	.509	.011
Tuberculosis incidence (per 100,000 people)	−.732	.003	.518	.000
Lifetime risk of maternal death (%)	−.668	.001	.612	.000

Source: Authors' own computation.

towards achievement of SDG 3 targets and the outcomes are also confirmed by the correlation results which clearly demonstrate that there is a negative correlation among the selected dependent and independent variables which are statistically significant at 5% level.

The results indicate that as the government expenditure's relation to the healthcare sector increases, it helps in the reduction of spread of diseases and resulting mortality rate which in turn helps in the improvement of good health and well-being of the masses and to efficiently achieve the SDG 3 targets.

Government Schemes Related to Good Health and Well-Being in India

According to the Economic Survey of India, 2020, public healthcare spending in India is just over 1% (1.5%) of its GDP, which is drastically low with respect to the country's population and demographics. In this context, the Budget 2021–2022 allocated Rs. 2, 23,846 crores towards the healthcare and wellness sector. This also includes Rs. 35,000 crores for COVID-19 vaccination, on a rolled-out basis across the nation since the beginning of this year, that is, January 2021. In the context of the severe spread of the COVID-19 pandemic, a 137% increase in funds allocation in the healthcare sector is seen as compared to the budget last year.

According to the Ministry of Health and Family Welfare, Government of India, there has been a 55.75% increase in the number of MBBS seats in the last six years, that is, from 2014 to 2020, across the country. In the same period, 179 new medical colleges, both government and private, have been established throughout India. On the other hand, focused schemes and policy measures implemented by the central and state governments have helped in strengthening the healthcare infrastructure and promoting wellness among the masses, especially in rural India who are deprived of basic healthcare support.

According to the India VNR2020, NITI Aayog, Government of India, in providing universal access to affordable healthcare services, India has made remarkable progress under the National Health Policy (2017) which is considered to be instrumental in achieving significant progress in several areas – improving child and maternal health, reducing mortality, improving life expectancy and strengthening the defence against major communicable diseases. Ayushman Bharat, the world's largest health protection programme, launched by the central government provides inclusive healthcare to at-risk facilitated 10 million beneficiaries.

Pradhan Mantri Jan Aarogya Yojana is also considered to be a significant policy measure in the healthcare sector which provides health coverage to 100 million vulnerable families up to Rs. 5 lakhs per family per year for hospitalization. The Pradhan Mantri Jan Aushadhi Pariyojana is also launched in India which provides quality medicine at affordable prices. To improve the maternal health and well-being of the women and children, the

Reproductive, Maternal, Newborn, Child and Adolescent Health (RMNCHA) strategy was implemented.

In the context of the women's health, Janani Suraksha Yojana (conditional cash transfer for institutional delivery) has extended support to underprivileged mothers and has proved to be effective in reducing lifetime risks of maternal death in rural India. Moreover, National Health Mission has also created a strong workforce of frontline workers – the ASHA, Auxiliary Nurse-Midwife (ANM) and Anganwadi Workers (AWWs), and with the help of the *Gram Panchayats* – are involved in awareness creation, promoting health support and healthcare and women sanitation service delivery activities.

Mission Indra Dhanush, a focused initiative for universalizing immunization among children and the Integrated Child Development Services (ICDS) Scheme have helped to increase immunization in children aged between 9 and 11 months by approximately 3.1%, from 88.66% in 2016–2017 to 91.76% in 2018–2019. The percentage of receipts of all basic vaccinations among children aged 12–23 months have also increased from 44% in 2005–2006 to 62% in 2015–2016, which has helped in reducing the under-five mortality rate as well as neonatal mortality rate.

Cross-Country Analysis of South Asian Countries

South Asian nations have shown considerable progress in the areas of poverty alleviation, access to education and agricultural advancement, and resilience towards climate change. But, still many countries are struggling in reducing inequalities, promote healthcare and well-being, sanitation and in generating sufficient employment (Kumar et al. 2016, Leal Filho et al. 2020 and Ogu et al. 2016).

According to the Sustainable Development Report 2020, the overall SDG ranking (out of 193 UN Member States) of Bhutan is 80, which is the first rank among South Asian countries. The Maldives ranks 91, ranking second in South Asia. Sri Lanka secured the third position among South Asian countries with an overall ranking of 94. The overall ranking of Nepal is 96 with a South Asian ranking of four. Bangladesh stood 109th in the overall ranking with a South Asian ranking of five. India's rank is 117, with a South Asian ranking of six. The overall ranking of Pakistan is 134, which is seventh rank among South Asian countries. Afghanistan's overall rank is 139th with a South Asian ranking of eight.

The cross-country analysis among South Asian countries with respect to the indicators related to SDG 3 among the nations is explained with the help of the results given in Table 13.2.

The above ANOVA table clearly indicates that all the F values are significant at a 5% level and hence indicates that there are statistically significant variations of the indicators values among South Asian countries with respect to the study period, that is, from 2000–2001 to 2020–2021. This

Table 13.2 Single-Factor ANOVA Table

Variables	F	Sig.	Decision (5% Level)
Age-standardized mortality rate attributed to non-communicable diseases – female (per 1,000 live births)	135.65	.000	Accept
Age-standardized mortality rate attributed to non-communicable diseases – male (per 1,000 live births)	205.06	.000	Accept
Neonatal death (per 1,000 live births)	73.53	.000	Accept
Infants lacking immunization – DTP (% of one-year-olds)	149,201.28	.000	Accept
Infants lacking immunization – measles (% of one-year-olds)	65,086.95	.000	Accept
Mortality rate – female adult (per 1,000 people)	3,023.53	.000	Accept
Mortality rate – male adult (per 1,000 people)	3,245.90	.000	Accept
Mortality rate, under-five (per 1,000 live births)	7,473.66	.000	Accept
Mortality rate – infant (per 1,000 live births)	16,978.07	.000	Accept
Malaria incidence (per 1,000 people at risk)	11,3386.79	.000	Accept
Tuberculosis incidence (per 100,000 people)	11,3386.79	.000	Accept
Lifetime risk of maternal death (%)	11,143.20	.000	Accept

Source: Authors' own computation.

signifies that there is significant variation in the performance of South Asian nations in respect of the selected indicators, that is, to achieve the SDG 3 targets. The derived results are given in Table 13.3.

The mean rank table related to the indicators of SDG 3 computed from the year 2000–2001 to 2020–2021 indicates that there is variation in the performances of South Asian Countries. Afghanistan has constantly secured the eighth rank, that is, the last rank in most of the above indicators, except tuberculosis incidence and female adult mortality rate, which means its efforts have a positive impact, for example, on reducing tuberculosis incidence in its country as compared to other nations.

Bangladesh has successfully achieved the first position in reducing age-standardized mortality rate attributed to non-communicable diseases (male) and second position in reducing age-standardized mortality rate attributed to non-communicable diseases (female) as well as its efforts have positive impacts on its overall performance.

The performance of Pakistan has mixed implications and which is reflected in its overall performance. In the case of India also, the performance is mixed and more improvements are required. Bhutan, Maldives, Sri Lanka and Nepal are in a much better position in ensuring better health and promoting well-being among their people as compared to other South Asian Counties.

Table 13.3 Mean Ranks of Indicators of SDG 3 (2000–2001 to 2020–2021)

Variables	Country							
	Afghanistan	Bangladesh	Pakistan	India	Nepal	Bhutan	Sri Lanka	Maldives
Age-standardized mortality rate attributed to non-communicable diseases – female (per 1,000 live births)	8	2	7	4	5	6	1	3
Age-standardized mortality rate attributed to non-communicable diseases – male (per 1,000 live births)	8	1	6	7	5	3	4	2
Neonatal death (per 1,000 live births)	8	6	7	5	4	3	1	2
Infants lacking immunization – DTP (% of one-year-olds)	8	4	7	6	5	3	1	2
Infants lacking immunization – measles (% of one-year-olds)	8	4	7	6	5	3	2	1
Mortality rate – female adult (per 1,000 people)	7	3	4	5	6	8	1	2
Mortality rate – male adult (per 1,000 people)	8	2	4	6	5	7	3	1
Mortality rate, under-five (per 1,000 live births)	8	5	7	6	4	3	1	2
Mortality rate – infant (per 1,000 live births)	8	4	7	5	3	6	1	2
Malaria incidence (per 1,000 people at risk)	8	3	6	7	4	2	5	1
Tuberculosis incidence (per 100,000 people)	4	6	8	7	3	5	2	1
Lifetime risk of maternal death (%)	8	4	5	3	7	6	1	2
Mean rank (using Friedman test rank)	7.58	3.67	6.25	5.58	4.67	4.58	1.92	1.75
Friedman Test Statistics								
N	Chi-Square			df		Asymp. Sig.		
12	57.417			7		.000		

Source: Authors' own computation.

Friedman Test Results

The variation in the mean rank performances with respect to the selected indicators of the SDG 3 among South Asian countries related to the study period is statistically analyzed with the help of the Friedman Test is explained below.

The Friedman test mean rank validates the above results that the Maldives is the best performer among South Asian countries, followed by Sri Lanka, Bhutan and Nepal. India's mean rank is 5.58 which is better compared to Pakistan and Bangladesh. The SDG 3 indicators performance of Afghanistan is the lowest with a mean rank of 7.58 among South Asian nations.

The Chi-square value, also known as Friedman's Q is 57.417 and indicates that the ranks are placed apart from each other with an Asymptotic Significance value of 0.000 which is less than 0.05. Hence, it can be concluded that there is a statistically significant variation in the indicator's mean ranks both with respect to South Asian counties and the study period. This signifies that the performance of South Asian countries with respect to SDG 3 differs among themselves. The possible reasons may be due to the effectiveness of the policy measures, loopholes in policy implementation, population size, standard of living, socio-economic inequalities, etc.

Conclusion and Recommendations

India is the second-largest country in terms of population and the largest democracy in the world. The steps taken for the achievement of SDG targets by India are significant to the world as it represents a major section of the world. On the basis of the results drawn, it is evident that the efforts made by both the central and state governments in the form of health sector expenditure in India had helped to improve the overall health and well-being of the masses.

Despite these efforts, India is still struggling to improve its position in achieving the SDG 3 goals and its overall SDG rankings. This is a matter of concern and India needs to be more focused on properly and efficiently implementing the policies rather than merely announcing them. Moreover, expenditure on healthcare needs to be more prioritized and should increase the percentage of funds allotted to the healthcare sector out of the total allocations.

The cross-country analysis reveals that countries with smaller populations and resources such as Maldives, Sri Lanka, Bhutan and Nepal are in a better position compared to India and other countries. In this context, regional inter-governmental platforms such as ASEAN and SAARC must enhance their efforts towards the achievement of the SDGs. Cross-country learning and experiences, information, ideas, technology and knowledge, etc., need to be shared to develop strong partnerships and promote best practices among the member nations (Rahman et al. 2020, Sachs et al. 2019 and Shahbaz et al. 2021).

A developing country like India with such a large population has, to some extent, improved its healthcare but more of such focused initiatives and increased infrastructural investments are required. Proper healthcare and sanitation along with mother and childcare awareness need to be more effectively expended among the rural population. In this context, the role of ASHA, ANN, ANW, etc., frontline health workers along with the efforts of the *Gram Panchayats*, are significant and more emphasis needs to be given to enhance the number and reach of the frontline workers in the rural areas.

The performance of South Asian countries in implementing SDGs with their respective policies and strategies will decide the pace and extent of achievement of the 2030 Agenda. Asian countries need to learn from other countries' SDG adoption process and implementation, mobilization of funds, use of innovative technologies and effective monitoring of the data to promote good health and well-being among its citizens.

In various ways, regional collaboration and integration may be an effective complement to national efforts in South Asia to achieve the SDG 3 targets. In this context, there is a need to formulate and implement a strengthened regionally coordinated strategy aimed at maximizing the potential of regional value chains which can aid in the development of productive capacity in providing healthcare services among South Asian nations. Regional production networking in the context of healthcare products is required within South Asia along with improved transportation connections, as well as cross-border transportation and trade facilitation to ensure the overall well-being of South Asian nations.

Limitations and Future Research Scope

The present study is based on the analysis of the performance of South Asian countries with respect to SDG 3, that is, health and well-being. More nations across the globe can be included and more SDGs can be analyzed. The present study is based on 20 years' data. The study period can be extended and more sophisticated statistical tools can be applied.

References

Aayog, N. I. T. I. (2017, July). Voluntary National Review Report on Implementation of Sustainable Development Goals. *United Nations High Level Political Forum.*

Abel, G. J., Barakat, B., Samir, K. C., & Lutz, W. (2016). Meeting the Sustainable Development Goals leads to lower world population growth. *Proceedings of the National Academy of Sciences, 113*(50), 14294–14299.

Agarchand, N., & Laishram, B. (2017). Sustainable infrastructure development challenges through PPP procurement process: Indian perspective. *International Journal of Managing Projects in Business, 10*(3), 642–662.

Amin-Salem, H., El-Maghrabi, M. H., Rodarte, I. O., & Verbeek, J. (2018). *Sustainable development goal diagnostics: the case of the Arab Republic of Egypt.* The World Bank.

Armeanu, D. Ş., Vintilă, G., & Gherghina, Ş. C. (2018). Empirical study towards the drivers of sustainable economic growth in EU-28 countries. *Sustainability*, *10*(1), 1–22.

Asadullah, M. N., Savoia, A., & Sen, K. (2020). Will South Asia Achieve the Sustainable Development Goals by 2030? Learning from the MDGs Experience. *Social Indicators Research*, *152*(1), 165–189.

Aziz, N., He, J., Sarker, T., & Sui, H. (2021). Exploring the Role of Health Expenditure and Maternal Mortality in South Asian Countries: An Approach towards Shaping Better Health Policy. *International Journal of Environmental Research and Public Health*, *18*(21), 11514.

David, M. (2018). Sustainable Development Goals (SDGs)-Challenges for India. *Indian Journal of Public Health Research and Development*, *9*(3), 1–5.

Dhaliwal, L. K. (2019). Health in Sustainable Development Goals: Issues before India. *Research Journal of Humanities and Social Sciences*, *10*(2), 298–304.

Gautham, M. S., Gururaj, G., Varghese, M., Benegal, V., Rao, G. N., Kokane, A., & Shibukumar, T. M. (2020). The National Mental Health Survey of India (2016): Prevalence, socio-demographic correlates and treatment gap of mental morbidity. *International Journal of Social Psychiatry*, *66*(4), 361–372.

Gupta, R. P. & Biswas, B. (2021). Social Infrastructure Financing in India-An Empirical Study. *The Journal of Indian Institute of Banking and Finance-Bank Quest*, *92*(2), 33–38.

Haldar, S. K., & Hembram, S. (2020). *Health Progress in India with Respect to Millennium Development Goals: Are Health Targets of SDGs Achievable? An Empirical Study at Sub-National Level*. Cham: Sustainable Development Goals Springer, 41–55.

Khalid, A. M., Sharma, S., & Dubey, A. K. (2021). Concerns of developing countries and the sustainable development goals: case for India. *International Journal of Sustainable Development and World Ecology*, *28*(4), 303–315.

Khetrapal, S., & Bhatia, R. (2020). Impact of COVID-19 pandemic on health system and Sustainable Development Goal 3. *Indian Journal of Medical Research*, *151*(5), 395–399.

Kumar, N., Hammill, M., Raihan, S., & Panda, S. (2016). Strategies for achieving the sustainable development goals (SDGs) in South Asia: lessons from policy simulations. *South and South-West Asia Development Papers*.

Leal Filho, W., Brandli, L. L., Salvia, A. L., Rayman-Bacchus, L., & Platje, J. (2020). COVID-19 and the UN Sustainable Development Goals: Threat to Solidarity or an Opportunity? *Sustainability*, *12*(13), 1–14.

Ogu, R. N., Agholor, K. N., & Okonofua, F. E. (2016). Engendering the attainment of the SDG-3 in Africa: overcoming the socio-cultural factors contributing to maternal mortality. *African Journal of Reproductive Health*, *20*(3), 62–74.

Panda, B. K., & Mohanty, S. K. (2019). Progress and prospects of health-related sustainable development goals in India. *Journal of Biosocial Science*, *51*(3), 335–352.

Pandey, A. K. (2019). Impact of Health on Sustainable Development in India. *International Conference on Recent Trends in Humanities, Technology, Management and Social Development (RTHTMS 2K19); KIET School of Management*, Ghaziabad, UP, India, 9 (Special Issue), 38–43.

Paul, B., & Sana, A. K. (2018). Infrastructure Investment and Economic Growth in India: An Empirical Analysis. *Vidyasagar University Journal of Commerce*, *23*, 1–14.

Rahman, M., Khan, T. I., & Sadique, M. Z. (2020). SDG Implementation progress: What does the Asian experience reveal? *Southern Voice*, Occasional Paper Series. No 67, June.

Razzaq, S., Ahmad Maisam Najafizada, S., Sheel Acharya, S., Ellepola, Y., Chaudhry, K., Tabassum, R., & Kunwal, N. (2020). National Level Preparedness for Implementing the Health-related Sustainable Development Goals (SDGs) in Seven South Asian Countries: Afghanistan, Bangladesh, Bhutan, India, Pakistan, Nepal and Sri Lanka. *Global Policy*, 11(1), 191–201.

Sachs, J., Schmidt-Traub, G., Kroll, C., Lafortune, G., & Fuller, G. (2019). *Sustainable Development Report 2019*. New York: Bertelsmann Stiftung and Sustainable Development Solutions Network.

Shahbaz, M., Sharma, R., Sinha, A., & Jiao, Z. (2021). Analyzing nonlinear impact of economic growth drivers on CO_2 emissions: Designing an SDG framework for India. *Energy Policy*, 148, 1–23.

United Nations. (2017). Economic and Social Commission for Asia and the Pacific. Achieving the Sustainable Development Goals in South Asia: Key Policy Priorities and Implementation Challenges. *UN*.

http://hdr.undp.org/en/content/human-development-index-hdi
http://niti.gov.in/sdg-india-index
https://www.indiabudget.gov.in/economicsurvey/
https://www.mohfw.gov.in/
https://www.sdgindex.org/

14 Transformation of Microfinance and Financial as well as Social Inclusion in India

Sudhakar Patra

Introduction

Microfinance in India has come in a protracted manner. It commenced as an opportunity to supply finance to the unserved hundreds comprising the lowest of the socio-financial pyramid and steadily grew to become out to be a device for inspiring their social widespread and running their manner out of poverty. It is one of the maximum vital cogs of the finance enterprise due to the fact this quarter meets the credit score wishes of lots of aspiring microentrepreneurs. Compared to standard fashions of financing, microfinance is an altogether one-of-a-kind ball recreation because it needs a one-of-a-kind attitude and abilities. Here, a capacity client's capability, abilities and enterprise model, and "now no longer" his/her assets decide his/her credibility and eligibility for any mortgage amount. The quarter has helped hundreds of thousands of poor families within the remotest regions to offer lifestyles to their goals by offering them the way to meet them. With a sustainable boom and modest return, the words, this survived simply as "now no longer-for-income endeavor, has attracted numerous multinational and non-public fairness traders over the last decade".

In this extremely good journey, there were many highs and lows. The quarter-skilled exponential boom in 2015–2020 has made India one of the world's biggest developing markets. However, it encountered a primary disaster all through 2010 and thereafter it nearly destroyed; however, during the last decade, it has slowly honestly made a stable comeback. With the evolution of the regulatory framework, the microfinance institution (MFI) quarter has witnessed an orderly boom and consolidation. This has helped the world mature and end up as an imperative torchbearer of the maximum valued purpose of our economy, that is, inclusive finance. The introduction of the Micro Units Development and Refinance Agency (MUDRA) Bank as an investment automobile for MFIs within the Union Budget 2015–2016 has come as a primary shot within the arm of this quarter (ASSOCHAM, 2016). The dynamism within the quarter has simply been given with eight huge MFIs getting the license to transform into small finance banks (SFBs). When those banks get entry to inexpensive finances compete with MFIs, the MFIs might reinvent themselves to hold their relevance. They will discover new approaches to

DOI: 10.4324/9781003245797-15

decrease their working value thru enterprise reengineering and technological adoption. The key variable in this equation could be technology. Besides technology, MFIs have mounted new structures for partnership and collaboration wherein they make use of their sources as much as most useful levels.

Methodology of the Study

India is home to a developing and revolutionary microfinance region. With a big part of the world's negative economic and financial outlooks, India is in all likelihood to have a big capacity call for microfinance. For this reason, it makes experience to recollect the changing face of microfinance in India to shed light on similar adjustments within the area everywhere in the world The entire information on the evolution and nature of a country's monetary system, law and government's mindset toward the microfinance region is essential to apprehend the character of the arena in any country. Such knowhow permits one to apprehend the forces that form its boom and additionally the elements that avert it. Against this backdrop, the goal is to have a look at the traits of the microfinance region in India and its effect on the socio-financial improvements of people with financial backwardness. The chapter has also discussed the evolution and transformational journey of the microfinance sector in India. In the end, the study brings out the various challenges faced by the sector in India and possible solutions to overcome the problems.

Data Source

The present study relies on secondary sources of data collected from "Microfinance Pulse" published by Small Industries Development Bank of India (SIDBI), "Bharat Microfinance Report 2020" published by NABARD, "Micrometer" published by Microfinance Institutions Network (MFIN), Inclusive finance India Report 2019 and various publications/reports available at RBI, C-GAP, Microsave, etc. The study considered the time period from FY 2015–2016 to 2020–2021. Techniques of simple statistics have been applied to analyzing the data and getting the results to derive a logical conclusion. The analyzed data has been presented based on the objectives of the study in the form of tables and graphs, which are described, interpreted and conclusions drawn thereafter. The related data are also obtained from the sources such as Microfinance Information Exchange Inc (2006), Microfinance Pulse (2020), MFIN Micrometer (2020), Reserve Bank of India (1999), Sriram (2017), SIDBI (2001), The Bharat Microfinance Report (2020), United Nations Capital Development Fund (UNCDF) (n.d.).

Transformation Journey from NGO-MFIs to SFB/Universal Bank

With a view to meeting the challenges of uneven spread leading to exclusion, the financial system witnessed the emergence of Microfinance Intermediaries. The microfinance sector has grown up rapidly due to a

Transformation of Microfinance, Financial and Social Inclusion

combination of governmental support, implementation of technological enhancements and support provided by the banking sector.

i **Initial Period (1970–1989)**

- The term Microfinance emerges on the scene – Prof. Muhammad Yunus (Bangladesh) started shaping the modern microfinance modern movement.
- SEWA Bank owned and managed by women to provide financial services to women in the unorganized sector.
- Roots of Microfinance in India – Shri Mahila Sewa Sahakari Bank (SEWA Bank), Gujarat.
- Micro Finance in India started evolving around the self-help group (SHG) concept – pre-dominantly an NGO-driven intervention in the financial inclusion space supported by NABARD.
- NABARD advocates the SHG model as an important tool for poverty alleviation. Other government agencies follow.
- Mysore Resettlement and Development Agency (MYRADA), one of the early innovators of the concept of SHGs.

ii **Change (1990–2006)**

- SIDBI emerges on the scene – The Market Maker (1990).
- NABARD started the SHG Bank Linkage Programme (SBLP) (1992).
- Launch of SIDBI Foundation for Micro Credit (SFMC) (1999).
- Sa-Dhan, the association of Community Development Institutions comes into existence (1999).
- With the view to draw upon the international experience and bring in the microfinance best practices within the country, the "National Micro Finance Support Programme (NMFSP)" was launched by SIDBI in collaboration with DFID, UK (2000).
- RBI includes MFI lending within the priority sector and recognizes it as a tool for financial inclusion (2004).
- The United Nations (UN) declares "The International Year of Micro Credit" (2005).
- The Grameen Bank and its founder, Prof. Muhammad Yunus, were jointly awarded the Nobel Peace Prize (2006).

iii **Growth and Crisis (2007–2010)**

- MFIN, the association of NBFC-MFIs comes into existence (2009).
- Andhra crisis unfolds – sector slips into the abyss (2010).

iv **Consolidation and Maturity (2011–2020)**

- RBI grants approval for the conversion of Bandhan Financial Services Pvt. Ltd., the largest MFI in India at that time, into a Universal Bank (2014).

- RBI vide press release dated Nov. 26, 2013 issues guidelines for the creation of Self-Regulatory Organizations (SROs) for NBFC-MFIs (2014).
- MFIN was formally recognized by RBI as an SRO, (2014).
- RBI accords SRO status to Sa-Dhan (2015).
- PM launches Micro Units Development & Refinance Agency Ltd. (MUDRA) as a wholly owned subsidiary of SIDBI to fund the unfunded (2015).
- RBI accords in-principle approval to 10 entities to set up SFBs – 9 out of the 10 entities, including 8 MFIs, existing partners who have been nurtured and supported by SIDBI over the years (2015).

SHG Model and Building of Social Infrastructure

The role of SHG as a legitimate player in the financial inclusion space was recognized in 1992. The SHG movement put women at the core. By design and practice, SHGs got to be identified as a financial inclusion program targeted predominantly towards women, unlike all other previous programs that were probably gender-neutral in intent but tended to have more male customers. SHG-Bank linkage program which started as a bank outreach program for harnessing the flexibility of the informal system with the strength and affordability of the formal system, through the passage of time metamorphosed into a holistic program for financial, economic and off-late social capital building in rural areas. As on March 31, 2020, there were 102.43 lakh SHGs out of which 31.46 lakh SHGs had outstanding bank loans of Rs. 1,08,075 crore. During FY19, Banks disbursed Rs. 58,318 crore loans to 26.98 lakh SHGs and the total deposits of SHGs with banks was to the tune of Rs. 19,592 crore (Table 14.1). The average disbursement per SHG has been on an increasing trend and amounted to Rs. 2.46 lakh as on March 2020.

Commercial banks continue to play a leading role serving 53.5% of the total number of SHGs followed by RRBs with 31.8% and cooperative banks with 14.7%. The NPA percentage of SHG loans with banks stood at 4.19%. There is a steady decline in NPA amount by 5.19% in FY20 to Rs. 10,671 crores over the previous FY (Source: Bharat Microfinance Report, 2020).

MFI Industry Overview

As on March 2020, the microfinance industry has a total loan portfolio of Rs. 2,22,926 crore. This represents a growth of 53% over FY19. Banks hold the largest share of the portfolio in microcredit with a total loan outstanding of Rs. 90,613 crores. Banks thus account for 40% of the total industry portfolio, which includes both direct and indirect lending through BC partnerships. NBFC-MFIs are the second largest provider of microcredit with a loan amount outstanding of Rs. 71,342 crores, accounting for 32%

Table 14.1 Operational Highlights of SHG Model

Indicators	2020 (Rs.)	2019 (Rs.)	Change
Total no. of SHGs linked	102.43 lakh	100.14 lakh	⇧
No. of Families reached	133 million	130 million	⇧
Total savings of SHGs	26,152 cr	23,324 cr	⇧
Total no. of SHGs Credit linkage	31.46 lakh	26.98 lakh	⇧
Gross loan outstanding	1,08,075 cr	87,098 cr	⇧
Total loan disbursed	77,659 cr	58,318 cr	⇧
Average loan disbursed per SHG	2,46,849	2,04,314	⇧
Average loan outstanding per SHG	1,90,373	1,71,554	⇧
NPA (%)	4.19	5.20	⇩

Source: Compiled by the author from the Bharat Microfinance Report (2020).

Table 14.2 Industry Growth and Market Share by Lender Type from FY16 to FY20

Particulars	March 2016	March 2017	March 2018	March 2019	March 2020
Bank	21,175	33,176	43,914	59,999	90,643
SFBs	–	32,384	23,160	27,085	39,225
NBFC-MFIs	24,322	31,992	45,794	66,661	71,342
NBFCs	6,156	6,974	12,740	17,574	19,875
Not-for-Profit MFIs	26,470	1,467	1,616	7,228	1,841
Total Industry	78,123	1,05,994	1,27,223	1,78,547	2,22,926
Y-o-Y growth rate (%)		36	20	40	53

Source: Compiled by the author from the data of SIDBI Microfinance Pulse.

of the total microcredit universe. SFBs have a total loan amount outstanding of Rs. 39,225 crores with a total share of 18% (Table 14.2). NBFCs account for another 9% and Not-for-Profit MFIs account for 1% of the industry portfolio.

The number of loans disbursed increased approximately by 25% from FY19 to FY20. Thirty to forty thousand loan categories have witnessed the highest increase from 18 lakh loans disbursed in FY18 to 29 lakh loans disbursed in FY19, the disbursements have increased by 56% on a Y-o-Y basis from FY18 to FY19.

Current Status of the Microfinance Sector and Geographical Range

Microfinance which started with NGOs at the forefront has increasingly become more and more mainstream with formal banking. In the last five years, Bandhan, the largest MFI became the universal bank, eight large MFIs were converted to SFBs and there were many deals of banks taking over MFIs viz. IDFC Bank acquiring Grama Vidiyal, RBL Bank acquiring Swadhaar Finserve, Kotak Mahindra Bank taking over BSS Microfinance, India Infoline acquiring Samsata Microfinance, Muthoot Finance picking up a significant stake in Belstar Investment. etc. With Bharat Financial Inclusion Ltd. (formerly SKS Microfinance), the current largest MFI having been taken over by IndusInd Bank, the bank's share in the overall mF portfolio will further go up.

The top 10 states account for 85% of the microfinance industry's gross loan portfolio. West Bengal and Tamil Nadu contribute 31% of the top 10 states. Amongst the top states, West Bengal, Tamil Nadu and Bihar have a portfolio of more than 20,000 crores each, indicating a highly concentrated market (Table 14.3).

As per available industry data as on March 2020, in terms of regional distribution, the active microfinance clients in the East & North East account for 40%, South 27%, North 11%, West 14% and Central 8%. As per the latest credit bureau data, Microfinance is currently spread across 593 districts in the country. However, around 111 districts each have a portfolio outstanding of less than Rs. 10 crore. Further, about 80% of the microfinance portfolio is accounted for by 213 districts. The aspirational districts account for 12% of pan India's outstanding balance and 90+ delinquencies are at 0.43%. The data shows that there is still a huge scope for expansion and growth of microfinance services in the country. However, the rates of growth in many of the concentrated geographies have been above the national/state average.

Table 14.3 Portfolio Outstanding Trends – Top 10 States

Top 10 States	March 2016	March 2017	March 2018	March 2019	March 2020
West Bengal	10,148	15,166	19,589	26,987	31,814
Tamil Nadu	11,042	15,055	18,828	24,611	32,501
Bihar	5,312	8,465	11,685	18,036	26,505
Karnataka	8,078	9,903	11,030	15,294	19,362
Maharashtra	8,091	9,674	8,903	12,420	16,659
Assam	3,726	5,471	7,966	12,021	11,594
Orissa	3,789	5,166	8,166	11,412	13,391
Uttar Pradesh	7,175	8,072	8,425	10,812	15,549
Madhya Pradesh	5,325	6,043	7,303	9,905	13,556
Kerala	2,967	3,839	5,772	6,942	9,572
Total Top 10 States	65,654	86,854	1,07,668	1,48,440	1,90,503
All India	78,123	1,05,994	1,27,223	1,78,547	2,22,926
Market Share of Top 10 States (%)	84	82	85	83	85

Source: Compiled by the author from the data of MFIN Micrometer, Issue 33, March 2020.

Shifting Trends of Microfinance Borrowers (Rural to Urban)

Since its inception, the Indian MFI quarter has been perceived as a predominantly rural targeted quarter, in large part distinct from the MFI quarter in Latin America in addition to components of America and Africa. However, recently, MFIs have shifted their cognizance from rural hinterlands to city pockets. The industry's outreach to the city customers has changed into growing state every 12 months and in FY15, for the primary time in its records Indian MFIs suggested extra city customers than rural ones (ASSOCHAM, 2016). The proportion of city clients has appreciably declined from 62% in FY16 to 39% in FY17 (Figure 14.1). This shift within the consumer base of MFI has been because of numerous factors – sturdy boom of city-targeted MFIs; shift in the commercial enterprise version of many MFIs and reluctance of banks to lend to small borrowers.

Many MFIs have modified their operations to a city-centric enterprise version to cut-down working fees and maximize operational efficiency. Many banks strengthen small debtors via MFIs to fulfil their objectives of precedence quarter lending. MFIs cannot rate greater than 12% over the value of loans taken from banks whilst solving the mortgage rate for small debtors and hence, the profitability of MFIs relies closely on their operational efficiency. The upward push in city customers of MFIs additionally underlines the reluctance of banks to lend to small debtors. Despite the presence of banking infrastructure in city areas, there's a sturdy call from the unorganized quarter and migrants for microfinance loans.

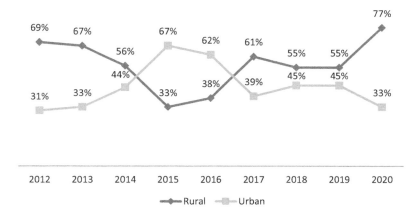

Figure 14.1 Trends in rural–urban share of MFI borrowers.

Source: Compiled by the author from the data of the Bharat Microfinance Report (2020).

Credit Plus Activities by MFIs

Improved human capital could enable microfinance clients to service bigger loans, which ultimately would enhance the financial performance of MFIs, by reducing the risk of default. Realizing that microcredit though critical but addresses only one of the many problems the poor come across, MFIs across the country are revisiting their strategy to offer a wide variety of financial and non-financial products and services to the poor to improve their lives. These services, besides credit, include savings, insurance, pension, remittance, business development services, training, financial literacy, and health and social services.

These services either tend to be funded through donations or customer service charges while some MFIs even cross-subsidize their parallel services. Even MFIs, have diversified their credit products to include renewable energy, water, sanitation and affordable housing. Many MFIs have been providing microinsurance products. As per available data, 19 MFIs have reached 79.42 lakh clients for life insurance, 14 MFIs have reached 22.18 lakh clients for health products and 43 MFIs have reached 224.13 lakh clients for non-health products.

Impact of Microfinance on Socio-Economic Development

Socio-economic development referred to financial expansion, economic growth and improvements in the general well-being of the people. Microfinance helps in the empowerment of the poor by improving their access to the formal credit system through various microfinance innovations in a cost-effective and sustainable manner, provision of various financial services like savings, credit, money transfers and insurance in small doses for the poor to enable them to raise their income levels and improve living.; eradicating poverty and unemployment; promoting children's education; improving health outcomes for women and children and empowering women (Brigit, 2006); Collins et al., 2010; Manahan, 2015; Legerwood, 1999). In 2002, the UN (2002) affirmed that almost one-fifth of the population of the world were living below the poverty line, i.e., their earnings were below 1$ a day, microfinance has helped people in combating poverty. The UN claims that the aims of the Sustainable Development Goals (2016), which are substantially eradicating poverty with other human development goals, can be achieved through the noteworthy contribution of microfinance. Microfinance can have both social and economic effects on society and individuals.

However, critiques raise several questions on the relevance and contribution of microfinance to socioeconomic development. But, programme reviews across the world have proved that finance is a much-required service to the poor and vulnerable sections of the society and also helps in improving their living standards. Credit and savings are used not only to smooth consumption, but also to deal with emergencies like health problems and to

Transformation of Microfinance, Financial and Social Inclusion 229

accumulate larger sums for meeting their life cycle requirements like business opportunities and paying for expenses like education, weddings or funerals.

Similarly, SIDBI commissioned a seven-year impact assessment study in India to assess, on a national scale, the development impact of microfinance in relation to different product designs and delivery systems in various parts of the country. The study revealed an increase in income of the customers, enterprise activities, positive changes in livelihoods patterns by giving impetus to enterprise activity, inculcating savings habit, acquisition of productive assets, less dependence on moneylenders on costly services, increased involvement of women in asset ownership and enhanced food security – from one or two meals a day to three meals a day (SIDBI, 2008). Further, the UN recognized the positive impact of inclusive finance on the overall reduction in poverty and stated in one of its reports that inclusive finance, including safe savings, appropriately designed loans for poor and low-income households and for micro-, small- and medium-sized enterprises and appropriate insurance and payments services can help people to enhance incomes, acquire capital, manage risk and come out of poverty (United Nations, 2006). However, these claims have been contested by a majority of researchers because scientific testing of the impact of microfinance is quite difficult. This is mainly because of the challenges associated with identifying controls group for comparison in microfinance. Despite this fact, some of the world's leading international organizations – ACCION International (n.d.), FINCA, Grameen Foundation, Opportunity International, UNITUS and Women's World Banking – have come together, accepted, reinforced and summarized the impact of microfinance based on their work experience in a paper and signed it jointly which is as follows: (a) Facilitating economic transactions; (b) managing day-to-day resources; (c) accessing services that improve quality of life; (d) protecting against vulnerability; (e) making productivity-enhancing investments; (f) leveraging assets; and (g) building economic citizenship.

Challenges to Microfinance: Anticipated and Unforeseen

Microfinance, which began out as a small-scale philanthropic motion to offer credit scores to the needy, has grown fantastically in current years and is being taken into consideration as a sizeable device for poverty remedy throughout the international. The microfinance quarter in India has grown unexpectedly over the past decade, albeit there are some demanding situations which want to be investigated critically for ensuring sustainability of the world.

    i   Concentration Risk: Microfinance outreach in India is remarkable for its choppy geographic coverage. Even with excessive penetration States, underserved wallet exists, in which microfinance penetration is pretty skinny and elevated outreach is substantially needed.

ii Multiple Borrowings and Over Indebtedness: More range of MFIs favour performing within side the equal vicinity and goal the equal set of terrible. Though it amounts to comfort in operations, it in the end ends in the troubles of a couple of lending and overburdening of households.

iii Higher Rates of Interest: The hobby prices within side the microfinance quarter are sure to be better compared to the hobby prices within side the banking quarter. This is in the main due to the fact the MF commercial enterprise is labour-intensive; the range of debtors is excessive ensuing in sizeable transaction and tracking fees and present door-step banking to their clients.

iv Credit Squeeze: The fashion being witnessed within the quarter is that Banks want to lend to the pinnacle 10 or 15 MFIs and now no longer disperse their portfolio too broadly. This, from the factor of view of banks is comprehensible because it obviates the want to screen many MFIs.

v Contagion Effect: Earlier, maximum reimbursement troubles in microfinance had been commonly limited to occasions that now no longer have an effect on markets at the local or countrywide levels. Recent occasions in Andhra Pradesh and Karnataka have set up that interdependencies among organization individuals have a drawback to it.

vi Credit – A Mixed Blessing: Using the channels of microfinance to supply items and offerings to low earnings populace has ended up with a promising opportunity these days as there are large operational advantages of having access to a present distribution community as an alternative to getting to construct one from scratch.

vii Fast-developing MFIs, elevating fairness and quasi-fairness capital is crucial to leverage its increase. MFI managers want a good way to determine the proper price of fairness products, which includes dilution of possession and control, and investors' expectancies of percentage appreciation and/or dividends.

viii Good Governance through Regulatory Control: The absence of the right regulatory framework and supervision mechanism for the world is a primary trouble which is constraining the orderly increase of the world (Singh, 2010). The want for law is all of the greater emphasis because the extent of monetary transactions of the MFIs has been developing unexpectedly over the past five years.

Key Policy Recommendations

i As microfinance keeps growing, it will likely be crucial to make sure this increase is inclusive, with higher geographical insurance to deal with the call for economic offerings in underserved States and districts.

ii MFIs ought to result in transparency concerning hobby costs and different expenses charged to the clients. While there may be transparency in the hobby rate, transparency in working value is required.
iii Strong control in addition to sturdy forums of administrators in MFIs can offer oversight and continuity and construct properly organizational cultures that preserve the middle talents of the organization and lead it forward.
iv Microfinance gamers should go "past lending" and provide a complete suite of microbanking merchandise viz. insurance, pension, payments, deposits and different simple funding advisories.
v Proper technology may result in huge adjustments within the manner microfinance is presently being carried out and, within the process, might also additionally convey stronger outreach and value reduction.
vi Good governance should be practised at the group level as well as its linkage with the banking system to have better social development.

Conclusion

Growth in the sector is required not only for MFIs but also because unserved and underserved markets continue to remain large. However, the exponential growth in the sector has led to questions being asked about microfinance business models and their ability to sustain client relationships in the long run. The areas that have been particularly in focus are client over-indebtedness, coping strategies in cases of crisis, transparency in loan pricing and reporting to funders, governance, etc. Hence, responsible and orderly growth is the call of the hour considering the current status of microfinance. It is important to increase the provision of microfinance to have better financial inclusion and social development using proper governance mechanisms.

References

ACCION International (n.d.) Accessed from: https://grantspace.org/resources/knowledge-base/microfinance/

ASSOCHAM (2016). Evolving landscape of microfinance institutions in India, July, India, https://forum.valuepickr.com

Brigit, H. (2006). "*Access for all building inclusive financial systems*" Consultative Group to Assist the Poor (CGAP), Accessed from: https://www.cgap.org/research/publication/access-all-building-inclusive-financial-systems

Collins, D., Morduch, J., & Rutherford, S. (2010). *Portfolios of the Poor: How the World's Poor Live on $2 a Day*, Princeton University Press.

Legerwood, J. (1999). Sustainable banking with the poor, "Microfinance Handbook" An Institutional and Financial Perspective, The World Bank, pp 1, https://openknowledge.worldbank.org/handle/10986/12383

Manahan, H. (2015). Private Equity Investment in Microfinance in India, *Michigan Business and Entrepreneurial Law Review*, 4(2), pp. 294.

MFIN Micrometer Various Issues 2020.

Microfinance Information Exchange Inc (2006). 2005 MIX Global 100: MFI league Tables, pp. 6.

Microfinance Pulse (2020). SIDBI-Equifax Quarterly Newsletter.

Reserve Bank of India (1999). Task Force on Supportive Policy and Regulatory Framework for Micro Finance in India, https://www.rbi.org.in/scripts/BS_ViewBulletin.aspx?Id=1347

SIDBI (2001). Assessing Development Impact of Micro Finance Programmes: Findings and Policy Implications from a National Study of Indian Micro Finance Sector, Access from: http://www.spandanaindia.com/pdfs/SIDBI_Impact_study.pdf

SIDBI (2008). SIDBI Annual Report, Government of India, https://www.sidbi.in/files/financialreport/Sidbi-Annual-Report-2008-09.pdf

Singh, P. (2010). Understanding the structure of Microfinance Institutions in India and suggesting a regulatory framework.

Sriram, M.S. (2017). Inclusive Finance India Report, An ACCESS Publication

The Bharat Microfinance Report (2020). New Delhi, November.

United Nations (2006). Report of the Secretary-General, 2nd November, No. A/61/556, https://www.un.org/en/ga/contributions/financial.shtml

United Nations Capital Development Fund (UNCDF) (n.d.). International Year of Microcredit 2005. Accessed from: http://www.gdrc.org/icm/glossary/

15 Knowledge Deprivation Index

Measurement for the UG Students in Purulia and Paschim Bardhaman Districts of West Bengal, India

Saptarshi Chakraborty and Chandan Bandyopadhyay

Introduction

COVID-19 (SARS-CoV-2) since its outbreak in Wuhan, China, in December 2019 spread to every corner of the world. In India also, it has affected more than 30 million people with more than 4 lakh people losing their lives due to this viral effect. Understanding the WHO guidelines that the virus can spread over by contact or by droplets coming out from the mouth and nose of the corona-affected persons, the Government of India, like other countries, had imposed lockdowns from 24th March 2020 onwards. Since then, we experienced phases of 'unlock' periods followed by 'new normal' situations. Those activities which remained stopped or closed during the total lockdown period gradually resumed their normal activities. Industrial production, transportation, amusement, tourism, etc., became normal slowly, but the educational institutions remain closed to date. All institutions like primary schools, secondary schools, colleges, universities and every type of educational institution, be it private or public, were barred from campus classes. But these institutions resorted to a new method of teaching and learning and that was through online mode. In this chapter, the aim is to find whether such an online process really compensated the campus mode, and if not, then by how much it differs. For this, we find a formula for measuring the deprivation index and calculate it on the basis of the collected data.

Deprivation is the concept of excluding someone from enjoying certain opportunities that are however enjoyed by the other privileged section. In the aforesaid online method or process of teaching and learning, there may be deprivation. For availing online classes, a student requires at least a smartphone with an internet connection facility. In this new system teachers have to modify their classes and share to the students via different media like WhatsApp, Google Meet, Zoom and YouTube. Hence, both teachers and students have to adapt to this new system of education. The outcome is unavoidable considering the general rural nature, economic status, mental setup and infrastructure of our country.

Here deprivation as in all cases corroborates to lack of income also. During the lockdown, many people lost their jobs, many had to bear with

DOI: 10.4324/9781003245797-16

curtailment of wages or salaries and many had to face irregularities in payments. People engaged in agriculture also faced market imperfections in selling their products. These constraints forced their living conditions into a miserable situation where people were unable to arrange sufficient two square meals for all family members. Besides, many families were affected by coronavirus (SARS-CoV-2) infections, thereby meeting expenditure for health-related issues; the out-of-pocket expenditure in this new case may be high enough that one has to curtail his/her consumption expenditure or one may withdraw his savings, if any, from banks or one may take loans. In every possible case, people were drained of their money. For availing online education, a student needed a smartphone and a net connection and the parents have to support their sons and daughters by any means. But many times, students are not lucky enough to own a net connected smartphone, thereby deprived of the online class taken by the teacher.

Literature Review

Kumar and Krishna (2010) focused on the impact of the e-learning environment on teacher effectiveness, with reference to Personal Effectiveness, Teaching Skill and Research and academic activities. According to the study, technology increases the efficiency of teachers by giving them varied opportunities. The trend of using e-learning as a learning and teaching tool is now rapidly expanding into education. They measured the effectiveness of the technology by developing a research tool which was administered to 250 teachers serving in colleges of engineering and technology and university departments. The finding of the study reveals that teacher effectiveness of the teachers, on the whole, is high with the assistance of an e-learning environment.

Mohammad (2012) examines the impact of e-learning and e-teaching in universities, from both the student and teacher perspectives. It is shown that e-teachers should focus not only on the technical capacities and functions of IT materials and activities, but must attempt to more fully understand how their e-learners perceive the learning environment. His paper indicates that simply having IT tools available does not automatically translate into all students becoming effective learners. More evidence-based evaluative research is needed to allow e-learning and e-teaching to reach their full potential.

Saba (2012) presents a model approach to examine the relationships among e-learning systems, self-efficacy and students' apparent learning results for university online courses. Independent variables included in this study are e-learning system quality, information quality, computer self-efficacy, system use, self-regulated learning behaviour and user satisfaction as prospective determinants of online learning results. An aggregate of 674 responses from students completing at least one online course from Wawasan Open University (WOU), Penang, Malaysia, were used to fit the path analysis model. The results indicated that system quality, information quality and computer self-efficacy all affected system use, user satisfaction and the self-managed learning behaviour of students.

Gaikwad and Randhir (2015) highlighted the importance of e-learning in the modern era. According to their paper, if properly planned and executed then e-learning is an effective tool for the development of the educational sector in India. e-learning is learning and utilizing electronic technologies to access educational curriculum outside of a traditional classroom. It also summarizes several opinions regarding the comparison between traditional learning and modern learning technique. The research focused on classroom learning and e-learning in India as the main wheel of development of education.

Kaabi and Alsulimani (2018), in their paper, showed the effect of e-learning on teachers' motivation in Jeddah University. Before implementing an e-learning framework in Jeddah university, a questionnaire is established to highlight the ability of teachers to use this new way of education or not. The results show that the teachers have a favourable attitude towards the use of e-learning and new technologies to enhance education.

Salamat et al. (2018) studied the effects of e-learning on students' academic learning. They conducted their study on 205 students from the University of Lahore, Pakpattan Campus. Graduate students formed the population and a simple random sampling technique was used for data collection. The data was analyzed and used the statistical techniques of frequency and percentage score. The study found that e-learning provides time flexibility to the students and it motivates students to do their own work without others' help. It was also that students feel comfortable when they use the internet. The study concluded that e-learning is a system that provides time flexibility to the students for their learning and motivates students to do their work without others' help. It is also concluded that students feel comfort in browsing and surfing the internet.

Muthuprasad et al. (2021), in their article, found that the majority of the students in their study area have a positive inclination towards the online mode of learning due to flexibility and convenience. However, the students also preferred to reorder video uploading content along with quizzes and assignments at the end of the sessions. The students also reported problems related to technology due to weak network connectivity as well as the inefficiency of the teachers to handle ICTs. Mishra et al. (2020) made a study on online TLM adopted by Mizoram University for teaching as well as for the examination processes. Their objectives were to find various forms of TLMs, to study the perceptions of teachers and students on this new method of learning and also to examine the challenges faced by both the groups in the adoption of the method. All the teachers used the University portal of Learning Management System but only 60% of the students used this University LMS. Several platforms like Google Meet, Zoom and Cisco-Webex were also used for online classes. In their study authors found that the students are ready to adapt the new method of learning for completion of their syllabus and also the teachers are ready to welcome the Ministry of

Human Resource Development (MHRD) and University guidelines to conduct online classes and also to share their study materials on the university portal and also directly to the students through email and social media. Debbarma and Durai (2021) have conducted a survey to find the impact of online classes on the students of the North East states of India. Their study strongly revealed that there were educational disruptions in the academic life of those students. The most highlighted problem is the lack of mental readiness to welcome this new digital learning in place of face-to-face interactive offline classes. There were some other obstacles like poor network connection, teachers' inability to perform or adopt new technological teaching aids which also disrupted the learning process. Besides, the students also faced some psychological problems due to fear of COVID, due to delays in returning home town (for those who were in hostels), due to uncertainties related to examinations, campus placements and declaration of results.

According to a new joint report from UNICEF and the International Telecommunication Union (ITU), two thirds of the world's school-age children – or 1.3 billion children aged 3–17 years – do not have internet connections in their homes. The report 'How Many Children and Youth Have Internet Access at Home?' notes a similar lack of access among young people aged 15–24 years, with 759 million or 63% unconnected at home. UNICEF Executive Director, Henrietta Fore said, 'That so many children and young people have no internet at home is more than a digital gap – it is a digital canyon' (UNICEF, 2020).

Dhawan (2020) researched on online learning during the time of COVID-19. It is true that educational institutions (schools, colleges and universities) in India followed traditional methods of learning, that is, they follow the traditional set-up of face-to-face lectures in a classroom. However, many academic units have also started blended learning. This pandemic situation challenged the education system across the world and forced educators to shift to an online mode of teaching overnight. Many academic institutions that were earlier reluctant to change their traditional pedagogical approach had no option but to shift entirely to online teaching–learning.

Hindustan Times (3 June 2020), reported on *Online Learning: Digital Divide Hurting Economically Disadvantaged Students*. According to this report, those with no access to smartphones or computers will not benefit from quality education as their peers will, which will push them behind in their studies. The only source of learning for students during the pandemic is through mobile, SMS (Short Message Service), television, radio or social media. For students from families that can afford it, keeping up with their studies is not much of a problem. But what happens to those who cannot afford a Wi-Fi connection at home, let alone a smartphone?

Hanushek and Woessmann (2020) focused on the economic impact of learning losses in the OECD Report. The different ways of estimating the economic costs of the pandemic for current students provide consistent estimates of today's learning challenges. The costs of school closure and the associated learning losses go beyond the lower incomes that this cohort of students can expect. A less skilled workforce also implies lower rates of national economic growth. Roughly speaking, research in the economics of education shows that each additional year of schooling increases life income by an average of 7.5–10%.

Though the objective of this chapter is similar to that of Sundaram and Tendulkar (1995) and Chakraborty (2010a, 2010b, 2020), there are a few differences too. First, Sundaram and Tendulkar (1995) studied the problem on a large scale mainly on an inter-state basis in the case of shelter deprivation while this chapter uses similar tools in the case of knowledge deprivation. Second, this chapter has a different conceptual structure regarding the aggregation of individual indices.

Basic Structure and Methodology

Formulation and calculation of knowledge deprivation of a group[1] of students $N = \{1, 2... n\}$ who are owing to corona, lockdown and thereby shift of mode from campus to online forms the principal interest of our study. Let d denote the degree of such knowledge deprivation for group N such that d is an increasing function of d_i (i = 1, 2,..., n) where d_i denotes the degree of individual i's knowledge deprivation. Hence, we may write d = $F(d_1, d_2, d_3, ..., d_n)$. We assume that d_i lies in the interval [0,1] and an individual is said to be deprived if and only if $d_i > 0$. However, it is to be admitted that this chapter does not distinguish between individuals who do not suffer from knowledge deprivation but who have different levels of achievement in terms of knowledge. The intuitive conclusion about this formulation is that the degrees of 'overachievements' in terms of housing, of individuals, who are not deprived in terms of housing, are irrelevant for the purpose of measuring the housing deprivation of the group. This is, of course, exactly analogous to the literature on poverty measurement where no distinction is made between the different non-poor individuals.

It is obvious that in judging the standard of knowledge available to the students in an institution, one has to take into account many different attributes, some of which are common to all globally while there may be many others which may be specific to that institution or geographical area which is in consideration. Indeed, this multiplicity of the relevant attributes, together with the quantitative nature of some of these attributes, constitutes a major source of complexity in evaluating the standard of knowledge and its deprivation. To judge the deprivation of knowledge of the students in a group considered, this chapter takes into consideration a set of various different relevant attributes[2] Z (relating to the criteria adequacy, effort, opportunity, preference). For every individual i ∈ N and for every attribute x, let $y_i(x)$ denote i's actual consumption of attribute x. since many of the attributes are qualitative rather than quantitative in nature, we are to assume and assign a relevant real number[3] to denote its level. Let for every attribute x, let r(x) denote the benchmark level of the consumption of attribute x, that is, r(x) is the level of consumption which is considered satisfactory. For example, if x_i is 'how did reduction in syllabus benefit you', then r(x) is 'to a large extent' which this chapter considers the best possible alternative. But then, as these are qualitative in nature, they are denoted by **b(x)**, which then is converted, to a real number r(x) by a rule to be discussed later. It follows that individual i's consumption of attribute x is satisfactory if and only if $y_i(x) \geq r(x)$. We assume that for every $i \in N$, the degree of housing deprivation, d_i, is a function of $y_i(x)_{x \in z}$ $r(x)_{x \in z}$. Thus, the function can be written as

$$d_i = f\left(y_i(x)_{x \in z}, r(x)_{x \in z}\right) \quad (15.1)$$

The Criteria and the Attributes

Though there are numerous attributes which are relevant in judging the standard of knowledge and its deprivation of students, this chapter focuses on and considers a set of only 41 such attributes. These attributes are partitioned into four groups each of which is called a **criterion**. The partitioning of the attributes is not entirely arbitrary; it has an intuitive basis in so far as the attributes in each criterion relate to a specific intuitive aspect of knowledge. The four criteria henceforth will be called adequacy (A), effort (E), opportunity (O) and preference (P). Following are the explanations of each criterion and its elements.

> **Knowledge Adequacy (A):** It is expected that even when there is corona and an unavoidable shift of mode of education from campus to online owing to lockdown, the basic objective of educational institutions is to provide sufficient facilities not only to get the studies going but actually to ensure that proper and timely deliberation of knowledge is not deprived to students. This aspect has been tried to capture by this particular criterion. This chapter considers a set $\{a_1, a_2 \ldots a_{14}\}$ of the following 14 attributes for this criterion to explain the knowledge adequacy of a house.

i) Home is Rural/Urban/Semi-Urban area (a1)
ii) Parent's Occupation (a2)
iii) Time spent on online classes (hours/day) (a3)
iv) Reading Materials were given during lockdown. Were these of much help to you? (a4)
v) Did you get sufficient numbers of electronic notes during the lockdown? (a5)
vi) Did webinars during lockdown enrich you? (a6)
vii) Other than college classes, which of these have you experienced? (a7)

viii) How much did the online course of study during lockdown increase your knowledge? (a8)
ix) Did lockdown make your course lengthy? (a9)
x) Did the use of the INTERNET during this period enrich you? (a10)
xi) DATA PACK was necessary for class, was this COSTLY for you? (a11)
xii) During lockdown, class TIMINGS were very flexible. Did this help you? (a12)
xiii) College FEES was affordable or not (a13)
xiv) Device by which online class is done (a14)

However, it is to be admitted that many other attributes could have been included into this criterion for its exhaustiveness and field data is collected from students (respondents), who actually may not be the best judge of their own derivation. Hence, one has to depend on their value judgements. Moreover, it is also a fact that it is difficult for them to judge all aspects correctly as some attributes[4] cannot be truly understood just by seeing them superficially.

Effort (E): Supply of knowledge is all in vain when no initiative is taken to make use of it. An adequate quantum of knowledge and its means imparted by the institutions and government is necessary but such facilities have to be actually properly received and utilized by the students. This chapter considers such attributes clubbed under the criterion 'Effort'. It is a set $\{e_1, e_2 \ldots e_{10}\}$ of following ten attributes:

i) No. of Days on Online Classes per week (e1)
ii) Time spent on own learning (hours/day) (e2)
iii) Time spent on surfing the internet for study materials (hours/day): (e3)
iv) Time spent on social media (hours/day) (e4)
v) Time spent on sleeping (hours/day) (e5)
vi) Time spent on conversations with family members (hours/day) (e6)
vii) Time spent on online coaching class, if any (hours/day) (e7)
viii) During this difficult phase, did your motivation for education decrease? (e8)
ix) During this difficult phase, did your willpower decrease? (e9)
x) Did the use of the INTERNET have any negative effect on you? (e10)

It is tempting to assume that in view of the reality of rural India, one can afford to ignore the online infrastructure facilities. However, given that such facilities are important for seeking knowledge during pandemic, this chapter seeks to capture the concept of 'absolute deprivation' rather than 'relative deprivation. Given this, the fact that most of the rural population of India does not have proper online facilities at home is not a compelling reason for not including such facilities as a relevant attribute.

Opportunity (O): Apart from the normal demand (Effort) and supply (Adequacy) of knowledge, it is also important whether the education environment is proper and conducive in a sense that whether the new online mode of education really compensated for the campus mode and whether it could open enough opportunities for the students. Taking this into consideration the criterion of opportunity is considered with a set $\{o_1, o_2 \ldots o_{14}\}$ of the following 12 attributes:

i) Were you affected by COVID? (o1)
ii) Were ANY of your family members affected by COVID? (o2)
iii) The library could not be used during lockdown. Did it affect you? (o3)
iv) The syllabus was reduced. Did this help you? (o4)
v) Do you think that curtailed syllabus will reduce job market value? (o5)
vi) Enrichment through programmes/courses like SWYAM, TV and Community-Radio (o6)
vii) Do you think online Exams evaluated you properly? (o7)
viii) Did studying in online mode during the pandemic increase your technical know-how? (o8)
ix) Did the online mode of teaching during lockdown make your studies easier? (o9)
x) Practical classes were not possible during lockdown; has this hampered your study? (o10)
xi) Projects/Excursions were not possible during lockdown. Has this hampered your study? (o11)
xii) 'Online education' was as if a 'doorstep delivery' of knowledge; do you feel good about it? (o12)

Preference (P): We believe that no knowledge touches our hearts and brains unless we enjoy our learning. Here, we club together some attributes which, individually, may not be essential as any of those included in adequacy, effort and opportunity, but which are important for enjoyable teaching–learning. This criterion of preference encompasses:

i) Online class during lockdown was the only choice and how much did I enjoy it? (p1)
ii) Do you think the Online mode of exams is better? (p2)
iii) Should the Online Exams system be continued even after the lockdown? (p3)
iv) How far do you think is the Online mode better than the Campus mode? (p4)
v) How will you OVERALL grade this ONLINE system? (p5)

It is to be admitted that many other attributes could have been included into these criteria for its exhaustiveness, but this chapter considers the above set of attributes merely as a case study. However, one can add many other attributes that may be suitable for a particular place or group where the actual survey and the study are to be done. It implies that this chapter focuses mainly on how to calculate the deprivation rather than on what are the best criteria for such calculation.

Numerical Representation of Consumption Levels

Some of the attributes, like 'No. of Days on Online Classes per week (e1)' and 'time spent on own learning (hours/day) (e2)', come with obvious numerical measures for corresponding consumption levels. In contrast, the attribute 'During this difficult phase, did your will power decrease? (e9)' does not have any such obvious measure and is judged qualitatively by saying whether it is 'more' or 'less'. But for numerical analysis, the issue is how to transform such qualitative data into some numerical value. Note that numerical measures that seek to capture qualitative judgements cannot have a compelling obviousness of the 'natural' numerical measures available in the case of an attribute such as the 'time spent on own learning (hours/day)'. They must involve judgements and, to that extent, they must involve an element of arbitrariness. However, so long as the underlying judgements are made clear, they do serve a useful purpose.

> **Specification of Achievement Levels**: For an attribute **x**, the different possible qualitative levels have to be specified. As, for example, for criterion **A** (Adequacy) and a_6 (Did webinars during lockdown enriched you?), one can consider four levels of achievements listed in ascending order:
>
> i) Not at all ($a_1.1$)
> ii) Not much ($a_1.2$)
> iii) To a considerable extent ($a_1.3$)
> iv) Very much ($a_1.4$)

In general, for any given attribute x, one has to distinguish in quantitative terms, **t[x]** levels of possible achievements (x.1), (x.2), ..., (x.t[x]). This chapter identifies[5] the different qualitative levels of achievements for the attributes considered.

> **Benchmarks for the Different Attributes**: For every attribute x, a qualitative 'benchmark' level, b[x] has to be specified, such that any student that falls short of that benchmark is deprived in terms of x. As for the attribute 'Did webinars during lockdown enriched you?' (a_6), we consider the achievement level $a_1.3$ to be the benchmark so that any household achieving only $a_1.1$ and $a_1.2$ will be considered to be deprived in terms of a_6. Thus $b[a_1]$ is $a_1.3$.

Specification of Numerical Scores: let i be a given individual and x be a given attribute. Suppose the level of i's achievement in terms of x is **x.k** and b[x] is **x.k**. The achievement score $y_i(x)$ for x is to be specified as (k − 1) and the numerical benchmark score r(x) for x to be (k − 1). Consider the following example. Suppose, in terms of the attribute 'Did webinars during lockdown enriched you?' (a_6), student i's achievement level is 'Not much' ($a_1.2$). Then, i's achievement score $y_i(a_1)$ is given by (2 − 1) = 1 and noting $b[a_1] = a_1.3$, the benchmark score of a_1 is (3 − 1) = 2. At the risk of emphasizing the obvious, it may worth be explaining the intuitive procedure underlying this method for specifying $y_i(x)$ and r(x). The procedure is actually the procedure for assigning rank numbers under the well-known **Borda**[6] rule (Young 1974), supplemented by the rule of normalization. Since there are four possible achievement levels for the roof a_1, the rank numbers for them range from 1 to 4, a higher number being assigned to a higher achievement level; likewise, the rank number assigned to the benchmark level $b[a_1] = a_1.4$ is 4. These numbers are then normalized by deducting 1 from each of them so that the lowest possible achievement level ($a_1.1$) is assigned the number 1 and the benchmark level $b[a_1]$ is represented by the benchmark score 3.

Function f: Given the scores $y_i(x)$ and r(x) for each attribute x, the overall deprivation d_i of individual student i can be obtained by a three-stage technique. First, for every individual i and every attribute x, his or her deprivation in terms of that attribute can be represented as

$$d_i(x) = \begin{cases} 0 & \text{if } y_i(x) \geq r(x) \\ \dfrac{r(x) - y_i(x)}{r(x)} & \text{if } y_i(x) < r(x) \end{cases} \quad (15.2)$$

where individual i is said to be deprived of the attribute x if $y_i(x) < r(x)$ and thus $d_i(x) > 0$. Intuitively, an individual is deprived in terms of attribute x if and only if i's achievement score falls short of the benchmark score for x. further, the degree of deprivation, if any, is the shortfall from the benchmark score expressed as a percentage of the benchmark score.

Once the level of deprivation of an individual is obtained for each attribute $d_i(x)$, the deprivation of individual i for each criterion $d_i(X)$ can be obtained by the following two alternative measures:

$$d'_i(X) = \frac{\Sigma d_i(x)}{|X|} \quad (15.3)$$

$$d''_i(X) = \begin{cases} 0 & \text{if } \sum \dfrac{r(x) - y_i(x)}{r(x)} \leq 0 \\ \dfrac{\sum \dfrac{r(x) - y_i(x)}{r(x)}}{|X|} & \text{if } \sum \dfrac{r(x) - y_i(x)}{r(x)} > 0 \end{cases} \quad (15.4)$$

The two alternative ways of computing the degree of deprivation in terms of X differ insofar as $d''_i(X)$ allows deprivation in terms of one attribute in X to be compensated by over-achievement in terms of another attribute in X, where $d'_i(X)$ does not allow for such compensation or trade-off. Therefore, if one uses $d'_i(X)$ as a measure of i's deprivation in terms of X and i happens to be deprived in terms of any attribute in X, then i will turn out to be deprived in terms of criterion X, no matter how high i's achievements in terms of the other attributes in X may be. However, for this chapter, we will not consider the compensation issue as we believe that such an exercise is not plausible with this present study.

The overall deprivation of an individual i is assumed to be a weighted average of the deprivations of i in terms of each of the four criteria. However, since for every criterion X, there may be two conceptually different measures of deprivation $d'_i(X)$ and $d''_i(X)$, there must be two different distinct versions of the overall deprivation d_i for individual i.

$$d'_i = w(A) \cdot d'_i(A) + w(S) \cdot d'_i(E) + w(E) \cdot d'_i(O) + w(C) \cdot d'_i(P) \quad (15.5)$$

$$d''_i = w(A) \cdot d'_i(A) + w(S) \cdot d'_i(E) + w(E) \cdot d'_i(O) + w(C) \cdot d'_i(P) \quad (15.6)$$

where w(A), w(E), w(O) and w(P) are non-negative weights adding up to 1. These weights can be considered equal and taken to be each equal to ¼ (or in any other proportion as the investigator perceives about the importance of the criterion). Suppose the investigator opines that 'comfort' is not that much essential, he may consider w(A) = w(E) = w(O) = 2/7 and w(P) = 1/7.

Aggregation of Individual Deprivation Levels

Once derived as a measure of the housing deprivation of every individual in N, the process to measure the housing deprivation of the group N is similar to measuring the income poverty of a group, given the percentage shortfall of each individual from the poverty threshold. For this, the three measures can be used: the **Sen Measure**, the **Quadratic Measure** and the **Simple Average** each of which can be based either on $(d'_1, d'_2, ..., d'_n)$ or on $(d''_1, d''_2, ..., d''_n)$. Thus there are actually six different measures of housing deprivation on N. Measures based on $(d'_1, d'_2, ..., d'_n)$ are termed as **Type – I** and those based on $(d''_1, d''_2, ..., d''_n)$ are termed as **Type – II**.

Let **J** be the set of all I in N such that $d'_j > 0$. Let **p** be the cardinality of J. Index the individuals in J as j(1), j(2), ..., j(p) in such a way that $d'_{j(1)} \leq d'_{j(2)} \leq ... \leq d'_{j(p)}$. For all I in J, the rank of i, denoted by q(i), is defined to be **v** where $I = j(v)$. Then,

$$\text{Sen Measure (Type – I)} = \frac{2\sum_{i \in J} q(i).d'_i}{n(p+1)} \qquad (15.7)$$

$$\text{Quadratic Measure (Type – I)} = \frac{\sum_{i \in J}(d'_i)^2}{n} \qquad (15.8)$$

$$\text{Simple Average (Type – I)} = \frac{\sum_{i \in J}(d'_i)}{n} \qquad (15.9)$$

Type – II measures can be defined similarly in terms of d''_i. The Sen measure was first introduced in his classic paper, *Poverty: An Ordinal Approach to Measurement* (Sen, 1976). The Quadratic measure is a distinguished element of the class of poverty measures considered by Foster, Green and Thorbecke (1984). The Simple Average is just the aggregate of all deprivations divided by the total number of individuals in the group under consideration but this measure has serious limitations insofar as the intuitively compelling 'transfer axiom'.

In this chapter, we consider only Sen Measure of Type – I. However, one can find all other measures which have their own interpretations.

Data Levels

Data is collected from students of two districts, namely, Purulia and Paschim Bardhaman, of the state of West Bengal, India, during June 2021 from various undergraduate colleges. Two[7] questionnaires[8] had been formulated in Google Forms. The choice of these districts is primarily to consider the varsity of students with respect to economic status, rural–urban location, reach of online facilities, etc. There have been 761 respondents and the data has been compiled in an e-location[9], which can be accessed on request from the authors of this chapter.

Outcomes of the Study

Data collected from students have been compiled and converted to numerical values as per the rule stated earlier. To make analysis simple and considering the nature and category of respondents, this chapter assigned equal weights to all four criteria. Moreover, it is also believed that, for the sample for which this present study has been done, overachievement in one attribute may not plausibly be compensated with underachievement of other attributes. Hence, this chapter considers only Sen Measure of Type – I to aggregate the deprivation indices and calculated it in accordance with the methodology discussed above. This chapter also considers the weights of the four criteria in the manner: w(A) = 0.4, w(E) = 0.2, w(O) = 0.25 and w(P) = 0.15 which is arbitrary but based on intuitions of the authors regarding the nature and characteristics of the respondents. However, it is to be admitted that the weights can well be estimated through another survey or literature, which may well be an extension of this chapter. Some basic results are portrayed in Table 15.1.

It has been obtained that for the group taken and the attributes considered, d = 39.84. It implies that the respondents are **39.84%** deprived of knowledge as per this study. However, it is to be admitted that all the respondents are college undergraduate students and their responses are purely based on their value judgements. It is their feel, their choice and their way of thinking. This needs to be taken into consideration before making any judgement because it is obvious that some students will feel less deprived, though they actually are not, when asked about certain issues. This chapter wants to find out the 'knowledge deprivation', which for attributes like 'Do you think online Exams evaluated you properly? – o(7)', 'Do you think that curtailed syllabus will reduce job market value? – o(5)' or 'Do you think Online mode of exams are better? – p(2)', students rank the available options (not at all, a little bit, much, very much) in an order which makes their life temporarily easy whereas they actually choose to sacrifice 'knowledge' in the long run.

As far as the socio-economic structure of the surveyed area is concerned, the online mode of education may be helpful to the female students who can attend their classes sitting at home; otherwise, they may be forbidden to go to college campus regularly, may be due to cost of transportation or may be due to their helping hand extension to household chores and care work. The same may be true for those male students who cannot afford transport costs regularly and who are engaged in some part-time jobs. This issue has been addressed here in this chapter and the same study has been calculated for female students only. It has been found that the deprivation now is **d = 38.98**. It implies for the respondents, **38.98%** of female students are

Table 15.1 Deprivation index across sex and areas

Group	Deprivation Index
TOTAL	39.84
MALE	43.28
FEMALE	38.98
RURAL	42.59
URBAN	38.29

Source: Authors' calculations.

deprived of knowledge as per this study. It has also been found that the deprivation for male students only is d = 43.28. It implies that for the respondents, 43.28% of male students are deprived of knowledge as per this study. Though online mode may be beneficial to female students, this chapter will still not be in favour of this mode as its demerits are far more detrimental to society as a whole.

This chapter is not just to calculate the deprivation index of the group considered. It is also to create an alarm that if this online mode is continued and implemented even after the lockdown then there will be inequality in the distribution of knowledge. One such deprivation is certainly with respect to location, specifically rural or urban. On calculating the knowledge deprivation index only for the rural areas, it has been found that the deprivation index is d = 42.59. It implies for the respondents, 42.59% of rural students are deprived of knowledge as per this study. It has also been found that the deprivation for urban students is d = 38.29. It implies that for the respondents, 38.29% of urban students are deprived of knowledge.

Conclusion

From our analysis, it is found that as the knowledge deprivation index of the total group of respondents is about 40%, it matters so far as the future of students is considered. However, that does not mean that all students are 40% deprived of knowledge. It is the average deprivation of the group considered. Owing to corona and lockdown, the mode of study has shifted from 'campus' to 'online' and the deprivation, so obtained, can also be viewed as 'deprivation of knowledge' owing to the changeover to 'online mode'. It was also found that, intra-group, viz. male–female, rural–urban, etc., inequality widens with such a changeover and hence, such an online mode should not[10] be continued once the pandemic is over.

This chapter admits that the so-called 'online' mode of education is unavoidable in pandemic situations, but strongly believes that such a mode must be temporary as that of the corona phase. When things get normal, we must revert back to the campus mode as from the social point of view, inequality may also be intensified and aggravated and may encourage corporatization of basic education system, which is generally believed to be profit-oriented and hence corporate sector may gradually and eventually capture the whole process of teaching, learning and evaluation which will be detrimental to the society as a whole. Knowledge will lose its essence and dignity. It may just be a marketable object that too for those who can buy it. Corona waves will pass on but let not the campus be washed away.

This study can be extended, upgraded and customized as per need, location, attributes and criteria and thereby opens up various further research agendas like (a) how much are economically backward students deprived of knowledge owing to the online system, (b) whether infrastructure is responsible for knowledge deprivation, (c) which aspects of online mode may be continued even after lockdown and which aspects must be terminated and

(d) how should Govt. frame policies if the tail of corona effect is not as short and temporary as it seems.

Notes

1 This chapter considers a group of students or undergraduate students from two districts of the state of West Bengal, India, primarily with varied rural–urban orientation and income status.
2 See Section "The Criteria and the Attributes".
3 For the rule for deciding what real number is to be assigned, a rule is to be used that has been discussed later in this chapter.
4 For example, if a student is asked whether online exam has deprived you, the student will certainly not truly consider whether this Open-Book system of examination really increases his/her job market value.
5 See e-location: https://docs.google.com/spreadsheets/d/1D9H4JOLzF6Ns9yg0x 5VRIsQhjEZzxjpTaAD40nIXdII/edit?usp=sharing
6 Famous rule for assigning numerical ranks to qualitative data
7 One in English and the other in vernacular (Bengali)
8 English (https://forms.gle/9T4z8r4PyTMQ4C8UA) and Bengali (https://forms.gle/MV4KGhBftuejZPQk8)
9 Please mail any of the authors to access the data.
10 Provided the Govt. takes proper correctional measures to combat it

References

Chakraborty, S. (2010a). Positive discrimination in rectifying housing deprivation inequality: Caste may not be the basis. *Asian Journal of Research in Social Sciences and Humanities*, 3(9).

Chakraborty, S. (2010b). Necessity of estimation of housing deprivation: Rule out the rule of thumb. *PANCHAKOTesSAYS*, 1(3).

Chakraborty, S. (2020). Economic Convergence and Real Dimensions: The C …, Megacities and Rapid Urbanization: Breakthrough… (ISBN13: 9781522592761), 288–313.

Debbarma, I., & Durai, T. (2021). Educational disruption: Impact of COVID-19 on students from the Northeast states of India. *Children and Youth Services Review*, 120, 1–6.

Dhawan, S. (2020). Online Learning: A Panacea in the Time of COVID-19 Crisis. *The Journal of Educational Technology Systems (ETS)*, https://doi.org/10.1177/0047239520934018

Foster, J., Green, J., & Thorbecke, E. (1984). Notes and comments: A class of decomposable poverty measures. *Econometrica*, 52, 761–765.

Gaikwad, A., & Randhir, V. S. (2015). E-Learning in India: Wheel of Change, *International Journal of e-Education, e-Business, e-Management and e-Learning*, 6(1), 40–45.

Hanushek, E. A., & Woessmann, L. (2020). *The Economic Impacts of Learning Losses*. OECD.

Kaabi, H., & Alsulimani, T. (2018). The effect of E-Learning on Teachers' Motivation: A case study in Jeddah University. *International Journal of Management & Information Technology*, 14, 3316–3327.

Kumar, R. M. & Krishna, K. R. (2010). Impact of E-Learning on Teacher Effectiveness. *Journal of Educational Technology*, 7(3), 63–68.

Mishra, L., Gupta, T., & Shree, A. (2020). Online teaching-learning in higher education during lockdown period of COVID-19 pandemic. *International Journal of Educational Research Open*, 1.

Mohammad, M. (2012). The Impact of e-Learning and e-Teaching. *World Academy of Science, Engineering and Technology International Journal of Educational and Pedagogical Sciences*, 6(2).

Muthuprasad, T., Aiswarya, S., Aditya, K. S., & Jha, G. K. (2021). Students' perception and preference for online education in India during COVID-19 pandemic. *Social Sciences & Humanities Open*, 3, 1–11.

Saba, T. (2012). Implications of E-learning systems and self-efficiency on students' outcomes: a model approach. *Human-centric Computing and Information Sciences*, 2, 1–11.

Salamat, L., Ahmad, G., Bakht, I., & Saifi, I. L. (2018). Effects of E–Learning on Students' Academic learning at University Level. *Asian Innovative Journal of Social Sciences and Humanities*, 2(2), 1–12.

Sen, A. (1976). Poverty: An ordinal approach to measurement. *Econometrica*, 44, 219–231.

Sundaram, K., & Tendulkar, S. (1995). On measuring Shelter Deprivation in India. *Indian Economic Review*, 30, 131–165.

UNICEF (2020). "How many children and young people have internet access at home? Estimating digital connectivity during the COVID-19 pandemic." UNICEF, New York, 2020.

Young, H. P. (1974). An axiomatization of Borda's rule. *Journal of Economic Theory*, 9(1), 43–52. doi:10.1016/0022-0531(74)90073-8.

Index

Accountability 31, 33–36, 43, 45, 59–61, 63–65, 75, 79, 94, 130–131, 139, 149, 163, 165–166, 168–170, 209
Accredited Social Health Activist (ASHA) 206, 214, 218
Adult literacy 6, 62
Africa 6, 8, 10, 20, 41, 43, 47–48, 51, 53, 55–56, 60, 70, 72–73, 92, 95–98, 106–110, 114, 122, 138, 161, 168, 174, 177, 184–185, 219, 227
African Development Bank 98, 107
Akaike information criterion (AIC) 180
Andhra crisis 223
Anganwadi Worker (AWW) 215
ANOVA 211, 214–215
Applications of governance 160
Asian Development Bank (ADB) 44, 54, 142, 147, 181
Augmented Dickey Fuller (ADF) 51, 79–80
Autoregressive distributed lag (ARDL) 79–80, 98
Auxiliary Nurse-Midwife (ANM) 214

Bidirectional causality 47
Bureaucracy 9, 11, 13, 33–34, 49, 65, 70, 75, 129, 162
Bureaucratic corruption 9–12, 20

Carbon Dioxide (CO2) Emissions 149, 153–154, 156, 207, 220
Census 118, 124, 199
Centre for Monitoring Indian Economy (CMIE) 180, 201
Challenges to Microfinance 229
Cointegration 50–52, 101–103, 108
Commons 5, 22–23, 29–33, 35–39, 156, 171

Commons governance 30, 35–36
Construction sector 191, 194–197
Control of Corruption (CC) 42, 45, 47–49, 52, 54, 60–61, 63, 65, 75, 95, 98–99, 101, 104–107, 109, 149, 170
Control of corruption 5–6, 42, 45, 47–49, 52, 54, 60–61, 63, 65, 75, 95, 98–99, 101, 104–107, 109, 149, 170
Corruption Perception Index (CPI) 76, 79, 85, 95, 149
Council of Europe (COE) 59, 70
COVID-19 168, 188–190, 199–201, 204, 206–208, 213, 219, 233, 236, 247–248
COVID-19 Pandemic 188–190, 200, 204, 206, 208, 213, 219, 248
Credit 132, 174, 188–190, 204, 221, 223–226, 228–230
Cumulative Sum (CUSUM) 79, 81–82, 84–85

Debt Autonomy (DA) 112, 115
Deprivation index 233, 245–246
Destabilizing Effect of Corruption 18
Developed Economies 1, 173, 179–180, 184
Developing Economies 77, 108, 181
Direct tax 13–14, 17–18
Domestic Capital Formation (DCF) 179
Dynamic Panel 7, 49, 55, 96, 108, 179–184, 187

Error Correction Model (ECM) 79–80, 97, 178
Error Correction Term 87, 89
Educational Expenditure 77–81, 84, 90–91, 98, 109, 176

250 Index

Expenditure Ratio 112, 114
European countries 48, 50–54
Expansive corruption 10
Emerging Market Economies 6, 140–141, 143, 145–151, 153–155, 157, 190
Environmental Quality (EQ) 6, 38, 140, 143–145, 147–149, 154, 156–157
Economic growth 2, 5, 7–8, 10, 19, 41–42, 47–49, 55–58, 60, 66, 70–72, 74, 76–79, 89–90, 92–93, 95–99, 104, 106–111, 124–125, 140, 142–148, 156–157, 159–163, 171, 173–176, 178, 184–187, 206–208, 219–220, 237
Economic Pie 17, 19
Economic development 1, 4–8, 20, 24, 42, 55–56, 74, 76, 80, 97, 108–109, 133, 142, 145–146, 156–157, 159, 163, 171, 173–182, 184, 186, 205, 228
European Union (EU) 2, 5, 9–10, 12, 20, 41, 43, 45–55, 57, 59, 70, 81, 86, 108–109, 112, 116, 126, 128, 138, 174, 178, 185–187, 189–190, 192, 198, 204, 219, 221, 224

Financial Inclusion 223–224, 226, 231
Fiscal Decentralization 6, 111–119, 121–125
Fiscal deficit 17, 201
Fixed Effect Model 68–69, 10
Foreign direct investment (FDI) 79, 179, 187

Gender equality 1
Generalized Entropy 116
Generalized Method of Moments (GMM) 5, 6, 7, 43, 50, 52–53, 96, 100–101, 105, 113, 118, 119, 123, 145, 149, 151, 179–184, 184
GINI 112, 118, 121, 142, 144, 149, 150–155, 202
Globalization 7, 29, 59, 72, 108, 128, 175, 184
Goal 3 2, 11, 19, 205–206
Good governance 3–8, 37, 42–45, 47, 52, 54–56, 58–61, 63–67, 69–76, 85, 93–95, 98, 105–107, 126, 137–138, 157–159, 161–163, 165–166, 170–171, 174–175, 184, 230–231
Governance attributes 33, 35

Governance index 63, 66, 109
Governance Indicator 8, 47, 56, 60–61, 64–65, 71, 75, 78–79, 84, 90–91, 110, 138, 143, 157, 168–170, 177, 179, 186–187
Governance reforms 42–43, 158–159, 161, 163, 165, 167, 169, 171
Governance structures 26–27, 29, 31, 33–34, 37, 48, 143, 154
Government Expenditure 20, 46–47, 89, 95, 97–99, 104–105, 107, 109, 117, 119, 122, 175–179, 184–186, 207, 210, 213
Government Expenditure on the Social Sectors 179
Governments Effectiveness (GE) 76
Grameen Bank 223
Gross Domestic Product (GDP) 6, 17, 48–54, 58, 62–63, 76–81, 83–89, 91, 93, 98–99, 101, 104–106, 112, 114, 117, 119–122, 142–145, 176, 178–180, 189, 193–194, 197–198, 201–202, 208, 211, 213

Health Expenditure 11, 77, 79–81, 84, 95, 97, 104, 178, 185, 188–189, 197–200, 219
Healthcare 1–2, 75, 97, 109, 135, 175, 177–178, 184, 188, 197, 205–206, 208–215, 217–219
Human Development Index (HDI) 61–63, 65, 68–69, 71, 74–75, 125, 143, 145, 148–156, 156–157, 185, 220

ICTs 235
Im, Persaran and Shin (IPS) 50–51, 102
Income inequality 60, 111, 113, 116–117, 119, 121–123, 125, 142, 144, 147–149, 153–154, 156–157, 176, 195
Index of social development (SDI) 48
Indirect tax 14, 17–18
Individual deprivation levels 243
Inequality 3–8, 11, 19, 56, 60, 92, 108, 111–119, 121–123, 125, 142, 144, 147–149, 153–154, 156–157, 161, 176, 188–191, 193, 195–197, 199, 201, 203, 246–247
Institutional corruption 11
Institutional informality 5, 22–23, 25, 27, 29, 31, 33, 35, 37, 39
Integrated Child Development Services (ICDS) 214

International Development Association
  (IDA) 94, 108
International Labour Organisation
  (ILO) 55, 201
International Telecommunication
  Union 236

Job creation 2, 122
Job opportunities 42

Karachi Electric Supply Corporation 132
Keynesian paradigm 12
Keynesian theory of unemployment 46
Knowledge Adequacy 238
Knowledge Deprivation Index 233, 246

Lagrange Multiplier (LM) 79–86, 88, 98
Leave-One-Out (LOO) 118
Levin-Lin-Chu (LLC) 179–181
Life expectancy 11, 62, 145, 174, 178

Macroeconomic Stability 2, 14, 164
Material wellbeing 19
MENA 47, 56, 96, 109, 142, 156
Micro Units Development and
  Refinance Agency (MUDRA) 221,
  224
Microfinance 125, 221–224
Microfinance Institutions (MFIs)
  221–228, 230–231
Microfinance Institutions Network
  (MFIN) 222–224, 226, 232
Microfinance Pulse 222, 225, 232
Millennium Development Goal (MDG)
  4, 77, 89, 143, 157, 178, 207, 219
Ministry of Human Resource
  Development (MHRD) 236
Modified Fundamental Index of Fiscal
  Decentralization (MFDI) 6, 30, 112,
  114, 116–117, 119–123

National Accountability Bureau (NAB)
  130–131
National Bank for Agriculture and
  Rural Development (NABARD)
  222–223
National Institution for Transforming
  India (NITI) 118
National Security Council 136
National Unity Government 134
Net State Domestic Product (NSDP) 143
Non-governmental Organization
  (NGO) 131–132, 184, 222–223,
  225

Offline learning 236, 246
Online learning 7, 234, 236, 247
Ordinary Least Square (OLS) 50, 59,
  98, 100, 118, 143–144, 178
Organisation for Economic
  Cooperation and Development
  (OECD) 72, 78, 90, 117–118, 124,
  142, 156, 222, 236, 247
Overall deprivation 243

Panel Vector Auto Regression (Panel
  VAR) 148–150, 153, 157
Panel vector error correction 47
Pedroni 50–51, 101–103
Political corruption 126–127, 138
Political economy 9, 11, 19–22, 109,
  124, 126, 130, 138, 156, 159, 171,
  185–186, 204
Political finance 160
Political stability 5, 45, 47–49, 52, 54,
  61, 63–66, 79, 149, 169–170
Political Stability and Absence of
  Violence 47–49, 52, 54, 61, 63,
  149, 170
Poverty 6, 8–10, 41–43, 55–56, 60–61,
  66, 70, 72–73, 92–94, 97, 107–109,
  111–125, 133, 161–163, 171, 174,
  186, 205, 214, 221, 223, 228–229,
  237, 243–244, 247–248
PPP 62, 112, 209, 218
Principal Component Analysis (PCA) 5,
  62, 66–68
Private governance 34
Property rights 30–34, 38–39, 65–66,
  159, 162
Public governance 31, 97, 109
Public space 5, 22, 26–27, 38–39
Public Space Governance Framework
  (PSGF) 26
Purchasing power parity 62

Quantitative easing 204

Random Effect Model 69
Recession 5, 14–15, 19, 189, 194
Redistribution of Income 5, 10,
  17–19
Regulatory Quality 42, 60–61, 63, 65,
  75, 93, 149, 170
Revenue Autonomy 112, 114–115
Rule of Law 2, 5–6, 42–43, 45–48, 52,
  54, 60–61, 63–66, 69, 93–95,
  98–99, 101, 104–107, 128, 136,
  146, 149, 162, 165, 167–170

South Asian Association for Regional Cooperation (SAARC) 178, 186, 217
Index of social development (SDI) 48
Small Industries Development Bank of India (SIDBI) 222–225, 229, 232
Size of the government 6, 112
Skilled and Unskilled Labour 195, 197
Small and Medium Enterprises 201
Short Message Service (SMS) 236
Social Expenditure Database (SOCX) 78
Social sectors 1, 74, 78, 85, 90, 92, 177, 179, 211
STATA 49, 120–121, 150, 155
Self Help Groups (SHGs) 223–225
Sen's measure 244–245
Social credibility 5, 22, 37
South Asia 4, 7, 56, 118, 124, 131–132, 138, 161, 205–207, 209–211, 214–215, 217–220
Sub-Saharan Africa (SSA) 5, 50–54, 60
Social Sector Spending 1, 3, 5–6, 77, 92–93, 95, 98, 100–101, 104–107
Social sector development 1, 5, 41–43, 46, 48–50, 52–56, 90
Social Infrastructure 1, 7
Sustainable Development Goals (SDGs) 1, 2, 4, 7–8, 41, 97, 109, 141, 168, 205–210, 218–220, 228
Sustainable Growth 3, 6, 60, 85, 92–107
Socio-economic development 7, 42, 133, 177, 228
Sustainability 2, 8, 24, 30–31, 38, 45, 98, 107–108, 123, 125, 141, 146–148, 153, 157, 163, 209, 219, 229

Tax immunity 12
Transfer Dependency Ratio 115
Transparency International 9, 21, 79, 85, 90, 128–129, 133–134, 139, 168
Two-stage least square (2SLS) 50, 100

Unemployment 4, 7, 19, 42–50, 52–56, 95, 98–99, 101, 104–106, 133–134, 175, 201, 204
UNEP 146
UNICEF 41, 56, 236, 248
Unit root 50–51, 79, 101–102, 155–156, 179–181, 185–186
United Nations Development Programme (UNDP) 42, 44–45, 48–49, 56–57, 61–62, 74, 94, 110, 142, 147, 156, 220
United Nations University 55
Urban Open Space (UOS) 22–34, 36–38
Urban Open Space governance 28, 31
Urbanization 22, 29, 188, 199–200, 203–204, 247
User-centric functional credibility 29

Variance decomposition 150–151
Vector Auto Regression (VAR) 47, 149–151
Vector Autoregression 97, 140, 148, 151, 155
Vector Error Correction Model (VECM) 47, 178
Voice and Accountability 60–61, 63–65, 75, 79, 149, 168, 170
Volume of International Trade 179

Wald test 79, 81, 83–84, 182–183
WHO 210, 233
World Bank 8, 10, 44, 57, 61, 65, 70–73, 75, 79, 90–93, 96, 98, 110, 112, 114–115, 118, 123, 136, 139, 157–158, 162, 169–173, 177, 179, 184, 186–187, 189, 218, 229, 231
World Development Indicators (WDI) 48–49, 79, 98, 110, 149, 157, 179, 181–184, 187
Worldwide Governance Indicator (WGI) 8, 61, 63, 75, 79–81, 83–110, 134, 149, 157, 179–187
WWF 146